A COMPLETE GUIDE

LIGHTHOUSES & LIGHTS

OF NOVA SCOTIA

E.H. RIP IRWIN

NIMBUS
PUBLISHING

Acknowledgements

Nimbus Publishing Limited
PO Box 9166
Halifax, NS   B3K 5M8
(902) 455-4286

Printed and bound in Canada
Design: Kathy Kaulbach, Paragon Design Group

Cover: Sambro Island lighthouse, the oldest operating lighthouse in North America.
Photo credits: p.12, A.L. Hardy; p.97, Captain Mel Lever; p.1, p.168, Tim Randall; p.15, p.25, p.72, unknown. All other photos: Rip Irwin. Original postcards appear on p.6, p.26, p.77.

National Library of Canada Cataloguing in Publication Data

Irwin, E. H. Rip
Lighthouses and lights of Nova Scotia : a complete guide / E.H. Rip Irwin.
Includes index.
ISBN 1-55109-426-6
1. Lighthouses—Nova Scotia. I. Title.
VK1027.N6I79 2003   387.1'55'09716
C2003-901939-X

We acknowledge the financial support of the Government of Canada through the Book Publishing Industry Development Program (BPIDP) and the Canada Council for our publishing activities.

First, I wish to acknowledge Chris Mills, a fellow lighthouse enthusiast and friend since 1986. For several years, he was the only person I knew who shared my interest in lighthouses. In those days, any thought of their preservation was practically non-existent, but by 1993 public awareness was picking up. I wish to acknowledge Patricia MacDonald and another very good friend, Graham McBride, who with Chris Mills and I founded the Nova Scotia Lighthouse Preservation Society on July 20, 1993. The society was incorporated on August 31, 1994.

A special word of thanks goes to all the members of the Canadian Coast Guard at Dartmouth, who were helpful to me in so many ways: Carl Goodwin, Ken Hamilton, Joe Leclair, Captain Mel Lever, Dan MacNeil, Dave Smith, Eric Stevens, Danny Veniot, and the man who arranged for me to go on Sable Island, Larry Wilson. I'd also like to thank technicians Wayne Dedrick, Bud O'Halloran, and Peter Tapper—and Cathy Ferguson and Bonnie LeBlanc in records. I must also thank the guys from Search and Rescue at Sambro: Chris Flemming, Stephen Beazley, and Ken Mills; they took me to Sambro Island several times in the Coast Guard cutter *Sambro*, in the days before I had my own Zodiac.

Some of the lightkeepers who made me welcome at the stations that were still manned include: Harvey and Marion Huskins, Battery Point Breakwater; Blair Cameron and Bert Fleet, Beaver Island; Frank Kozera, Black Rock Point; Angus Smiley, Boars Head; Gilbert Ingersoll, Brier Island; Lawrence Morris, Cape d'Or; Lawrence Wentzell and Walter Goodwin, Cape Forchu; John Gwynn, Cape North;

Foster Welsh, Caribou; George and Ethel Locke, Chris Mills, Cross Island; Paul Finck, Charles and Beatrice Finck, and Violet Finck, who celebrated her one hundred and eighth birthday on January 8, 2002, East Ironbound Island; Patsy and Yvonne LeFort, Enragee Point; Robert and Gerry Spears, Fourchu Head and Scatarie Island; Pete Welch, Grand Passage; Earl Flemming and Danny Lowe, Gull Rock; Ingram and Lynne Wolfe, and Thom and Anne Drew, Mosher Island; Ivan and Mildred Kent, Musquodoboit Harbour Range; Carl and Brenda Goyetche, Point Aconi; Hector Lowe and Glen McCabe, Port Bickerton; Carmand Frankland, Prim Point; John and Marjorie Fairservice, Gerry O'Neill, and Kelly Brown, Sambro Island; Brian Stoddard, and James and Mary Nickerson, Seal Island; John Fairservice and Wally MacLeod, St. Paul Island Northeast; John and Gloria MacQuarrie, and Ernie Keefe, White Head Island; Bill Baker, who, although not an official lighthouse keeper, owns Henry Island and cares for the lighthouse as if it were his own.

It is unlikely that I would have ever given serious thought to putting together a book on Nova Scotia lighthouses had it not been for my friend Del Lowe. He has been supporting this notion since 1996, and finally got me on track to go ahead. Thank you for your support, Del.

Finally, I wish to thank the staff of the Japan Camera shop in Truro, particularly Sheri Ellis, who has done the bulk of my photographic processing over the years, taking care to ensure that the results are the best they can be. Before that, Cathy Scullion and Beth Delaney provided me with equally excellent service.

Table of Contents

Map of Lighthouses & Lights		iv
Preface		vi
Introduction		vii
Glooscap Trail		1
Evangeline Trail		11
Lighthouse Route		27
Halifax Metro		69
Marine Drive		81
Cape Breton Island		111
Sunrise Trail		163
Glossary		179
Bibliography		180
Index		181

LIGHTHOUSES & LIGHTS
OF NOVA SCOTIA

164

Amherst

Pugwash

001

Cape Chignecto

004 005

002

003

Parrsboro

006

007

008

014

009

015

016

017

Wolfville

011

010

019

022

018 020

023

Bridgetown

013

021

Digby

012

024

Windsor

025 028

Glooscap
Trail

026 029

027

030

031

Halifax
Dartmouth

069

Mahone Bay

068

Halifax

Dartmouth

081

072

Lunenburg

067

080

083

Lighthouse
Trail

064

066 070

073

082

071

075 077

084

Yarmouth

065

074

079

032

062

076

038

063

078

033

059 061

034 035

060

058

036

040

Liverpool

057

039

056

041

Shelburne

055

044

052

054

043

047

042

037

051

053

045

050

046

048 049

Glooscap Trail 1
001	Apple River	.2
002	Ile Haute	.2
003	Cape d'Or	.3
004	Spencers Island	.4
005	Port Greville	.4
006	Cape Sharp	.5
007	Parrsboro	.6
008	Five Islands	.7
009	Bass River	.8
010	Burntcoat Head	.9
011	Walton Harbour	.10

Evangeline Trail 11
012	Mitchener Point	.12
013	Horton Bluff	.12
014	Black Rock	.13
015	Margaretsville	.13
016	Port George	.14
017	Hampton	.14
018	Prim Point	.15
019	Digby Gut	.16
020	Victoria Beach	.16
021	Bear River	.16
022	Schafners Point	.17

023	Annapolis	.17
024	Boars Head	.18
025	Grand Passage	.19
026	Brier Island	.19
027	Peter Island	.20
028	Gilbert Point	.21
029	Belliveau Cove	.22
030	Church Point	.22
031	Cape St. Mary	.23
032	Cape Forchu	.23
033	Bunker Island	.26

Lighthouse Route 27
034	Green Island	.28
035	Candlebox Island	.28
036	Pease Island	.29
037	Seal Island	.30
038	Tusket River	.32
039	Whitehead Island	.32
040	Abbott's Harbour	.33
041	Pubnico Harbour	.34
042	Bon Portage Island	.35
043	Stoddart Island	.36
044	Woods Harbour	.37
045	West Head	.37
046	Cape Sable	.38
047	Seal Island Light Museum	39

048	Baccaro Point	.40
049	The Salvages	.41
050	Cape Negro Island	.42
051	Cape Roseway	.43
052	Sandy Point	.44
053	Gull Rock (Lockport)	.45
054	Carter Island	.47
055	Little Hope Island	.47
056	Port Mouton	.48
057	Western Head	.50
058	Coffin Island	.50
059	Fort Point	.52
060	Medway Head	.53
061	Port Medway	.54
062	Mosher Island	.55
063	West Ironbound Island	.56
064	Battery Point Breakwater	.57
065	Cross Island	.58
066	Gunning Point Island	.59
067	Westhaver Island	.60
068	Kaulbach Island Range	.61
069	Quaker Island	.61
070	East Ironbound Island	.62
071	Pearl Island	.64
072	Indian Harbour	.65
073	Peggy's Point	.66
074	Betty Island	.67
075	Terence Bay	.68

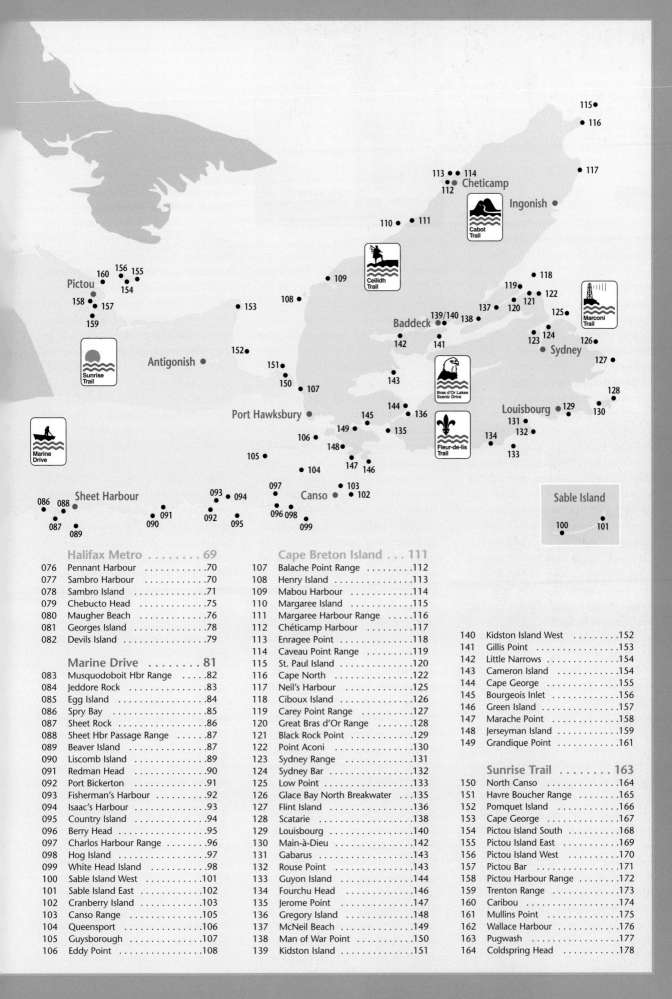

Sable Island

Halifax Metro 69

076 Pennant Harbour 70
077 Sambro Harbour 70
078 Sambro Island 71
079 Chebucto Head 75
080 Maugher Beach 76
081 Georges Island 78
082 Devils Island 79

Marine Drive 81

083 Musquodoboit Hbr Range 82
084 Jeddore Rock 83
085 Egg Island 84
086 Spry Bay 85
087 Sheet Rock 86
088 Sheet Hbr Passage Range 87
089 Beaver Island 87
090 Liscomb Island 89
091 Redman Head 90
092 Port Bickerton 91
093 Fisherman's Harbour 92
094 Isaac's Harbour 93
095 Country Island 94
096 Berry Head 95
097 Charlos Harbour Range 96
098 Hog Island 97
099 White Head Island 98
100 Sable Island West 101
101 Sable Island East 102
102 Cranberry Island 103
103 Canso Range 105
104 Queensport 106
105 Guysborough 107
106 Eddy Point 108

Cape Breton Island . . . 111

107 Balache Point Range 112
108 Henry Island 113
109 Mabou Harbour 114
110 Margaree Island 115
111 Margaree Harbour Range 116
112 Chéticamp Harbour 117
113 Enragee Point 118
114 Caveau Point Range 119
115 St. Paul Island 120
116 Cape North 122
117 Neil's Harbour 125
118 Ciboux Island 126
119 Carey Point Range 127
120 Great Bras d'Or Range 128
121 Black Rock Point 129
122 Point Aconi 130
123 Sydney Range 131
124 Sydney Bar 132
125 Low Point 133
126 Glace Bay North Breakwater . . .135
127 Flint Island 136
128 Scatarie 138
129 Louisbourg 140
130 Main-à-Dieu 142
131 Gabarus 143
132 Rouse Point 143
133 Guyon Island 144
134 Fourchu Head 146
135 Jerome Point 147
136 Gregory Island 148
137 McNeil Beach 149
138 Man of War Point 150
139 Kidston Island 151

140 Kidston Island West 152
141 Gillis Point 153
142 Little Narrows 154
143 Cameron Island 154
144 Cape George 155
145 Bourgeois Inlet 156
146 Green Island 157
147 Marache Point 158
148 Jerseyman Island 159
149 Grandique Point 161

Sunrise Trail 163

150 North Canso 164
151 Havre Boucher Range 165
152 Pomquet Island 166
153 Cape George 167
154 Pictou Island South 168
155 Pictou Island East 169
156 Pictou Island West 170
157 Pictou Bar 171
158 Pictou Harbour Range 172
159 Trenton Range 173
160 Caribou 174
161 Mullins Point 175
162 Wallace Harbour 176
163 Pugwash 177
164 Coldspring Head 178

Preface

Five Islands lighthouse

I SERVED IN the Royal Canadian Navy from February 1951 until my retirement from the service as chief petty officer first class in 1975. During that time, I served on ten different warships, and nothing ever stirred me so much as the first glimpse of the Sambro lightship or Sambro Island lighthouse after a lengthy time away. From that moment, I anticipated the warmth of my home and loving family more eagerly than in all the preceding days and nights, when everything in the world was always just over the horizon.

I often wondered about lighthouses and the people who manned them, especially wave-swept towers such as the Eddystone lighthouse at the approaches to Plymouth, England, and the Bell Rock lighthouse located about 17 nautical miles off the entrance to Scotland's Firth of Tay and Dundee. Although lighthouses always seemed somewhat mysterious, and often conjured up visions of stormy seas and heroic deeds, I must admit I had not much more than a passing interest in them until 1985, when I first became aware of automation and the de-staffing of lighthouses. Thinking that this meant lighthouses would cease to exist, I decided to spend the summer photographing them while they were still around.

Of course, I soon learned that automation didn't necessarily mean the end of the lighthouse—not right away anyway. However my interest had been sparked and the summer project turned into an eight-year odyssey. I had not realized that there were over 160 lighthouses in Nova Scotia alone, 68 of them on islands. The more of them that I got to see, the more I became obsessed with the idea of actually touching and photographing every one. This was finally accomplished with my landing on Flint Island in October 1993. I had visited 53 of the islands all alone in a 4.25-metre Zodiac, and camped on many of them for several days and nights. I must have looked suspiciously like a drug-runner to the Coast-Watch people, because on a few occasions I was stopped by the RCMP, Coast Guard, and once by a Fisheries and Oceans officer. The funny part was that the drug-runners probably thought I was a member of the Coast Guard or police. Looking back, it seems that every trip was an adventure, and despite being scared out of my wits a few times, I think of those trips as some of the best times of my life.

I have visited hundreds of lighthouses in these last 17 years, photographing, researching, and recording everything I can find on them. The history and lore of the lights continues to fascinate me, and I am bound and dedicated to their preservation. In 1993, three friends, Patricia MacDonald, Chris Mills, Graham McBride, and I founded the Nova Scotia Lighthouse Preservation Society and I became its first president. One of our first projects, and the one for which I am most proud, was having Sambro Island lighthouse, at the approaches to Halifax Harbour, recognized as the oldest lighthouse in North America, and successfully lobbying to have it listed on the National Register of Historic Buildings.

Subsequent to being designated a "classified building," it was listed by the International Association of Lighthouse Authorities as one of the world's one hundred most important lighthouses.

With ongoing automation, de-staffing, and divestiture of lightstation buildings and effects, as well as rapid technological changes in optics and fog alarms, I couldn't record every-thing that has happened to each lighthouse over the years. Some of the descriptions and photographs may already be somewhat different from how they would appear now. In fact, some lighthouses may no longer exist at all. This book is meant to be "a snapshot in time," a record of our lighthouses that will serve as a benchmark for what will be changed, what will be lost, and what will be preserved for future generations. What is a lighthouse and what is simply a light? My definition of a lighthouse would be "a structure supporting a light in a lens contained within a glazed lantern room for the purpose of providing the mariner aid to safe navigation." What about a skeleton mast or a fibreglass tower with a bare waterproof lamp on top? These I call simply "lights." Some people agree with me, others don't—it is not easy to get a consensus on the subject. The book is titled *Lighthouses and Lights* to show that there is an arguable distinction. As for which of the sites here are lighthouses and which are lights, I leave that for you, the reader, to decide according to your own definitions.

If you have never given a thought as to the purpose of lighthouses, their construction, the lightkeepers' lives or how they kept the lights, the historic significance or the lore of the lights, a visit to almost any lighthouse site will invariably reward your effort with a spectacular view of the sea and coastline.

Before you visit a lighthouse, consider the weather, tides, and the state of the sea. The information that I have provided regarding lighthouse visits, including directions, does not imply in any way that you have the right to access any property or site described in this book. I recommend that you always seek permission to enter lands or property to which access may be limited.

Happy lighthouse hunting.

Introduction

IT SEEMS WE ARE NOW entering the final years of the age of lighthouses, an era for which the chronological base was established in 280 B.C., when the world's first lighthouse was built in Egypt. The Pharos of Alexandria was 30 metres square at the base, rising to a height of 137 metres, with an open fire burning at the top that could be seen 47 kilometres away. Its massive size rivalled that of the Great Pyramid, and like the pyramid, was considered to be one of the seven wonders of the ancient world. It stood for over 1,500 years, until it was toppled by an earthquake early in the thirteenth century. Actually, two of the seven wonders of the ancient world were lighthouses. The other was the Greek Colossus of Rhodes, a 30-metre-tall bronze figure of Apollo, his legs astride and feet planted on piers at each side of the harbour entrance and one arm reaching upward holding a torch 50 metres above the harbour. Legend has it that the statue was hollow and one could walk up into its head and look out its eyes. Built in about 280 B.C., this structure lasted only about 56 years, when it fell during an earthquake in 224 B.C. However, some scholars dispute that fires were kept burning in its eyes or that the torch was ever a flaming beacon, and argue that there is no evidence to justify its inclusion among ancient lighthouses.

The Romans built about 30 lighthouses around the coasts of Europe, but as the Empire declined toward the end of the fifth century, anarchy reigned and eventually all lights were extinguished by pirates and raiders. It wasn't until near the end of the sixteenth century that a regularly maintained system of lights was re-established on Europe's coastline. The remains of one of the ancient Roman lighthouses still exist in England within the Dover Castle. The oldest operating lighthouse in the world is also one of the Roman lights, Corunna, on the northwest coast of Spain. Built in the third century, it is most often referred to as the Tower of Hercules. It suffered the same fate as all others at the fall of the Roman Empire, but the tower survived. Although no light was shown from it for hundreds of years, in 1682 it was restored as a lighthouse, and by virtue of this alone, qualifies as the world's oldest.

The first North American lighthouse was built on Little Brewster Island in Boston Harbour in 1716. During the American Revolution, while Boston was occupied by the British, American troops burned the tower. Repairs were attempted, but when the British fleet sailed from Boston in 1776, they blew up the lighthouse tower, totally destroying it. The stone tower that stands in its place today was completed in 1783 at a cost of £1,450. The second lighthouse in North America, the first in Canada, was built by the French at Louisbourg in 1734. Fire almost destroyed it in 1736, but it was rebuilt and a new, improved lantern was added. In 1758, during a siege, British bombardment so severely damaged the lighthouse that it was considered to be beyond repair. By the time a new one was built here in 1842, there were already 14 others strategically placed along the Nova Scotia coast, including one on Sambro Island, built in 1758. The second Louisbourg lighthouse was destroyed by fire in 1922, and the current tower, the third, was built in its place in 1923. The ruins of the two previous lighthouses have been stabilized and preserved by the Historic Sites and Monuments Board of Canada, and interpretive plaques were erected at the sites.

Because of the unfortunate circumstances that caused the destruction of the lighthouses in Boston in 1776, and Louisbourg in 1758, Sambro Island lighthouse became the oldest operating lighthouse in North America and remains so to this day.

In August 1996, an evaluation of the Sambro Island lighthouse and gas house was completed by the Federal Heritage Buildings Review Office. As a result, the lighthouse is now designated as a classified building—a federal building to which the minister of the environment has assigned the highest possible heritage designation. The gas

Seal Island lighthouse

house, although not nearly so highly rated, was nevertheless designated as a recognized building, the second highest heritage designation.

By 1835, there were 18 lighthouses in the Maritime provinces, 10 in the Bay of Fundy and 8 on the Atlantic coast. By Confederation, in 1867, there were 53 lighthouses lighting the 7,443 kilometres of Nova Scotia's coast, and in the decade that followed, when shipbuilding flourished, the number almost doubled, even into the Minas Basin, where high tides flooded the most unlikely looking mud flats with enough water to float the largest vessels of the day—for instance, the *William D. Lawrence*, which was built in 1874 at Maitland, and was the largest full-rigged ship ever built in Canada and probably the largest wooden sailing ship in the world at the time. Lighthouses were necessary to guide such vessels safely into harbours and anchorages, great ships such as the *E.J. Spicer* and the *Glooscap*, the *George T. Hay*, and, of course, the *Mary Celeste*, made famous because of the mysterious disappearance of its entire crew. On December 5, 1872, the ship was found at sea under full sail with not a living soul aboard, and so remains one of the great unsolved mysteries of the sea.

By the mid-1950s, over 350 lights lit the coast of Nova Scotia, including 170 conventional lighthouses and range lights of wood or concrete construction, Sambro Island lighthouse being the only remaining stone tower.

In 1968, the auditor general observed that too much money was being spent on the operation of lighthouses, and shortly thereafter, automation and de-staffing began. Some lighthouses were even taken out of service. With advanced technology, lighthouses were brought up to date with new equipment and remote monitoring systems,

resulting in less need for lightkeepers on many of the stations. In 1972, only 62 lightstations remained manned and in three years, from 1976 to 1979, the number of lighthouse keepers was reduced from 213 to 143, mostly through attrition, which meant 16 stations were de-staffed at that time. And so it went. By 1985, there were only 40 manned lightstations, in 1987 only 25 were still manned, 5 in 1990 and by 1993, there were no manned lightstations in Nova Scotia—whether we liked it or not.

Today, only one lightstation in the Maritimes remains manned, on Machias Seal Island, 10 nautical miles west of Southwest Head, Grand Manan Island, New Brunswick—and this only because of an ongoing territorial dispute with some residents of the state of Maine. They claim ownership of the lighthouse even though Canada first built one there in 1832 and has manned it continuously ever since.

Although we appear to be in the final years of operational lighthouses, the age of lighthouses has not yet passed, and they must not be allowed to slip into the hands of time. There are landfall lights, major and secondary coastal lights, and, to a greater extent, the little pepper-shaker harbour lights. Not all are as impressive or as old as Sambro, but each and every lighthouse is important in its own way and each has a story to tell. Every community lucky enough to have a lighthouse has a responsibility to work for its preservation.

No two lighthouses are exactly the same, but they each have one very significant thing in common, each is an important link to our past and embodies the maritime history of our country. We need to do whatever we can to save them.

Glooscap Trail

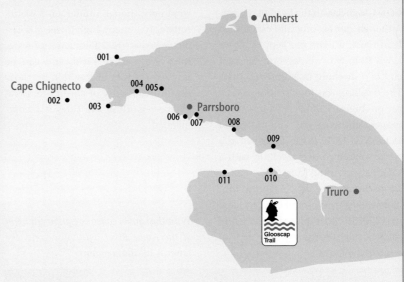

Amherst

001

Cape Chignecto

002 003 004 005

Parrsboro

006 007 008

009

011 010

Truro

Glooscap
Trail

001 Apple River 2
002 Ile Haute 2
003 Cape d'Or 3
004 Spencers Island 4
005 Port Greville 4
006 Cape Sharp 5
007 Parrsboro 6
008 Five Islands 7
009 Bass River 8
010 Burntcoat Head 9
011 Walton Harbour 10

Apple River

Ile Haute

001 The vicinity of Cape Capstan was once considered to be the only safe anchoring place from Cape Chignecto to the head of the bay. Although not an officially established lighthouse, a light was kept by Gaius Lewis from two windows on the west end of a dwelling in as early as 1848. The dwelling was totally destroyed by fire on August 9, 1869, at which time a proper lighthouse was built and lit on October 1, 1870. It was described as a white, oblong, wood dwelling with a square tower rising from the roof, and surmounted by an octagonal iron lantern. Just over a hundred years later, in 1972, it was replaced by a white square cement tower on the corner of a square building.

With the advent of automation and de-staffing, the lighthouse building was torn down, leaving only the somewhat ugly, though utilitarian, 3-metre-square, 10.7-metre-high tower. It is easily viewed across 2 kilometres of water from West Apple River, and can be reached on foot at low tide by those possessing a sense of adventure. Local advice regarding the tides is recommended.

With the square concrete equipment room of the Apple River lighthouse gone, the tower is all that remains.

002 This lighthouse was established on land that was discovered by Champlain in 1607 and named Ile Haute, meaning "high island." Located about 10 kilometres SSW of Cape Chignecto, it is only 2.8 kilometres long by about 0.8 kilometres wide, with cliffs over 96 metres high. There is evidence that the island was visited by pirate Edward Lowe in the early 1700s, and in June 1952, Edward Snow, an American historian, found a human skeleton and eight Spanish doubloons there.

In 1878, Captain Nelson Card became the first to keep the light in the original lighthouse: a square tower with sloping sides, 16 metres base to vane, with a dwelling attached.

APPLE RIVER

ESTABLISHED:	1870
CCG LIGHT #:	163
POSITION:	45° 28' 24.5" N
	64° 51' 25" W
	On Cape Capstan
LIGHT:	Flashing white;
	F0.5/E3.5
AHW:	21.6 metres
NOM. RANGE:	6 nautical miles
HORN:	None
DESCRIPTION:	White square tower,
	10.7 metres high

This utilitarian tower replaced the original Ile Haute lighthouse after it burned down in October 1956.

Cape d'Or

Unfortunately, the lighthouse was destroyed by fire in October 1956 and was replaced by the utilitarian 12.2-metre steel skeleton tower that is still there today. This new light was fuelled by acetylene gas, a reliable illuminant that required no lightkeeper, thus John Fullerton was the last to keep the light. Today, one can still see the old lighthouse foundation, along with the broken remains of the long-focus catoptric (reflector-type) optic, which came crashing down through the burning tower to the depths of the basement below.

Day trips to the island can generally be arranged during the summer months from Harbourville, on the south side of the bay, or from Advocate Harbour on the north side.

003 A steam fog-whistle was put into operation here in 1874. The tall, iron smokestack gave mariners a bearing while negotiating the 6-knot tidal current around the cape in daylight, but a light was needed after dark.

Finally, in 1922, a 6.7-metre-tall pepper-shaker-type tower was moved from Eatonville to Cape d'Or, where it was mounted on a 2.5-metre-high red wooden trestle about 30 metres away from the fog-alarm building. The lightkeeping duties were taken over by Malcome McLeod.

The present-day lighthouse, unmanned since 1989, continues to flash its warning across the waters from a modern 250-millimetre airport beacon. Every year, thousands of visitors visit the site and enjoy the panoramic view from the headland, which rises 152 metres above the bay. The cape has been designated an international biological site, mainly because an arctic-alpine plant and several other rare species grow there. It is also a breeding habitat for many birds, including the peregrine falcon. One of the ex-keeper's dwellings now features a gift shop and a dining room called the Keepers Kitchen. For those discriminating guests who might appreciate peace and solitude under the rotating beam of a lighthouse, overnight accommodation can be provided in the second keeper's dwelling.

At Advocate, on Route 209, a sign points the way to Cape d'Or. Follow the twisting gravel road eight kilometres to the lighthouse.

ILE HAUTE	
ESTABLISHED:	1878
CCG LIGHT #:	164
POSITION:	45° 15' 02.5" N
	65° 00' 22.2" W
	Highest point of
	the island
LIGHT:	White flashing; F0.5/E3.5
AHW:	108.5 metres
NOM. RANGE:	Unknown
HORN:	None
DESCRIPTION:	Skeleton tower,
	12.2 metres high

CAPE D'OR	
ESTABLISHED:	1922
CCG LIGHT #:	167
POSITION:	45° 17' 30" N
	64° 46' 32" W
	End of the point
LIGHT:	White flashing light
	every 7.5 seconds
AHW:	24.1 metres
NOM. RANGE:	16 nautical miles
HORN:	B2, S3, B2, S3, B2, S48
DESCRIPTION:	White square tower on
	corner of square building

Photo of Ile Haute circa 1900.

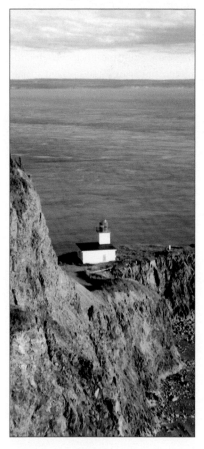

Cape D'Or lighthouse as seen from the top of the 152-metre headland.

Spencers Island

004 Spencers Island was a great shipbuilding port between 1861 and 1920. Over 30 deep-sea sailing vessels were built and slid down the ways here, including the *Glooscap*, which at 1,549 tonnes was the largest ship ever built in Cumberland County, and the brigantine *Mary Celeste*, found in 1872 near the Azore Islands under full sail and with the crew missing. A cairn near the lighthouse commemorates the *Mary Celeste* and gives a brief account of the ship's life.

Built near the water's edge by day labour at a cost of $645.87, the lighthouse was put into operation on July 15, 1904, under the care of Baxter McLellan, its first lightkeeper. The illumination apparatus was a seventh-order, 200-millimetre lens with a single-wick Aladdin's lamp.

When the lighthouse was taken out of service in 1987, a well-known local historian, Stan Spicer, led the community in acquiring it, and played a leading roll in its restoration and preservation. In 1995, it was opened as a museum, displaying pictures and other items that reflect the local Loyalist and shipbuilding heritage.

Turn off Route 209 at Spencers Island settlement. The lighthouse is right on the beach.

Spencers Island lighthouse now serves the community as a museum open to the public during the summer months.

SPENCERS ISLAND	
ESTABLISHED:	1904
CCG LIGHT #:	168
POSITION:	45° 21' 24" N
	64° 42' 38" W
	Spencer Island
	settlement
LIGHT:	Fixed white
AHW:	10.4 metres
NOM. RANGE:	8 nautical miles
HORN:	None
DESCRIPTION:	White pepper-shaker-type
	tower, 9.1 metres high

Port Greville

005 The site for the Port Greville lightstation was bought for $194.70, and for an additional cost of $790, John D. Reid of Wallace Bay, Nova Scotia, built the lighthouse. It was considered an essential aid to vessels and scows loading lumber and pulpwood, and gave support to the flourishing Wagstaff and Hatfield shipyard. The first lightkeeper was Ernest A. Hatfield, who was appointed in January 1908 at $180 per year.

When the shipyard closed in the mid-1970s, and with other marine activity failing, the Coast Guard discontinued the light. In 1981, the tower was sawed in half and trucked away to the Coast Guard College at Point Edward in Cape Breton, where it was restored as a very attractive centrepiece to an assortment of lights and buoys scattered around the grounds of the college.

It was fortunate that the lighthouse had not been entirely destroyed because when the Greville Bay Heritage

Port Greville lighthouse as it is now, at the Age of Sail Heritage Centre in Wards Brook.

Cape Sharp

Association opened the Age of Sail Heritage Centre nearby at Wards Brook in May 1995, it decided that the lighthouse would be a marvellous addition to the complex. The Coast Guard graciously donated the lighthouse, and with a lot of hard work by dedicated members of the association, it was brought back home and officially opened to the public in August 1998.

The Age of Sail Heritage Centre, including the Porthole Tearoom, is located right on Route 209 in the community of Wards Brook. This very interesting complex is a testament to what a small community can do to preserve the glory of its past. Well worth a visit.

006 Cape Sharp is so named because of its high elevation of 116 metres and extraordinarily sharp contours that project out into the Minas Channel at its narrowest point. From the lighthouse site, you can enjoy an unimpeded view of the Cape Split promontory looming up only 4.5 kilometres across the channel, and to the southeast, you can see the Blomidon Peninsula, the eastern end of the North Mountain Range.

Robert J. Ward, the first keeper of this light, lived in reasonable comfort, for the times, in a square two-storey dwelling attached to the square lighthouse. Eighty-seven years later, in 1973, a modern new bungalow was built for the lightkeeping family of

In 1973, this lighthouse was built to replace the original 1886 lighthouse. A new bungalow was also built for the lightkeeping family at that time, but it is now gone from the site.

PORT GREVILLE	
ESTABLISHED:	1908
CCG LIGHT #:	170
POSITION:	45° 24' 24" N
	64° 33' 02" W
	Bank of the shoreline
LIGHT:	Fixed red light
AHW:	18 metres
NOM. RANGE:	5 nautical miles
HORN:	None
DESCRIPTION:	White wooden pepper-shaker-type tower, 7.6 metres high

CAPE SHARP	
ESTABLISHED:	1886
CCG LIGHT #:	171
POSITION:	45° 21' 53" N
	64° 23' 34" W
	South extremity of the cape
LIGHT:	White occulting; F7/E3
AHW:	18.3 metres
NOM. RANGE:	11 nautical miles
HORN:	B4, S56
DESCRIPTION:	White wooden pepper-shaker-type tower, 10.7 metres high

Victor and Betty Elliott, and the new freestanding pepper-shaker-type light tower that is still there today. Victor and Betty left the station when it was de-staffed in February 1989, after 24 years of service. Shortly after, the dwelling was removed from the site, and today, only the tower and fog-alarm building remain.

It is only 1.3 kilometres to the lighthouse via a narrow gravel road from West Bay south of Parrsboro. Please note that it is very steep and must be hiked.

Parrsboro

007 A petition presented to Lieutenant-Governor Sir John Harvey in 1852 succeeded in getting a lighthouse built at Parrsboro to guide vessels into safe anchorage, there being no other between it and Apple River.

The beautiful original octagonal timber-frame tower with dwelling attached was soon occupied by the first lightkeeper, James R. Howard, and his family. Unfortunately, the entire station was built on the extremity of a sand and gravel spit, and in spite of elaborate and extensive breastworks, gales and high tides frequently caused severe damage, undermining the lighthouse until it was eventually destroyed in about 1945. A temporary pole light was installed at this time, and subsequent lights were shown from a skeleton tower, until the current lighthouse

Despite the construction of extensive breastworks to protect it, this beautiful 1852 timber-frame lighthouse at Parrsboro eventually succumbed to erosion caused by the extremely high tides of the Minas Basin.

PARRSBORO	
ESTABLISHED:	1852
CCG LIGHT #:	172
POSITION:	45° 23' 13.4" N
	64° 19' 01.8" W
	At entrance to harbour.
LIGHT:	Fixed green light
AHW:	8.4 metres
NOM. RANGE:	8 nautical miles
HORN:	B3, S27
DESCRIPTION:	6.4-metre-high square concrete tower on corner of square building

There were thirteen lighthouses built in this style in Nova Scotia, mostly in the 1960s.

was built in 1980. The lantern was installed by helicopter in 1983. The last keeper, Ronald A. Wood, kept this light from 1963 until it was de-staffed in 1987.

From 1827 to 1837, Abraham Gesner, a physician with a great love for geology and a fascination with the local coast, lived in Parrsboro, where he began the work that would lead him to the discovery of a means of distilling kerosene from coal. This fuel burned cleaner and brighter than any other illuminant in use at the time, revolutionizing the lighting of lighthouses worldwide.

The lighthouse can be viewed from either side of the harbour. On the west side, you can drive to the end of the

Five Islands

spit and walk out to the lighthouse. It is easiest to do this at low tide, but caution is advised if you plan to attempt to walk on top of the rock breakwater.

Parrsboro lighthouse. Note the airchime fog alarm trumpet on the gallery deck. The small window below the trumpet contains the sperrygraph fog detector that controls the fog horn automatically.

008 Glooscap, the mighty legendary figure of the Mi'kmaq, reigned from atop Cape Blomidon and controlled the Bay of Fundy tides, the highest in the world. According to legend, five islands were created when Glooscap, angry at Beaver, threw handfuls of sod at him; where the sod landed, the five islands came to be. In order from the farthest offshore, they are Pinnacle, Egg, Long, Diamond, and Moose islands.

The lighthouse tower that is still at the site today was built in 1914 under contract to A. L. Mury of West Arichat at a cost of $750. The first keeper, Cyrus MacBurnie, was hired at $115.67 per year.

The erosion of the bright red cliffs

The Five Islands lighthouse just before it was moved away from the eroding bank that threatened to topple it into the bay.

along this shore necessitated moving the tower in 1952 and again in 1957. When the Coast Guard finally extinguished this light in 1993, it was once again perilously close to being toppled by erosion. When a winter storm in 1995/96 caused the concrete retaining wall to collapse, the loss of the lighthouse appeared imminent. However, a

FIVE ISLANDS	
ESTABLISHED:	1914
CCG LIGHT #:	174
POSITION:	45° 24' 02" N
	64° 04' 08" W
	On extremity of
	sand point
LIGHT:	Flashing red light,
	now extinguished
AHW:	13.1 metres
NOM. RANGE:	6 nautical miles
HORN:	None
DESCRIPTION:	White wooden
	pepper-shaker-type tower,
	10.1 metres high

community group led by Ronald MacBurnie, whose family had kept this light for 50 years, and Anita Murphy came to the rescue. The lighthouse was purchased by the community, and on November 23, 1996, it was once again moved to a safe place on campground property about 80 metres from the shore.

Five Islands Provincial Park affords a wonderful view of the lighthouse and islands. Alternatively, turn off Route 2 on Sand Point Road and drive 2.2 kilometres to the lighthouse. Property owner Barry Walker says visitors are welcome during the summer months, but he asks that this private property be respected.

Bass River

009 Cobequid Bay continues to narrow significantly from Bass River to the head of the basin 30 kilometres to the east. Even fishermen and other local mariners are extremely careful here because of the numerous shifting sandbanks that dry at low tide. The lighthouse, then, was considered to be of vital importance. The first lightkeeper, David Vance, was appointed on October 24, 1907.

In recent years, due to a combination of the downturn in the fishery and a harbour plagued by tides that limit access to just a few hours of high water each day, the lighthouse was used less and less. This led to a de-activation of the light in about 1992, and shortly after it was declared surplus. In 1994, it was sold to private interests and attractively re-modeled as a cottage for the owners' use.

Heading west on Route 2, turn left about 400 metres past the Bass River fire hall onto Wharf Road. It is 1.6 kilometres to the beach near the lighthouse. Please respect private property.

The lighthouse at Bass River was originally a free-standing pepper-shaker-type tower that was deactivated and sold to private interests. Still on the original site, the building has been renovated to provide the owner with a beautiful summer home.

BASS RIVER

ESTABLISHED:	1907
CCG LIGHT #:	177
POSITION:	45° 23' 42" N
	63° 46' 54" W
	Point on west side
	of river mouth
LIGHT:	Fixed white light,
	now extinguished
AHW:	12.5 metres
NOM. RANGE:	Unknown
HORN:	None
DESCRIPTION:	White wooden
	pepper-shaker-type tower,
	9.8 metres high

Burntcoat Head

010 This site is proclaimed to have the highest tides in the world, rising 14.3 metres at neaps and 16.6 metres at spring tides. The first lighthouse was a square wooden dwelling with a square tower attached to the end. Its first lightkeeper, Nathan Smith, and all subsequent keepers would have witnessed the rise and fall of these mighty tides, which eroded the narrow neck of land around the lighthouse until it was eventually cut off from the mainland and could only be reached by climbing up the bank with a ladder. In 1913, it was torn down and some of the timbers were used to build a new lighthouse 152 metres to the east—a square wooden dwelling surmounted by an iron lantern.

The appointment of William Faulkner as keeper in August 1874 began a dynasty of Faulkner lightkeepers here, except for one 14-year period, ending in 1949. When William Bub Faulkner retired in 1949 after 31 years of service, the grateful government gave him a medal and a monthly pension of $12.08.

By 1972, the lighthouse had fallen into such a state of disrepair that it was purposely burned down and replaced

BURNTCOAT HEAD

ESTABLISHED:	1859
CCG LIGHT #:	No longer an active aid to navigation
POSITION:	45° 18' 37" N 63° 48' 25" W Northwest extremity of head
LIGHT:	None
AHW:	23 metres
NOM. RANGE:	Unknown
HORN:	None
DESCRIPTION:	White square wooden dwelling surmounted by a lantern, 11.88 metres base to vane

with a skeleton mast, then discontinued altogether a few years later. In 1992, when the Fundy Shore Ecotour was being developed, a community group led by Charlie McCulloch built a replica of the lighthouse on the same site as the 1913–1972 lighthouse, which opened to the public on Canada Day (July 1) 1995. A very pleasant picnic area and walking trails have also been developed around the site.

To get to the lighthouse, take the Burntcoat Loop off Route 215 at the community of Noel and watch for the sign.

This is a replica of the second Burntcoat Head lighthouse, 1913–1972, at the site of the highest recorded tides in the world. It is open to visitors during the summer months.

Walton
Harbour

011 On November 1, 1872, when this lighthouse was first lit, Timothy Parker had the distinction of being not only the first lightkeeper, appointed at $91.66 a year, but also the man that built it, at a cost of $620.

Walton was a busy and important small harbour where ships could load 2,250 tonnes of gypsum and barites between tides, as well as pulpwood and lumber. The lighthouse was needed to guide vessels into harbour when tides allowed. At high tide, there is a variable depth of water between 4.6 and 8.2 metres, but at low tide, a sand bar at the entrance dries out to a distance of 2 kilometres. In 1978, the gypsum quarry closed and commercial shipping stopped, marking the end of an era. The last lightkeeper, Arthur Sanford, extinguished the light, and in 1986 it was declared surplus and listed for disposal.

Then along came Ted Burgess and local historian Reg Clark to the rescue. After several years of lobbying, they were successful in acquiring the property, and in 1992 the lighthouse received heritage status. After a good deal of hard work, the lighthouse has been restored and developed into an interpretation centre with a nicely landscaped picnic area that is open to the public.

The lighthouse is easily located in the village of Walton at the end of Wier Road.

WALTON HARBOUR	
ESTABLISHED:	1872
CCG LIGHT #:	No longer an active aid to navigation
POSITION:	45° 14' 02" N 64° 00' 44" W East side of the mouth of the Walton River
LIGHT:	None
AHW:	18.3 metres
NOM. RANGE:	Unknown
HORN:	None
DESCRIPTION:	White wooden pepper-shaker-type tower, 9.4 metres high

There's an extraordinarily wonderful view of the tidal flats from the lantern room of this lighthouse at Walton Harbour. The lighthouse and picnic grounds are open to visitors during the summer months.

Evangeline Trail

012	Mitchener Point	12
013	Horton Bluff	12
014	Black Rock	13
015	Margaretsville	13
016	Port George	14
017	Hampton	14
018	Prim Point	15
019	Digby Gut	16
020	Victoria Beach	16
021	Bear River	16
022	Schafners Point	17
023	Annapolis	17
024	Boars Head	18
025	Grand Passage	19
026	Brier Island	19
027	Peter Island	20
028	Gilbert Point	21
029	Belliveau Cove	22
030	Church Point	22
031	Cape St. Mary	23
032	Cape Forchu	23
033	Bunker Island	26

Evangeline
Trail

Mitchener Point

Horton Bluff

012 The first lightkeeper to man this seasonal beacon was William A. Curry, who was appointed on June 15, 1908, at $180 per year. The original lighthouse was a square wooden tower, 12.8 metres high, with sloping sides. It showed a fixed white light from the lantern; a second light, fixed red, was shown from a window lower down the south side of the tower to mark the exact turning point for outbound vessels. The current light tower was erected in 1972, and although the colour of the lights has changed, they still serve the same purpose.

Look for the lighthouse road off Route 1, about 2.8 kilometres southeast of Hantsport on the west bank of the Avon River, directly across from the mouth of one of its tributaries, the Kennetcook River. Large tides in this

area make the river navigable as far as the town of Windsor, but as sea trade has diminished significantly, it is little used.

013 Situated on the west side of the Avon River, this light is visible in clear weather over the greater part of Minas Basin after passing Cape Blomidon, and is of great importance to mariners navigating by the numerous mud banks at this location. When Robert King became the first keeper, the light was simply shown from an upstairs window of his dwelling; there was no lighthouse. It is interesting to note that when the second keeper of this light, Charles E. Rathburn, died in 1879, his widow took over the lightkeeping duties. Four years later, in April 1883, the dwelling burned down. Five months later, a proper lighthouse was built with a beautiful little dwelling attached, in which Mrs. Rathburn lived and kept the light until 1921. The last keeper, William A. Crosby, recalls the

final days of the old lighthouse: after 78 years of service, its useful life ended; it was unceremoniously pushed over the cliff and burned.

Two new dwellings and a modern square concrete lighthouse were built in 1961, spelling the end of an era at Horton Bluff, when the lighthouse was also the lightkeeper's family home.

The lighthouse is just off Route 1, about 6 kilometres north of Hantsport.

HORTON BLUFF	
ESTABLISHED:	1851
CCG LIGHT #:	188
POSITION:	45° 06' 30.7" N
	64° 13' 31.2" W
	On bluff
LIGHT:	Fixed green light
AHW:	26.8 metres
NOM. RANGE:	Unknown
HORN:	B3, S27
DESCRIPTION:	White square concrete tower, 8.7 metres high, on square building with red vertical stripe

MITCHENER POINT	
ESTABLISHED:	1908
CCG LIGHT #:	186
POSITION:	45° 02' 38" N
	64° 08' 47" W
	On point of land west side of Avon River.
LIGHT:	Flashing red top light; fixed red lower light.
AHW:	23.5 metres
NOM. RANGE:	Unlisted
HORN:	None
DESCRIPTION:	Red circular fibreglass tower with two white horizontal bands, 9.1 metres high.

[TOP] In this picture of the 1883 lighthouse at Horton Bluff, the lightkeeper's daughter appears to be waiting on the gallery of the lighthouse tower for the arrival of her suitor, approaching in his surrey. Her mother waits at the gate either to greet him or to deny him entry; another daughter sits in the doorway, witnessing the event.

[LEFT] In 1961, this lighthouse replaced the one that was built in 1883 at Horton Bluff.

Black Rock   Margaretsville

014 This fibreglass tower is one of 14 currently in use in Nova Scotia. It is very different from the square wooden dwelling that served as a lighthouse and home to John Crotty from 1848 until he retired in July 1872 at 80 years old. He was succeeded by James Robinson, who served until 1885, and then by Charles Robinson, stretching the Robinson years of service to over 60 years. The old lighthouse showed a fixed white light from eight oil lamps fitted with 300-millimetre reflectors, from a three-sided bow window in the roof of the dwelling. This lighthouse served until 1967, when it was replaced by the existing light.

From Route 101, take Exit 15, drive north to Harbourville, then east to Black Rock.

Note the colour scheme of this Black Rock tower compared to that at Mitchener Point. This makes them easily identifiable from seaward in daylight hours.

BLACK ROCK	
ESTABLISHED:	1848
CCG LIGHT #:	193
POSITION:	45° 10' 12.8" N
	64° 45' 44.8" W
	South shore of
	Minas Channel
LIGHT:	White flashing light,
	F1/E2/F1/E8
AHW:	14.8 metres
NOM. RANGE:	10 nautical miles
HORN:	None
DESCRIPTION:	White circular fibreglass
	tower, 10.4 metres high,
	with two red horizontal
	bands

015 In 1859, Margaretsville was an important railway terminus connected by rail to all parts of the province and by steamboat service to Saint John, New Brunswick—but it needed a lighthouse. Along came Sir Brenton Halliburton, who donated the land on which a lighthouse was built to serve as a coast light and a leading mark for the harbour. There being no accommodation within the lighthouse, William Early, the first lightkeeper, lived in his own home about

The Margaretsville lighthouse, well appointed to receive visitors.

MARGARETSVILLE	
ESTABLISHED:	1859
CCG LIGHT #:	195
POSITION:	45° 03' 00" N
	65° 04' 00" W
	On extremity of point.
LIGHT:	White occulting light,
	F10/E3/F4/E3
AHW:	9.1 metres
NOM. RANGE:	12 nautical miles
HORN:	None
DESCRIPTION:	Square wooden tower
	with sloping sides and
	a wide black horizontal
	band, 9.4 metres high

one kilometre away. When his son John assumed the duties in 1887, he apparently renovated the second floor of the lighthouse to provide himself with quarters during bad weather.

Originally, to distinguish the light from others nearby, the Margaretsville lighthouse showed two lights—a white light over red—but being only a metre apart, they could not be clearly seen from a distance. Consequently, the lighthouse was moved and fitted with a new, improved iron lantern 2.4 metres in diameter and five oil lamps with 300-millimetre reflectors for greater range. The characteristic of the light was changed to fixed red. The oil lamps were converted to electric in 1960, and the characteristic was changed again, to white occulting. Shortly after, the light was de-staffed and the last lightkeeper, Gordon Aldred, was out of a job.

It is doubtful that anyone who visited this community with a camera ever left without photographing the lighthouse, so with tourism in mind, a community group added to the lighthouse's appeal by building a deck around the tower with benches to sit on and steps down to the beach. This lighthouse, the only one in Nova Scotia with a black horizontal band, bears a striking likeness to the one depicted on Canada's five-cent centennial (1967) postage stamp.

Take Exit 18A from Route 101 and drive north to Margaretsville.

Port George

Hampton

016 Showing a fixed green light from a catoptric apparatus, this lighthouse was erected on the outer end of the eastern pier and put into operation under the care of John McAndrew on April 1, 1888. It turned out to be like an April Fool's joke, however, because the dangerous condition of the western pier meant the lighthouse had to be moved to shore before its first year anniversary, and in the following March, it was moved back to its position on the eastern pier. At some unknown date, it was moved once again to its permanent position tight against the roadway. With both piers long gone and nothing but a launch ramp nearby, one wonders at the need for this lighthouse; however, it is a highly visible symbol of the community's marine heritage and worthy of preservation for generations to come.

From Exit 18 on Route 101, go north to Port George.

From Exit 18 on Route 101, go north to Port George.

PORT GEORGE

ESTABLISHED:	1888
CCG LIGHT #:	196
POSITION:	45° 00′ 25″ N
	65° 09′ 22″ W
	Near the haul-up slip
LIGHT:	Fixed red light
AHW:	9.4 metres
NOM. RANGE:	6 nautical miles
HORN:	None
DESCRIPTION:	White wooden pepper-shaker-type tower, 7.6 metres high

017 In late autumn 1911, contractor J. F. Titus of Hampton was putting the finishing touches on a new lighthouse, anticipating the appointment of its first keeper, Hebert Foster. The cost of the lighthouse was $585, not counting the cost of the site and inspection fees. Foster was appointed on December 2, 1911, at $190 per year.

The same lighthouse exists today, overlooking one of the most picturesque and snuggest little harbours on the Fundy shore. At Chute Cove, small vessels enter through a very narrow passage between two breakwaters into a haven where they can lie in perfect safety. At high tide, with the harbour at full flood, it is difficult to imagine that at low tide it dries completely and vessels lay aground. The phenomenon of tides can best be appreciated if you have the opportunity to visit long enough to see the harbour at both full flood and low water.

Hampton is 11 kilometres north from Route 1 at Church Street in Bridgetown.

HAMPTON

ESTABLISHED:	1911
CCG LIGHT #:	198
POSITION:	44° 54′ 20″ N
	65° 21′ 10″ W
	About 150 metres from the NE corner of the western breakwater
LIGHT:	Fixed white light
AHW:	21 metres
NOM. RANGE:	11 nautical miles
HORN:	None
DESCRIPTION:	White wooden pepper-shaker-type tower, 10.1 metres high

At the Hampton lighthouse, overlooking one of the prettiest and snuggest little harbours you are ever likely to see.

Prim Point

018 This important lighthouse guards the west point of the Digby Gut, a narrow opening 900 metres wide leading into Annapolis Basin. Although light lists indicate that a lighthouse was established here in 1817, there was, in fact, a lighthouse at this location in 1804, kept by J. Oliver, making it the first Nova Scotia lighthouse built in the nineteenth century, and the third after Sambro Island and Cape Roseway. Unfortunately, it burned to the ground in 1808. Although an earlier session of the General Assembly had granted a sum of £300 for the support and lighting of a lighthouse, and the House of Assembly had resolved that it should be applied toward replacing the

PRIM POINT	
ESTABLISHED:	1817
CCG LIGHT #:	201
POSITION:	44° 41' 28" N
	65° 47' 13" W
	Digby Gut, west point
	of entrance to
	Annapolis Basin
LIGHT:	Isophase white light,
	F3/E3.
AHW:	24 metres
NOM. RANGE:	13 nautical miles
HORN:	B3, S27
DESCRIPTION:	Square white concrete
	tower on corner of square
	concrete building; red
	vertical stripe on each
	side of the tower

destroyed lighthouse, it was not until 1817 that it was finally built. By this time, four other lighthouses had been constructed, making Prim Point the seventh in order of seniority. It was a square dwelling with a pentagonal lantern at its north end, and painted white with red vertical stripes on the north end and two sides. Richard Bragg was keeper of this light from 1821 until 1839, and was succeeded by his son

Frederick Bragg for another 33 years, until 1872, for a total of 51 years under the care of the Bragg family.

This lighthouse was destroyed by fire on March 16, 1873. It was replaced the following year by a square wooden tower with sloping sides and a dwelling attached. The same red vertical stripes adorned this lighthouse, making it appear, from a distance, the same as the previous lighthouse. As with the Bragg clan, another dynasty emerged to tend this lightstation for another 88 years—the Ellis family, beginning with Captain William Ellis in March 1875 and ending with Janet Wilson, the daughter of Leander Ellis, Captain William Ellis's son. For 29 years, she shared the lightkeeping duties with her husband, Frank Wilson, until he passed away in May 1963. As a point of interest, Captain Ellis discovered a comet in July 1887, which is known to this day by astronomers worldwide as the Ellis Comet.

A tragedy occurred on December 3, 1883, when the government steamship *Princess Louise*, while under tow by SS *Newfield*, broke its tow and was driven onto the rocks about two kilometres west of the lighthouse. Of the ten crew members, only two were rescued by the lightkeeper's son Leander. In 1914, another vessel, the sailing ship *Donahoe*, was wrecked near the lighthouse while trying to pass the point in a wicked howling nor'easter.

[ABOVE] *Marking the entrance to Annapolis Basin, this lighthouse served at Prim Point from 1874 until it was replaced in 1964.*

[LEFT] *Notice that this current lighthouse at Prim Point uses the same vertical red stripe daymark as its predecessor, and the one before that.*

The last keeper, Carman Frankland, kept the light from June 1963 until the lighthouse was destaffed in 1987. During that period, he saw many changes take place. Once an efficient, fully staffed, operational station, the station became automated then became unmanned. May 13, 1964, was a very sad day, Frankland recalls, because that's when a huge bulldozer pushed the venerable 90-year-old lighthouse over the bank—another piece of our historic past gone forever. The square concrete lighthouse of today is the same one that went into service in 1964.

There's easy access to the lighthouse by road. Drive north from Digby, along the shore road to the point.

Digby Gut

Victoria Beach

Bear River

019 Originally established with a fog bell on the balcony of a building, the Digby station had no light until 1963, when one was shown from atop a steel skeleton mast on the north end of the building, where it continues to shine to this day. In 1980, the fog bell was changed to an electronically operated horn.

The light is situated 1.2 kilometres north of Victoria Beach, where there's a pathway to a very steep bank down to the light. However, the road to the bank is a right-of-way through private property so permission should be sought to proceed.

A very steep path leads down to this light. The helicopter landing pad seen here makes life a little easier for the maintenance crew. Doesn't much resemble an aid to navigation, but the light and electronic horn seen mounted on the mast just below the light serves the purpose.

DIGBY GUT	
ESTABLISHED:	1915
CCG LIGHT #:	202
POSITION:	44° 41' 17" N
	65° 45' 37" W
	On the east side of
	the Digby Gut
LIGHT:	Fixed white light
AHW:	13.4 metres
NOM. RANGE:	Unknown
HORN:	B1, S14
DESCRIPTION:	White rectangular
	wooden building

020 The lighthouse at Victoria Beach was built by John Roney at a contract price of $497 on land nine metres above high water and 30 metres from the water's edge. It was put into operation on July 8, 1901, with James Hinds as the first keeper.

Visible from all points of approach by water, this light serves as a guide through the gut, and shows the way for small vessels seeking passage into the sheltered basin at Victoria Beach. Because of the extremely high tides and the narrow width of the gut, there's a strong current of four to five knots at both ebb and flood tides, so mariners find the lighthouse is also a useful guide

VICTORIA BEACH	
ESTABLISHED:	1901
CCG LIGHT #:	203
POSITION:	44° 40' 33" N
	65° 45' 15" W
	On the east side of
	the Digby Gut
LIGHT:	Occulting green light,
	F6/E4
AHW:	18.3 metres
NOM. RANGE:	6 nautical miles
HORN:	None
DESCRIPTION:	White wooden
	pepper-shaker-type tower,
	9.4 metres high

in avoiding the numerous eddies and whirlpools created by the swift current.

From Annapolis Royal, drive along the north shore of Annapolis Basin to the village of Victoria Beach.

021 John Roney, the same contractor that built Victoria Beach lighthouse, also built the Bear River lighthouse but for $494 (three dollars cheaper). It was built on the

point at the western entrance to Bear River. William Hunt was appointed the first keeper on April 10, 1905, at $150 per year.

With tourism in mind, local residents have done much to preserve the tower and enhance the site. A trail has been cleared, and stairs with landings have been built from the tower down to the water's edge 13 metres below.

About five kilometres east of Digby, take Exit 24 from Route 101 to Route 1, where a railway bridge and a highway bridge cross the Bear River. From here, if you look carefully, you should be able to see the lighthouse. Continuing about 400 metres from the stop sign, you should find a narrow lane and a short walk gets you to the lighthouse.

BEAR RIVER	
ESTABLISHED:	1905
CCG LIGHT #:	208
POSITION:	44° 37' 00" N
	65° 41' 07" W
	On Winchester Point
LIGHT:	Fixed red light
AHW:	21 metres
NOM. RANGE:	Unknown
HORN:	None
DESCRIPTION:	White wooden
	pepper-shaker-type tower,
	9.8 metres high

Schafners Point

Annapolis

022 This lighthouse was needed to mark the treacherous Goat Island shoals. Goat Island divides the Annapolis River into two channels—Schafners Point being the deepest one. However, the shoal, which dries at low tide, almost surrounds the island to a distance of about 730 metres, thus decreasing the navigable channel to something considerably less than it appears at high tide. The lighthouse was put into operation on September 24, 1885, and lightkeeping duties were assumed by Joseph R. Healy.

From the community of Granville Ferry, proceed west 11 kilometres to Port Royal National Historic Park, a reconstruction of the first permanent white settlement in Canada, established by Samuel de Champlain in 1605. All the buildings on the 8-hectare site have been faithfully reproduced in every detail, right down to the oak main gate and its Judas peephole.

SCHAFNERS POINT	
ESTABLISHED:	1885
CCG LIGHT #:	210
POSITION:	44° 42′ 35″ N
	65° 37′ 12″ W
	On the north side of
	the Annapolis River
LIGHT:	Fixed white light
AHW:	14 metres
NOM. RANGE:	6 nautical miles
HORN:	None
DESCRIPTION:	White wooden
	pepper-shaker-type tower,
	13.1 metres high

Right beside the roadway, there is an unencumbered view of the Annapolis Basin from this Schafner Point lighthouse.

Ask about the "Order of Good Cheer." The lighthouse is 800 metres from the park, right on the roadside.

023 This is the end of the line, so to speak—at least, the end of navigable waters, as there is a causeway and dam across the Annapolis River at this point. It is the site of the first tidal power project of its kind in North America.

The lighthouse was intended for vessels navigating the Annapolis River between Goat Island and Annapolis Royal. It was built at the water's edge

The Annapolis lighthouse is beside a boardwalk in a little park right on the main street of historic Annapolis Royal.

on the main street, on the site of the old Government House, which had burned down in 1833. The lighthouse was put into operation on July 30, 1889, with Michael Riordan its first lightkeeper.

Annapolis Royal was the most fought over place in the history of this country. Between 1630, when a new French fort was built here, and 1710, it changed hands between the French and English no less than five times and suffered several attacks by the Indians and pirate raiders. Until Halifax was

Boars Head

024 Petit Passage, between Digby Neck and Long Island, is just 400 metres across at its narrowest point, making it very difficult to see from seaward without a lighthouse to mark the entrance. The passage is important because it shortens the distance for vessels bound to and from the

---

ANNAPOLIS

ESTABLISHED:	1889
CCG LIGHT #:	211
POSITION:	44° 44' 40" N
	65° 31' 13" W
	Northeast of
	the government pier
LIGHT:	Fixed red
AHW:	9.1 metres
NOM. RANGE:	8 nautical miles
HORN:	None
DESCRIPTION:	White wooden
	pepper-shaker-type tower,
	8.5 metres high

founded in 1749, Annapolis Royal was the capital of Nova Scotia. Over 150 heritage buildings exist in this beautiful old town, including Fort Anne, a National Historic Site with battlements, moats, and ramparts; a museum and historical library in a reproduction of the British officers' quarters; and a powder magazine built in 1708, the oldest building in Canada outside Quebec.

Annapolis Royal is at the intersection of Route 1 and 8.

---

uated 15 metres from the edge of the cliff. Evidence of the old foundation can still be seen today. Henry M. Ruggles was appointed the first keeper in December 1864; he continued in this position for 37 years. Frank Ruggles followed him for another 29 years, until 1930.

Boars Head, so named due to the shape of the promontory on which it is built. Dual airchime horn emitters in foreground.

BOARS HEAD

ESTABLISHED:	1864
CCG LIGHT #:	216
POSITION:	Position 44° 24' 14.5" N
	66° 12' 55" W
	On the west side of the
	north entrance to
	Petit Passage
LIGHT:	Flashing white, F2/E10
AHW:	18.3 metres
NOM. RANGE:	12 nautical miles
HORN:	B2, S3, B2, S3, B2, S48
DESCRIPTION:	White wooden
	pepper-shaker-type tower,
	10.7 metres high

eastern parts of St. Mary's Bay by 10 to 15 nautical miles, and is the shortest route between Saint John, New Brunswick, and Yarmouth, Nova Scotia.

The first lighthouse to meet the need was a square wooden dwelling with a red iron polygonal lantern on the roof, ten metres high, base to vane, and sit-

The current lighthouse, built in 1957, can be seen as you approach the ferry wharf on Digby Neck. From the ferry that takes you across the passage, you'll recognize the distinctive animal profile of Boars Head, which is topped by the lighthouse. As you drive off the ferry, turn right and proceed a little more than a kilometre to the lighthouse. The last keeper, Angus Smiley, is no longer there to meet you and regale you with stories of his lighthouse-keeping days. One of the last lighthouse keepers in Nova Scotia, he accepted a transfer to Machias Seal Island, the last manned lighthouse in the Maritime Provinces, after Boars Head was de-staffed in September 1987.

Grand Passage

Brier Island

025 Leading into the communities of Freeport and Westport, this lighthouse marks the northwest side of the entrance to Grand Passage, a dangerous course through several ledges and shoals, made all the more hazardous by the 5- to 6-knot current created by the ebb and flow of the tides. When constructed in 1901, the lighthouse was a square wooden tower with sloping sides, painted white, and surmounted by an octagonal iron lantern painted bright red. It was built by Frank H. Piper of Westport for $897.50. A seventh-order dioptric lens cast a light eight nautical miles to all points of approach by water. Put into operation on January 12, 1901, Charles Buckman was appointed the first keeper and kept the light for over 40 years.

The old lighthouse was demolished in 1968 and the existing lighthouse was built in its place. Known locally as the North Light, it was kept for its last four years by Lawrence F. (Pete) Welch, who was born on Brier Island, and spent his whole life there. Considering that the first permanent settler was a man named Welch, it seems fitting that Pete was the last keeper on the island when the light was de-staffed in 1988. Pete laughingly told me that when he was a young boy, the lightkeeper had a lot of trouble with the fog bell at this station. When fog set in, the lightkeeper had to start the make-and-break engine that operated the machinery that rang the bell every five seconds in answer to a vessel's fog signal, but half the time he couldn't get the engine to start. He then had to go out on the rock with a huge mall and strike the bell by hand every five seconds until the vessel could find its way. This old fog bell is now mounted in front of the post office in Digby as part of a memorial to mariners who lost their lives at sea.

During the ten-minute crossing of Grand Passage on the ferry *Spray*, you can see Grand Passage lighthouse to the right, about 1.5 kilometres away, and to the left, Peter Island lighthouse about the same distance away. When you land from the ferry, turn right and follow the road to the Grand Passage lighthouse.

The waters around Brier Island are renowned as one of the best places in Nova Scotia for whale watching. These mammals can very often be seen cavorting near Grand Passage lightstation.

GRAND PASSAGE	
ESTABLISHED:	1901
CCG LIGHT #:	221
POSITION:	44° 17' 13" N
	66° 20' 31" W
	North point of
	Brier Island
LIGHT:	Flashing red light,
	F0.3/E9.7
AHW:	17.1 metres
NOM. RANGE:	12 nautical miles
HORN:	B3, S27
DESCRIPTION:	White square concrete
	tower on corner of white
	square concrete building

026 In 1806, the legislature of Nova Scotia granted the sum of £500 for the purpose of erecting a stone lighthouse on Brier Island. But two years later, after considering the state of the province, the government decided that a wooden lighthouse would probably do just as well and a sum of £200 was granted for that purpose. Five years later, another £100 was granted for the purpose of putting an iron railing around the top of the lighthouse to enable the keeper to clear

Known locally as "the western light," referring to the west side of Brier Island, this is the Brier Island light as it currently exists, with all the fog-alarm equipment fitted inside the tower.

snow and ice off the lantern. It is not clear who the first lightkeeper was, but a treasurer's account of February 27, 1811, shows that 47 pounds, 17 shillings, and 8 pence was paid to J. T. Hughes for lighting the lighthouse that year. One of the longest serving and more interesting lightkeepers was John Suthern, who kept the light from 1820 to 1883, a total of 63 years. He was given the position as a reward for good service in the Royal Navy. He had served in Admiral Nelson's fleet and later in the *Bellerophon*, the ship that carried Napoleon to exile on St. Helena Island. He was also the grandfather of Joshua Slocum, the first man to sail around the world alone.

The lighthouse was described as a white wooden octagonal tower, 16.8 metres high. In 1907, it was decided that the next time the lighthouse was painted, the tower should have three red bands to make it more visible in snowy weather. This lighthouse is known locally as "the western light," and is like a signpost of the sea, sepa-

BRIER ISLAND	
ESTABLISHED:	1809
CCG LIGHT #:	223
POSITION:	44° 14' 55" N
	66° 23' 32" W
	On the west point of
	the island
LIGHT:	White flashing,
	F2/E2/F2/E2/F2/E8
AHW:	29 metres
NOM. RANGE:	17 nautical miles
HORN:	B3, S3, B3, S51
DESCRIPTION:	White octagonal concrete
	tower with three
	horizontal red bands,
	18.3 metres high

rating the Bay of Fundy from the entrance to St. Mary's Bay on the south side of Digby Neck. This tower was destroyed by fire in February 1944. Later that year, the new lighthouse, as seen today, was completed.

The last lightkeeper of the western light was Gilbert Ingersoll. In 1966, he was appointed principal keeper with two assistants. In 1969, one assistant position was discontinued, then in 1979, the second one was cut, leaving Ingersoll alone to lament the passing of a way of life he had enjoyed for over 50 years—from 1936, when he was a 12-

year-old boy on Machias Seal Island, where his father was a lightkeeper, until 1987, when his own position became redundant after 21 years of keeping the light on the western end of Brier Island.

Westport is an important fishing port and has become a very popular centre for whale-watching tours. It is also home base to the Brier Island Ocean Study group, a registered charitable organization involved in whale research and educational programs. Brier Island is on the Atlantic flyway and the last landfall in western Nova Scotia. It is therefore a very popular gathering place for ornithologists, who list over 150 bird species annually.

From the ferry at Westport, turn left to about the centre of the village, then turn right onto Wellington Street and follow the road west out of the village for about 4.5 kilometres. Watch for signs.

027 This lighthouse was considered to be of great importance because it was situated where it could be seen from both ends of the passage. It was a large, two-storey dwelling with two dormer windows on each end of the roof, one looking north and the other looking south, and 7.3 metres apart. John D. Suthern was appointed keeper at £60 per year, with an additional £15 fuel allowance. He was also supplied with a 3.6-metre boat; the superintendent recommended that he be provided with a spy-glass, but it is not known whether he ever received one. Called the Westport lighthouse until about the turn of the century the name was changed to Peter Island, when W. Brooks of Digby built the current light tower in 1909 for $1,350. It has been known as such ever since.

Although the Peter Island light is described as flashing yellow, it seems to have more of an orange glow to it.

South Point is as close as you can get to Peter Island without a boat, but is close enough to be able to enjoy an unobstructed view of the island and lighthouse. There is a terrible current that streams through this narrow passage to the north at flood tide and to the south at ebb tide. The first thing you will probably notice on the point

Gilbert Point

PETER ISLAND

ESTABLISHED:	1850
CCG LIGHT #:	227
POSITION:	44° 15' 26" N
	66° 20' 16" W
	South entrance to
	Grand Passage
LIGHT:	Flashing yellow, F2/E3
AHW:	18.9 metres
NOM. RANGE:	8 nautical miles
HORN:	B2, S18
DESCRIPTION:	White wooden octagonal
	tower, 13.4 metres high

028 Built under contract by John Roney of Granville Ferry for the price of $1,193, Gilbert Point lighthouse was put into operation on August 18, 1904. The first keeper, Joseph W. Melanson, was paid $300 per year and faithfully kept the light until his death. His daughter Louise then assumed the duties and kept the light through the difficult years of World War Two.

As the age of sail came slowly and painfully to an end, and nothing came into the cove but an occasional trawler, some recreational sailboats, or sports fishermen in small open boats, there was really no more need for a light-

GILBERT POINT

ESTABLISHED:	1904
CCG LIGHT #:	231
POSITION:	44° 29' 42" N
	65° 57' 12" W
	On the extremity of
	the point
LIGHT:	Fixed red light
AHW:	12.2 metres
NOM. RANGE:	7 nautical miles
HORN:	None
DESCRIPTION:	Square wooden lantern
	rising from the red roof
	of a square wooden
	dwelling, 11 metres high

is the beachstone cairn with a bronze plaque honouring Captain Joshua Slocum, the first man to sail around the world alone. Westport was his boyhood home and first port of call in 1895, when he started his solo voyage of over 46,000 miles. Note that the ferry to Brier Island is named for Captain Slocum's ten-metre sloop *Spray*, in which he made his epic voyage.

For 12 years, until the light was automated in April 1984, Pete Welch acted as keeper. When he was a young boy, in about 1948, the old *Mohawk* used to run from Saint John to Yarmouth. Welch remembers "times when the fog was so thick you could bottle it, when the lightkeeper would hear her coming, and when she would blow her horn, he would take his big, square, hand-operated horn on top of the hill and pump it to blow in answer to the vessel's signal. Bring her right into the passage." In his day, the light and horn were controlled from a small building on South Point. The architectural feature that makes this lighthouse different from every other in Nova Scotia is the round gallery deck instead of the customary octagonal deck on an octagonal tower.

Turn left off the ferry and drive 1.5 kilometres to South Point.

The Gilbert Point lighthouse is designated an Historic Property, lovingly restored to display pictures and historic items pertaining to the service it provided. Inside, there's a small gift shop and tea room.

house. In about 1975, the lighthouse was discontinued and a skeleton tower was built nearby to show a light.

In 1982, the local communities came together to create the Gilbert Point and District Historical Society under Ernest Morrisey as president. After considerable restoration, the lighthouse has been designated a provincial heritage property and was opened to visitors in the summer of 1985. Inside, you will see pictures, documents, charts, drawings, and artifacts relating to the glorious shipbuilding era and history of this small community. There is also a small tea room and gift shop inside.

Off Route 101, just 1,200 metres down a gravel lane. Stop by, visit the lighthouse, have a picnic, look at the bay, sense the past, relax, and enjoy yourself.

Belliveau Cove

Church Point

029 Who better to be appointed first keeper of this light in Belliveau Cove than John H. Belliveau on February 16, 1889, at the princely sum of $80 per year?

BELLIVEAU COVE	
ESTABLISHED:	1889
CCG LIGHT #:	No longer listed
POSITION:	44° 23' 20" N
	66° 03' 45" W
	On the end of
	the east pier
LIGHT:	Fixed green
AHW:	7.3 metres
NOM. RANGE:	4 nautical miles
HORN:	None
DESCRIPTION:	White wooden
	pepper-shaker-type tower,
	6.7 metres high

There were small harbour lights all along the east shore of St. Mary's Bay in the early years of the twentieth century, but as the need for them diminished, they were extinguished, one by one, and Belliveau Cove light was gone before the Groundhog Day gale of 1976, which blew away the lighthouse at Sissiboo, 6 kilometres away.

The light was not, however, to remain unlit and lost to the community. It is now in the care and control of a concerned group of residents. It has been restored and is maintained in very good condition, an integral part of this well-protected and scenic little harbour.

The lighthouse is easily found within the village, just 100 metres off Route 1.

030 The original lighthouse was built by G. S. Parker at a contract price of $650, and described as a square wooden building 6 metres high, topped by a red iron 12-sided lantern.

CHURCH POINT	
ESTABLISHED:	1874
CCG LIGHT #:	235
POSITION:	44° 19' 55" N
	66° 07' 38" W
	East side of
	St. Mary's Bay.
LIGHT:	White occulting, F6/E4
AHW:	11 metres
NOM. RANGE:	11 nautical miles
HORN:	None
DESCRIPTION:	White wooden
	pepper-shaker-type tower,
	9.4 metres high

It was put into operation on September 25, 1874; Jeremiah McLaughlin was its keeper at a yearly salary of $200. There was no accommodation within the lighthouse, so McLaughlin lived in his own house some distance from the light. The following year, $500 was approved for the lightkeeper to build a dwelling attached to the tower. It is not known how well he managed, but after four years McLaughlin resigned and his job went to John H. Saulnier, who kept the light for 40 years. Accommodation was much improved in 1884, when

Church Point, the only lighthouse on a university campus in Canada. Too bad they don't take more pride in it.

two unfinished rooms upstairs in the dwelling were finally made habitable, much to the benefit of the family.

In about 1953, the dwelling, now 78 years old, was removed. The light was made unwatched, then discontinued altogether in 1984.

Church Point boasts the only French language university in Nova Scotia, Sainte Anne University, which in turn boasts the only university campus in Canada with a lighthouse. It has even named its campus newspaper *Le Phare de la Pointe* (Lighthouse Point). In 1986, after some successful fundraising projects by the university, restoration work began on the lighthouse. However, it didn't amount to much, and as late as 2000, the lighthouse was still in very poor condition, certainly not something of pride for the university.

Church Point can hardly be missed because standing right beside Route 1 is the largest wooden church in North America, which soars a full 56 metres into the sky and can be seen from many kilometres away. From Route 1, take Lighthouse Road 900 metres through the university campus to the lighthouse.

Cape St. Mary

Cape Forchu

031 The first lighthouse was a wooden octagonal tower 15.8 metres high, built on Cape St. Mary, where it would serve as a coastal light, guiding vessels into the bay, as well as those using Grand Passage and Petit Passage through the Digby Neck. This lighthouse also warns of a rocky ledge that dries at low tide and extends about 365 metres southward from the extremity of the cape, and a heavy rip tide that extends over one kilometre south-southwest. The lightstation consisted of a 7-metre by 10-metre dwelling a short distance from the light tower, and a good size barn. Maturin Robichau was appointed keeper in July 1868 at $516.38 per year.

For a short time in 1969, until the old lighthouse was torn down, the station

the cliffs are steep and range up to almost 20 metres in height. Care must be taken, especially if you have children or pets with you.

CAPE ST. MARY	
ESTABLISHED:	1868
CCG LIGHT #:	241
POSITION:	44° 05′ 9.2″ N 66° 12′ 39.6″ W East side of the bay
LIGHT:	Flashing white, once every five seconds
AHW:	27.4 metres
NOM. RANGE:	Unknown
HORN:	B4, S56
DESCRIPTION:	White square concrete tower on the corner of a white square concrete building, 8.7 metres high

was blessed with two lighthouses, the old timber-frame wooden tower and the new square concrete tower.

There is a shallow lagoon close by that dries a distance of about 500 metres at low tide— an excellent place to observe shore birds, especially during migration. The beach is a provincial picnic park.

Turn west off Route 1 at the village of Mavillette, which is about three kilometres from the lighthouse. Adjacent to the lighthouse property,

During migratory bird season, Cape St. Mary lightstation is a great vantage point from which to view the mud flats at low tide, alive with birds that provide quite a spectacle as they swarm and turn in the air at take-off and landing.

032 Cape Forchu, named by the French explorer Samuel de Champlain in 1604, means Forked Cape. It's actually an island surrounded by three different bodies of water, the Atlantic Ocean, the Bay of Fundy, and Yarmouth Harbour. It is now joined by a causeway to the mainland and accessible by car.

On March 16, 1839, the House of Assembly granted the sum of £250 to add to the £750 that had already been granted for the erection of a lighthouse at the entrance to Yarmouth Harbour. A temporary light was shown from 1839 until a permanent light was first lit on January 15, 1840, atop a beautifully proportioned, wooden, octagonal, timber-frame tower that stood 18 metres high. The first keeper was a Royal Navy pensioner, Commander James Fox, who died on March 27, 1840, only a few weeks after his appointment. His son, Cornelius John Thomas Fox, was subsequently appointed to the position and faithfully kept the light for 34 years.

In 1848, arrangements had to be made with Ezekiel Baker for the use of his land by the lightkeeper to obtain fresh water—the supply of which was limited and precarious in those days. The arrangement was authorized by the commissioner of lighthouses, provided it didn't cost in excess of £1 annually. Ezekiel Baker also petitioned for an annual remuneration for the use of the road that passed through his land to the lighthouse. It is not known if the arrangement was satisfactory to all concerned, but at one time there was a toll gate on the road to the lighthouse, and long after the gate was removed, the iron bolts could still be seen embedded in the large boulders that supported it.

Much to the chagrin of a vast number of people who would have preferred its restoration, the old light-

Two Crouse-Hinds 91.44-cm. airport beacons mounted vertically in the Cape Forchu lantern, offset in such a way that they provide a distinctive flashing characteristic as they revolve.

house was torn down after 123 years of service. Although the new tower, built in 1961, was less aesthetically pleasing to many, it did have its admirers. A striking design resembling, to some, an apple core, it is thought to be the second most photographed lighthouse in Nova Scotia, after Peggy's Cove.

Tens of thousands of ferry passengers see the lighthouse as they pass close by on one of the three ferries that operates between Yarmouth and Maine: the *Bluenose* to and from Bar Harbour, the *Scotia Prince* to and from Portland, and the *Cat* between Yarmouth and Bar Harbour. Able to travel at a speed of 88

kilometres per hour, the *Cat* is North America's first and fastest super car-ferry. Many ferry passengers, influenced by the scenic beauty, make the lighthouse their first stop in Yarmouth.

Two of the last regular lightkeepers, Lawrence Wentzell and Walter Goodwin, have both related stories to me of hurricane-force winds, when the only way they could move about outside was on hands and knees, with seas so high they swept up over the west side of the station and cascaded down the other side like a waterfall. Even in recent times, when the weather conditions haven't been so bad, several careless people were swept off the rocks into the sea—two of them to their death. Please be careful!

The lighthouse was de-staffed on July 1, 1993, and in 1994, a property lease was arranged by the Yarmouth County Tourist Association. Shortly after, Craig Harding and Gert Sweeney formed Friends of the Yarmouth Light Society and took over management of the station. After untold hours of toil, sweat, and tears—and thousands of dollars spent on restoration and preservation—they established a tea

[LEFT] *The original 1839 timber-frame Cape Forchu lighthouse.*

[BELOW] *The new Cape Forchu lighthouse has its admirers, and is probably the second most photographed lighthouse in Nova Scotia after Peggy's Point. It is one of only two hexagonal lighthouses in Nova Scotia.*

room and a gift shop in the newer lightkeeper's bungalow, and an impressive little museum in the old duplex dwelling. On June 1, 2000, at an international lighthouse conference at White Point Beach Resort in Nova Scotia, the Canadian Coast Guard transferred the ownership of an operating lighthouse to the municipality of Yarmouth. It was the first time such a transfer had ever been made.

From 1908 until 1962, the optic in this lighthouse was a second-order Fresnel lens, often described as beehive in shape, with eight panels containing 360 prisms, each geometrically different from the others, to refract and reflect 87 percent of the available light into a horizontal beam of great intensity. It is 1.4 metres in diameter, about 2.2 metres high, and weighs 1,500 kilograms. An absolute marvel of engineering and beautiful to behold, this lens can be seen in the Yarmouth County Museum.

To get to the lighthouse, find Route 304 out of Yarmouth and follow it south for about nine kilometres. Watch for signs.

Bunker Island

033 The Bug Light, as it is known locally, was built by Francis Ryerson. The original contract price of $2,875 to erect a pier and lighthouse on Bunker Island became $3,802.18 by the time it was put into operation on February 16, 1874, and Joshua Doane assumed the duties as lightkeeper at

BUNKER ISLAND	
ESTABLISHED:	1874
CCG LIGHT #:	263
POSITION:	43° 48' 44.5" N 66° 08' 36.5" W Southwest point of the island
LIGHT:	Fixed red
AHW:	9.8 metres
NOM. RANGE:	6 nautical miles
HORN:	B1, S14
DESCRIPTION:	White square concrete tower on corner of white square concrete building, 9.1 metres high, with red vertical stripe on the corner

$350 per year. The cost overrun was attributed to unexpected problems with building a cribwork about 7.3 metres high to support the small dwelling and tower. There was also a 4.6-metre station boat slung on davits attached to the top of the beacon.

Conditions at the station weren't ideal. The keeper lived in his own home on shore, but had to remain at the station at night and during rough weather in an upstairs room over the

oil stores. In 1885, a new dwelling had to be built upon the existing cribwork in an attempt to make it more habitable for the keeper and his family. Then in 1892, the cribwork was found to be rotten, so a new pier consisting of a steel cylinder filled with concrete had to be built, and the dwelling was moved onto it. A very good account of life on Bunker Island was written by Hazel B. Snow for the Atlantic Advocate in May 1965. She wrote about the Jules Cottreau family and how they spent 29 years, from 1930 to 1959, in this dwelling perched 7.6 metres above low water on a cylinder only 11 metres in diameter. The Cottreaus and their six children had to climb a vertical iron ladder to reach the dwelling—even their dog learned to climb the ladder. The Cottreau family often joked with people curious about their lifestyle by telling them that they raised all their vegetables on the Bug Light—with a block and tackle. When they retired in 1959, it was decided that a new lighthouse would be built but that it would no longer provide accommodation for a lightkeeper. This is the lighthouse that currently exists, although it originally had windows, and instead of a lantern atop the tower, there was a small skeleton mast. In 1984, the windows were closed in and the skeleton mast was replaced by a proper lantern.

This lighthouse, with its red vertical stripe, is clearly visible from the road out to Cape Forchu, but to get to it, go to the tiny community of Sand Beach, just south of Yarmouth, and look for a sign marked Bunker Island. Follow this single-lane dirt road about 700 metres to a gate where you can park, then walk five minutes to the lighthouse.

[BOTTOM] Also known as the "Bug Light," this new Bunker Island lighthouse in Yarmouth Harbour was built in about 1960. It can be reached on foot at low tide.

[TOP] The 1885 Bunker Island lighthouse had to be moved onto this new concrete-filled steel cylinder in 1892.

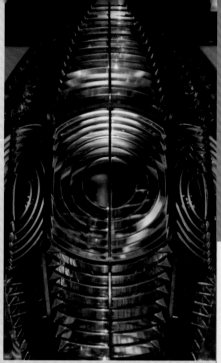

Lighthouse Route

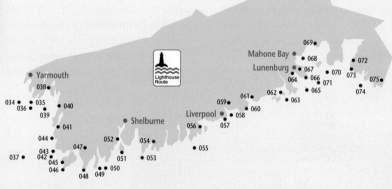

Lighthouse Route

034	Green Island	28
035	Candlebox Island	28
036	Pease Island	29
037	Seal Island	30
038	Tusket River	32
039	Whitehead Island	32
040	Abbott's Harbour	33
041	Pubnico Harbour	34
042	Bon Portage Island	35
043	Stoddart Island	36
044	Woods Harbour	37
045	West Head	37
046	Cape Sable	38
047	Seal Island Light Museum	39
048	Baccaro Point	40
049	The Salvages	41
050	Cape Negro Island	42
051	Cape Roseway	43
052	Sandy Point	44
053	Gull Rock (Lockport)	45
054	Carter Island	47
055	Little Hope Island	47
056	Port Mouton	48
057	Western Head	50
058	Coffin Island	50
059	Fort Point	52
060	Medway Head	53
061	Port Medway	54
062	Mosher Island	55
063	West Ironbound Island	56
064	Battery Point Breakwater	57
065	Cross Island	58
066	Gunning Point Island	59
067	Westhaver Island	60
068	Kaulbach Island Range	61
069	Quaker Island	61
070	East Ironbound Island	62
071	Pearl Island	64
072	Indian Harbour	65
073	Peggy's Point	66
074	Betty Island	67
075	Terence Bay	68

Green Island

Candlebox Island

034 Although a fog alarm was established at Green Island in 1919, it wasn't until 1964 that the lighthouse was built, which is surprising given the hazards of rocks, shoals, and ledges that lie within the general area. In particular, there is an exposed ledge that extends nearly 800 metres south of the island, and a bank with depths as little as one fathom, extending a further 800 metres.

GREEN ISLAND

ESTABLISHED:	1964
CCG LIGHT #:	272
POSITION:	43° 41' 22.8" N
	66° 08' 40.3" W
	Centre of island
LIGHT:	Flashing white, F2/E8
AHW:	25 metres
NOM. RANGE:	12 nautical miles
HORN:	B2, S18
DESCRIPTION:	White square tower on white square concrete building, 6 metres high

Green Island is not very large at 500 metres long by about 180 metres wide, with an elevation of 15 metres. The lighthouse is located at the highest point in about the middle of the island. There were two houses on the island until lightkeeper George Moulaison moved to Cape Forchu in 1981. These two dwellings were declared surplus and went to Crown Assets for disposal.

When it was determined that there were no prospects for the sale of either house, the RCMP was given permission to exercise their emergency response teams and demolition experts at the site. There is no sign of either dwelling today. Only the lighthouse and associated structures remain: a helicopter pad, fog-alarm building, solar equipment, and a battery room with a huge 2.75- by 8.5-metre solar array panel used to charge the batteries that operate the solar-powered light and electronic horn.

On a clear day, the lighthouse can be seen about 12 kilometres south of Cape Forchu. But for a closer view, it is usually possible to hire a boat at Pinkney Point Harbour to take you out to the island about seven kilometres away.

Although the dwellings and other buildings are gone from the Green Island lightstation, an addition was made to the lighthouse to contain the large bank of batteries and associated equipment needed to power the light and electronic fog horn. Note the large solar panel at the right of the picture and the fog-alarm trumpet on the gallery deck.

035 The original lighthouse was a square wooden tower with sloping sides, attached to a dwelling, and topped by a red iron lantern. Base to vane, it was 11.3 metres high. It was built on contract by John B. Porter of Belleville, Yarmouth County, at a cost of $2,248 and put into operation on February 1, 1893. The first lightkeeper was Benjamin LeBlanc, who was paid $300 per year.

One of the Tusket Island group, Candlebox is a round, low-lying island only about 70 metres in diameter, bounded on all but the western side by other islands such as Ellenwood, Owls Head, Turpentine, Eagle, Deep Cove, and Murder Island. Although the smallest of the group, Candlebox was considered the best place from which to show a light visible to vessels approaching either entrance of Schooner Passage, providing a strait lead through from the south.

CANDLEBOX ISLAND

ESTABLISHED:	1893
CCG LIGHT #:	280
POSITION:	43° 39' 44.5" N
	66° 02' 45.4" W
	North entrance to Schooner Passage
LIGHT:	Fixed red
AHW:	14.1 metres
NOM. RANGE:	8 nautical miles
HORN:	B3, S27
DESCRIPTION:	White square concrete tower on corner of white square concrete building, 11.6 metres high

After 70 years of guiding vessels through Schooner Passage, the old lighthouse gave way to a new modern structure, built just in time to welcome a new lightkeeper, Lester LeBlanc, from nearby Pease Island, in 1963. In 1981, Leforest (Huck) Norwood came to Candlebox as assistant keeper, and when Lester LeBlanc retired in 1985,

Pease Island

Like many locations, all that remains on Candlebox Island since automation and de-staffing is the lighthouse.

Huck became head keeper. As it turned out, he was the last keeper of this lighthouse, which was de-staffed on June 18, 1986. Norwood had a penchant for exercise, which he found most easily accomplished by jogging around the perimeter of the island 22 times a day, which, of course, is a great many laps over five years. An aerial photograph of the island taken two years after his departure clearly shows a well-worn path around the extreme outer edges of the island. The photo also shows there's nothing on the island but the lighthouse and helicopter landing pad.

The lighthouse can be seen 4.5 kilometres from the end of the road at Pinkney Point. Sometimes, given the right conditions, you might be able to persuade a local fisherman to take you for a tour of the islands.

036 Pease Island is one of the Tusket Islands group in Yarmouth County and was considered the best location for a lighthouse to guide vessels through the mass of islands and to mark the southern approaches to both Ellenwood Passage and Schooner Passage. It also marks dangerous rocks known as the Old Man and Old Woman. The Old Man, the largest of a cluster of rocks, becomes uncovered about one hour before low water, and Old Woman, near the centre of the shoal, becomes uncovered at about two hours ebb tide. Pease Island is almost 1 kilometre long with an average width of about 200 metres. Shallow saltwater ponds nearly bisect the island, and during stormy weather, the sea rolls completely across the middle and Pease Island effectively becomes two.

The lighthouse was built under contract by Israel Chute of Brookville for

PEASE ISLAND	
ESTABLISHED:	1879
CCG LIGHT #:	283
POSITION:	43° 37' 42.2" N
	66° 01' 38.5" W
	On extreme southeast
	point of the island
LIGHT:	Flashing white, F0.5/E5.5
AHW:	15.6 metres
NOM. RANGE:	7 nautical miles
HORN:	B3, S3, B3, S51
DESCRIPTION:	Round fibreglass tower,
	11.6 metres high

and a two-storey duplex dwelling were built in the early 1960s, described by the lightkeeper as "like a palace compared to the old place." The lighthouse was typical for the times, a square concrete tower on the corner of a square concrete building.

Since the station was de-staffed in 1986, it has fallen into a sad state of ruin and one cannot help but feel a

the sum of $1,848, and Thomas Baker was appointed keeper at $250 per year. The lighthouse was a square wooden tower with sloping sides, 12.8 metres high, and attached to the end of a rectangular dwelling. Like nearby Candlebox Island, a new lighthouse

This picture of Pease Island lightstation, taken in 1995, shows a large, 11.6-metre fibreglass freestanding tower. There are seven of these towers in Nova Scotia. Note also the large solar panel on the equipment room roof.

Seal Island

deep sense of melancholy for the loss of a way of life. Five or six dozen sheep occupy the island at the time of writing, and have pretty much made it their domain. Even the dwelling, having fallen victim to vandals and left to the elements, has been occupied by the sheep, who are no doubt happy for the shelter and bed down inside it at night. Who can blame them?

In about 1994, the tower was removed from the lighthouse building and replaced by a free-standing fibreglass tower with solar-powered light. The trumpet of a single Airchime electronic horn automatically emits its melodious warning out across the water.

A tour boat from Yarmouth takes passengers for a seaward view of five lighthouses in the area, including Pease Island. Check with the Yarmouth Tourist Bureau.

037 Seal Island, 31 kilometres west of Clark's Harbour, Cape Sable Island, is the largest of a group of five islands collectively known as the Seal Islands, originally named Iles aux Loups Marins by Samuel de Champlain in 1604. The other four islands are Mud, Round, Flat, and Noddy—all a continuation of the Tusket Islands to the north.

Seal Island, roughly 4.8 kilometres long by 1.6 kilometres wide, shares a reputation with Sable Island, Scatarie Island, and St. Paul Island, a killer of ships and for taking a horrendous number of lives— a graveyard of the Atlantic

This 1831 Seal Island lighthouse is the oldest timber-frame lighthouse in Nova Scotia, second oldest in all of Canada.

where lie hundreds of vessels of all shapes and sizes. One of the most compelling shipwreck stories concerns the British man-of-war, HMS *Blonde*, which in 1782 captured the American ship *Lyon* near Seal Island and took its crew members prisoner. No sooner had they set a course for Halifax on May 10, when the ship wrecked on the rock that

SEAL ISLAND	
ESTABLISHED:	1830
CCG LIGHT #:	289
POSITION:	43° 23′ 43″ N
	66° 00′ 48″ W
	South point of the island
LIGHT:	Flashing white,
	once every ten seconds
AHW:	31.1 metres
NOM. RANGE:	16 nautical miles
HORN:	B2, S3, B2, S3, B2, S48
DESCRIPTION:	White octagonal wooden
	tower with two red
	horizontal bands,
	20.7 metres high

now bears the name of its victim, Blonde Rock, about 5.6 kilometres south of Seal Island. Most of the 150 crew and 64 prisoners reached the shore, but, ironically, they were rescued by New England privateers, transported the British to the mainland in exchange for teh American prisoners' freedom.

Winifred Hamilton, a lifelong resident of Seal Island, compiled a list of 136 vessels known to have been lost on and around Seal Island. To be wrecked there in the winter months, before there were any people living on the island, meant certain death; those who made it to shore soon perished for lack of any kind of shelter. Mainland fishermen, on their first visit to Seal Island every spring, considered it their duty to gather all the bodies of the seafarers that were invariably found there, and give them a decent burial.

In 1823, two young families, the Hichenes and the Crowells, took it upon themselves to take up residence on Seal Island, in shacks that they built, and under deplorable conditions, to provide a lifesaving service. Ships were still wrecked there, but from the time these stalwart and determined families arrived, not a single shipwreck victim perished on shore. They successfully petitioned for a wharf that was built in

1827, and then immediately set out to have a lighthouse built. After several petitions to the government, they were successful in getting construction started in 1830 and the first light was lit on November 28, 1831. From that day, Richard Hichens and Edmund Crowell, for the first time, drew salaries of £30 annually. They took six-month turns keeping the light, thus allowing each family the opportunity to spend some time on the mainland.

The lighthouse is built on a rock foundation with 40-centimetre squared timbers, each 14.3 metres long, set upright at each of the eight corners to form an octagonal structure. Each side is 4 metres wide at the base, and 9.3 metres sloping to 4.1 metres in diameter at the gallery deck, and topped by a lantern 3 metres in diameter and 4.67 metres high. Base to vane, the tower is 20.7 metres high. The lantern deck is reinforced with heavy wooden natural knees, as seen in old wooden sailing ships. The entire tower is wood sheathed, cedar shingled, and painted white. In 1908, two 2.5-metre-wide red horizontal bands were painted on the top half of the tower to make it a more visible daymark, especially in winter when snow is on the ground. This lighthouse tower is the oldest wooden timber-frame lighthouse in Nova Scotia, and the second oldest in all of Canada.

Descendants of the island's first families continued to keep the light through several generations, ending with Winifred Hamilton (Crowell), daughter of John Crowell, who kept the light from 1899 to 1925 and was the great-grandson of Edmund Crowell, member of the original island family. Winifred remained on the island until her death in 1982, and her daughter, Mary (Hamilton) Nickerson, a direct descendant of Edmund Crowell, continued to live on the island year-round until the lightstation was finally de-

Most of the more powerful coast lights, such as on Seal Island, have installed these 91.44-centimetre double-ended rotating airport beacons in place of the first- and second-order Fresnel lenses.

The Fresnel lenses and pedestals were very heavy, requiring very strong support beneath them, such as these natural "knees" found in the service room below the lantern deck of Seal Island lighthouse. The same kinds of supports could be found in the hulls of sailing ships.

staffed. Her husband, James Nickerson, was one of the last rotational lightkeepers on the station.

There was no "last lightkeeper" on Seal Island. In 1986, the station went from having two resident keepers to using a four-lightkeeper rotational system. Two teams of two men each alter-nately served 28 days on and 28 days off. Chris Mills, Brian Stoddard, Lawrence Welch, and James Nickerson share the distinction of being the last to serve, when on October 17, 1990, after 160 years, Seal Island lighthouse became unwatched.

The fascinating and incredible story of Seal Island seems to have come full circle: it has gone from being totally uninhabited, through the building of a close-knit and vibrant island community with a church, school, general store, and lobster canning factory, back to being uninhabited again, at least during the winter months. It still comes alive in the springtime, however, when bird watchers and fishermen and their families come to visit, and during the summer, when those with summer homes come to stay.

Several good accounts about Seal Island have been written. Among them, an excellent book, *Vanishing Lights*, by fellow lighthouse enthusiast Chris Mills, who writes about his time as lightkeeper at the Seal Island light, and about other lighthouses in the Maritimes.

Trips can be arranged to Seal Island, but some advance planning is necessary. Contact either the Nova Scotia Lighthouse Preservation Society, or the Kenney family in Clark's Harbour.

Tusket
River

Whitehead
Island

038 Big Fish Island is located on the east side of the entrance to the Tusket River. A lighthouse was needed to guide fishermen and other small craft through the many low-lying islands and dangerous reefs in the vicinity, into the two narrow channels to Wedgeport and Lower Wedgeport Harbour. These channels are not deep and vessels are pretty much limited to those of 4.6 metres or less draught. There are not so many vessels now as there were in the years of the famous International Tuna Cup Match, which started in 1937 and continued until the

TUSKET RIVER	
ESTABLISHED:	1864
CCG LIGHT #:	294
POSITION:	43° 42′ 12.5″ N 65° 57′ 08″ W Southwest point of Big Fish Island
LIGHT:	White flashing, F1/E9
AHW:	18.6 metres
NOM. RANGE:	15 nautical miles
HORN:	B2, S28
DESCRIPTION:	White wooden pepper-shaker-type tower, 11.2 metres high

039 Whitehead Island is a treeless island located at the entrance to Argyle Sound, about 3.2 kilometres seaward from Abbott's Harbour. The original lighthouse was called the Argyle light and is still known locally by that name. The entire station was built and put into operation at a cost of $4,479.15. This included the lighthouse with dwelling attached, an oil store building, and boathouse. A 4.57-metre station boat was supplied at cost of $23, and the lucky lightkeeper was also provided with an $8 telescope. The lighthouse design was typical of many built around that time, and like all the others, leaked very badly, so the clapboard siding was replaced with cedar shingles, and shingles were recommended for all future construction. And, like on most islands, it was difficult to establish a freshwater well, so a system was devised to collect rainwater from the roof of the dwelling into a cistern in the basement. This became common practice on other islands and remained so until modern times.

All that remains of the Tusket River lightstation is the pepper-shaker-type lighthouse built on Big Fish Island in 1962 to replace the original lighthouse.

tuna became scarce in the early 1970s. The match was discontinued in 1976.

In November 1864, Joseph B. White was appointed as first keeper of this light, which was simply a dwelling with lights shown from two dormer windows 7.6 metres apart. The east-side window faced seaward, and the west-side window had a light looking up the river and a light looking out on the channel. In 1869, a combined boathouse and storage shed for the station boat was built at the northeast end

of the island, with a 400-metre road connecting it to the dwelling. In 1874, an oil shed was added to the station.

In 1962, a new pepper-shaker-type tower was built where the original lighthouse/dwelling stood, but today, all the other buildings are gone. Extensive repairs were done to the tower in 1995, so we can hope, though it is unwatched, that it will continue to show a light for many years to come.

Access by boat only or view the lighthouse from Lower Wedgeport Harbour, 1.6 kilometres away.

Isaac A. Montague was appointed first keeper on September 25, 1874. Unfortunately, he drowned the following year on October 13, while returning to the island from the mainland. H.H. Hamilton was then placed in temporary charge of the lightstation, and ended up serving there for 22 years until 1897.

When head keeper Reg Smith and assistant Walter Goodwin left the station after it was de-staffed in June 1986, there remained, besides the lighthouse, a square, two-storey dwelling, a bungalow-style dwelling, and a large shed, all in excellent condition. Attempts to sell these buildings at fair market value failed. Except for the 110-square-metre bungalow that was bought by Arnold D'Eon, they were all demolished. The condition of the sale was that the building had to be removed from the island, so D'Eon, with the help of two brothers and a friend, moved the dwelling down to the shore, loaded it onto a homemade barge hooked to their two boats, and towed it 20 kilometres up to Pubnico Harbour. It was reported that almost

everyone in the community lined the shores to witness this event. Even school students got part of the afternoon off to take in the sight.

Nothing is left on the island now but the lighthouse with all the necessary equipment contained within. A single Airchime trumpet mounted on the gallery deck provides a warning where the light cannot reach.

You can see the island and lighthouse from Abbott's Harbour, but you will need a boat if you want to get closer.

040 A lighthouse was required here to guide vessels into the narrow channel, which is less than 200 metres wide between Abbott's Harbour Island and the mainland, where there's an excellent and well-sheltered haven for small craft. Originally, there was just a small lantern hoisted temporarily on a mast 12 metres above high water on the south extremity of the island. In 1891, a permanent mast with a shed at its base was built at a cost of $125. Fishermen were dissatisfied with this light, however, so it was discontinued in 1897. A new location on the mainland at the south entrance to the

WHITEHEAD ISLAND	
ESTABLISHED:	1874
CCG LIGHT #:	295
POSITION:	43° 39' 45.6" N
	65° 52' 04.3" W
	On the south point
	of the island
LIGHT:	Fixed white
AHW:	30 metres
NOM. RANGE:	8 nautical miles
HORN:	B3, S27
DESCRIPTION:	White square concrete tower on corner of white square concrete building, 11.9 metres high

ABBOTT'S HARBOUR	
ESTABLISHED:	1884
CCG LIGHT #:	296
POSITION:	43° 39' 36.9" N
	65° 49' 14.1" W
	On the east side
	of the harbour
LIGHT:	Fixed green
AHW:	11.4 metres
NOM. RANGE:	8 nautical miles
HORN:	None
DESCRIPTION:	White wooden pepper-shaker-type tower, 9.6 metres high

harbour was thought to be more advantageous, so the light was moved again. Finally, in 1922, a disused lighthouse in Amherst, a simple wooden pepper-shaker-type tower, was moved to Abbott's Harbour to replace the pole light that had served the community for 38 years.

Guillaume Henry D'Entremont took this all in stride as he assumed the duties of keeping a lighthouse instead of the pole light, which he had done since May 22, 1888. The D'Entremont family kept this light for a total of 77 years, beginning with Garvaise D'Entremont, who was paid $20 for tending the pole light for the 1884 season. There hasn't been an official

Whitehead Island lightstation as it appeared in 1995, after automation, destaffing, and clearing off of the dwellings and all other auxiliary buildings.

Pubnico Harbour

keeper since John Joseph Surette finished in 1966, but the community keeps the lighthouse well maintained as part of a small picnic park called Parc du Phare.

To see the lighthouse, turn west onto a gravel road at West Pubnico and drive 1.5 kilometres to the park.

A nice little park and picnic area at the Abbott's Harbour lighthouse.

041 The original Pubnico Harbour lighthouse was a small dwelling with a small wooden lantern at one end. The lightkeeper, Maturin Amiero, and his family of eight suffered under very poor conditions and a lack of room at the lighthouse. Even the authorities acknowledged the terrible and cramped conditions. There was no cellar, nor could one be made. The oil for the light had to be kept in the dwelling, which further added to the discomfort. The keeper had to put up a small building, at his own expense, to use as a kitchen. His salary was £35 with a fuel allowance of £10—not enough for the basic necessities of life, let alone to try to improve the living conditions. The lighthouse stood on a narrow spit, which extend-

PUBNICO HARBOUR	
ESTABLISHED:	1854
CCG LIGHT #:	299
POSITION:	43° 35' 53.3" N
	65° 46' 55.5" W
	On beach point at east side of harbour entrance
LIGHT:	Occulting white, F6/E4
AHW:	12.2 metres
NOM. RANGE:	7 nautical miles
HORN:	B3, S3, B3, S51
DESCRIPTION:	Circular fibreglass tower, 11.5 metres high; the bottom half is white, the top half is red

ed a considerable distance into the harbour, and at high tide the water was within a couple of metres of the door, and storms always brought waves crashing against the house. As a result, the family couldn't keep a cow or have a garden. Water had to be brought in barrels by boat from the village more that a kilometre away, and, of course, there was no electricity. Realizing the lightkeeper's plight, the government granted him small amounts of money from time to time, and as he was also a carpenter, Amiero added rooms to the dwelling as his family grew, ending up with 22 rooms. In 1967, the station was finally taken down and replaced with a small square fog-alarm building with a skeleton tower on top to support the light.

In 1984, the skeleton tower was removed and replaced with a free-standing fibreglass tower that is aesthetically pleasing, at least. A bungalow was also built some distance up the hill from the lightstation, where the last lightkeeper, Merle Thomas, lived in comfort until the station was de-staffed on September 7, 1987.

Turn off Route 3 at the Yarmouth/Shelburne county line, which is marked with a sign, and drive on Lighthouse Road about 200 metres to a barrier for stopping vehicular traffic. Park here and walk about five minutes to the lighthouse.

A compact and functional lightstation, which is subject to flooding, at Pubnico Harbour. There is talk of closing it down and dismantling it.

Bon Portage Island

042 This light was meant to guide vessels into Barrington, West Bay, and Shag Harbour. Built on the south point of Bon Portage Island, the tower was a square wooden building with sloping sides, 8.5 metres high, and topped by a 10-sided iron lantern. The dwelling was attached to the lighthouse tower and a separate oil store building was built. The station was also provided with a 4-metre boat, and in 1878, a road was built from the lightstation to the landing, 1.2 kilometres away on the east side of the island.

The light was put into operation on November 25, 1874, with Arthur Wrayton as its first keeper, appointed at $350 per year.

Bon Portage Island, or "outer island" as it is known locally, was bought by Morrill Richardson, sight unseen, just before he and Evelyn Fox were married on nearby Stoddart Island in 1926. He also applied for the position of Bon Portage Island lightkeeper on the advice of Evelyn's brother, Ashford, who believed the position was about to become vacant. In 1929, Morrill was appointed, and he, Evelyn, and their baby, Anne, moved onto the island and together assumed the lightkeeping duties. In 1945, Evelyn Richardson wrote We Keep a Light, in which she gave a detailed account of the island, the lightstation, and the remote way of life that she, her husband, and their three children experienced. For all their years on the island, there was no electricity, which made life a bit difficult, but of greater necessity, she wrote, was a telephone or some other means of communicating with the mainland in times of emergency. The book won the Governor-General's Award for creative non-fiction, and although Evelyn Richardson went on to write several more books, We Keep a Light remains her most popular work and was reprint-

BON PORTAGE ISLAND

ESTABLISHED:	1874
CCG LIGHT #:	307
POSITION:	43° 27' 23.2" N
	65° 44' 36.2" W
	On the south point
	of the island
LIGHT:	Flashing white, F0.3/E9.7
AHW:	14 metres
NOM. RANGE:	16 nautical miles
HORN:	B2, S18
DESCRIPTION:	White square concrete
	tower on corner of white
	square concrete building,
	12.2 metres high

ed in 1995. Coincidentally, in 1946, shortly after her book was published, electricity came to the island and a radiotelephone was installed.

In 1949, a power-driven foghorn replaced the old hand-operated horn, qualifying the station for an assistant keeper. In 1955, a new dwelling was built, and in 1964, a second dwelling was built for an assistant, along with the new lighthouse that stands there today. The beautiful little fourth-order Fresnel lens that projected the Bon Portage light from 1946 until 1970 is now in the Seal Island Light Museum in nearby Barrington.

This certainly doesn't look like the lightstation that Evelyn Richardson writes about in her prize-winning book We Keep a Light, but it is Bon Portage, otherwise known as Outer Island. As described in her book, one of the Scottish boilers from the steamship Express, wrecked here in 1898, can be seen on the beach in front of the dwellings.

Nothing remains of the lightstation Richardson wrote about, but the island itself has changed very little and is still recognizable from her descriptions. Of note is her description of the wreck of the steamship *Express*, which occurred in September 1898—right beside the lighthouse. Over the ensuing years, the sea erased pretty much all the evidence of the wreck, except for two tough-made Scottish boilers, about which she writes: "We shall miss them when they are gone, their long, gallant struggle against overwhelming odds ended at last." Amazingly, the last time I was on Bon Portage, those boilers were still there, albeit battered and beaten by the sea for over a hundred years.

When the Richardsons moved to their retirement home in Barrington in 1964, all of the island except the lighthouse point was bequeathed to Nova

Stoddart Island

Scotia's Acadia University as a study area for a program on ecology and wildlife management. Acadia biologist Peter Smith says that the island is home to the largest colony of Leach's storm petrels (also known as Mother Carey's chickens) on the eastern side of the continent—about 50,000 breeding pairs. The island also has the only nesting colony of black-crowned herons in the province, and several common egrets. Thus the area is being put to good use and there's still a human presence even after the lighthouse's automation and de-staffing in October 1984. In June 1990, in honour of the Richardsons, the university officially named its facility the Evelyn and Morrill Richardson Biological Research Station. The Richardsons' two daughters, Anne Wickens and Betty-June Smith, were present at the dedication.

The light can be seen about 6 kilometres in the distance from the Chapel Hill Museum in Shag Harbour. To get any closer, you need a boat.

043 This lighthouse guides vessels into the anchorage of Stoddart Harbour and Shag Harbour Sound. The sound is a 2.2-kilometre-wide passage between Stoddart Island and Bon Portage Island. Referred to officially as Stoddart Island, it is more commonly known as Emerald Isle. Michael Wrayton, an Irishman, bought the island some time in about 1870, and it was he who changed the name to Emerald Isle. Evelyn Richardson refers to it by that name throughout, *We Keep a Light*. She had a very deep and abiding love for the island, as it was there in 1902 that she was born; her maternal grandfather, Captain Ephraim Larkin, was keeper of the island's light for over 23 years, and in

STODDART ISLAND	
ESTABLISHED:	1877
CCG LIGHT #:	308
POSITION:	43° 28' 35.2" N
	65° 43' 08.4" W
	On the northwest point
	of the island
LIGHT:	Flashing green, F0.5/E3.5
AHW:	8.3 metres
NOM. RANGE:	Unknown
HORN:	None
DESCRIPTION:	White wooden
	pepper-shaker-type tower,
	6.4 metres high

1926, she got married to Morrill Richardson there.

The establishment date recorded for this lighthouse is 1877, but a Department of Marine and Fisheries report dated October 29, 1875, states that a small beacon light had been erected that year. At first the light was going to be put in the window of Michael Wrayton's private house. But it was finally considered more advisable to put an old lantern that was in the lighthouse store on the top of an inexpensive wooden beacon, the cost of which was less than $150. For two

The squattest little lighthouse existing in this province is found here on Stoddart Island.

years, Wrayton kept the light at no charge. Then, influenced by ships' masters who attested to the great usefulness of the light, the department decided to pay Wrayton an annual amount of $100 per year when he was officially appointed keeper on May 7, 1877.

In 1886, a new tower was erected and the light was greatly improved. An oil store was also built, using materials from the old building. This lighthouse is rather squat—at 6.4 metres high, it is only about 1.8 metres taller than it is wide at the base.

Stoddart Island lighthouse can be seen from Prospect Point at Shag Harbour at a distance of about 1.6 kilometres.

Woods Harbour

West Head

044 Woods Harbour lighthouse was established to serve two purposes: first, to mark the dangerous ledge called Big Ledge, which is covered at high tide, and second, to mark the southern entrance to Cockerwit Passage between the Mutton Islands and the fishing community of Lower Woods Harbour on the mainland. The lighthouse was built in 1900 by day labour under the supervision of Amos McLellan at a cost of $1,478.10. It was a square wooden building with sloping sides surmounted by a red octagonal iron lantern, standing on a concrete pier built on the highest part of the ledge. A hand-operated horn was provided to answer vessels' signals. It was found necessary to build a breakwater to protect the foundation from the sea and serve as a boat harbour. The first lightkeeper, James E. Goodwin, was appointed on August 27, 1900, at a starting rate of $200 per year; he served until April 1930. Of course, the wages had increased considerably by then—he made up to $966 per year in 1930.

In about 1963, the lighthouse was rebuilt to what it is today: a square building with a flat roof surmounted by a red aluminum lantern, and the five windows boarded up.

The lighthouse is highly visible about 800 metres from the wharf in Lower Woods Harbour and Route 3, which passes nearby, but only accessible by boat.

This Woods Harbour lighthouse has an unusual configuration for a lighthouse— a square building with a flat roof and the lantern at its centre.

WOODS HARBOUR

ESTABLISHED:	1900
CCG LIGHT #:	312
POSITION:	43° 31' 10.5" N
	65° 44' 43" W
	On Big Ledge
LIGHT:	Fixed white
AHW:	6.3 metres
NOM. RANGE:	5 nautical miles
HORN:	B3, S27
DESCRIPTION:	White square tower with red upper portion, 6.3 metres high

045 Before West Head got a light, G. S. Parker built a white, wooden, pepper-shaker-type tower 11 metres high on the outer end of Brooklyn breakwater, Liverpool Bay, for $494. It first showed a light on November 18, 1878—two lights, to be precise, a green light across the channel, and a white light to seaward. In 1885, rough seas destroyed the Brooklyn Pier. The tower, having been securely bolted to 30-centimetre-square timbers and the bottom heavily ballasted with stone, survived the storm and was subsequently moved to West Head, Cape Sable Island, in 1888, where it marks the headland to the southern side of the western entrance to Barrington Passage.

WEST HEAD

ESTABLISHED:	1888
CCG LIGHT #:	320
POSITION:	POSITION 43° 27' 23.8" N
	65° 39' 16.9" W
	On West Head, Cape Sable Island
LIGHT:	Fixed red
AHW:	15.6 metres
NOM. RANGE:	6 nautical miles
HORN:	B2.5, S3, B2.5, S52
DESCRIPTION:	Two wide red horizontal bands on a white circular fibreglass tower, 6.1 metres high

The first lightkeeper was A. K. Smith, appointed on August 25, 1888. The Smith family continued to keep this lighthouse until 1937, when Fred Newell took over and passed on the responsibility to his son Herbert Newell. The last keeper, he witnessed the final days of the old 94-year-old lighthouse when it was bulldozed and burned in 1972 and a new circular fibreglass tower was erected nearby.

The beautiful 270-degree, fifth-order (375-millimetre) glass drum lens—complete with red mantle and iron

Cape Sable

A one-of-a-kind light tower at West Head on Cape Sable Island.

pedestal—was saved, and is now a valued artifact proudly displayed in the little Archelaus Smith Museum at Centreville, Cape Sable Island. Old-time fishermen still lament the loss of the lighthouse, which they often used to locate one of the better lobster fishing grounds. When they were on target, they would say, "Lighthouse over Uncle Nels!"

Turn south from Route 3 onto Route 330. Proceed across the causeway onto Cape Sable Island. At 11.4 kilometres, turn right and drive another 500 metres to the lighthouse.

046 Often mistakenly referred to as Cape Sable Island light, Cape Sable itself is a low sandy islet about 4.8 kilometres long and very narrow—only about 100 metres wide for most of its length. It is separated from Cape Sable Island by Hawk Inlet and Hawk Channel. Because it is so low lying, vessels would very often be in peril before the islet was even seen. The point must be rounded by all vessels approaching from the east and is the turning point for the Bay of Fundy. To do otherwise means vessels must pass far to the southward, relying on the lighthouse at the southern end of Seal Island and resulting in the loss of valuable time, and becoming subject to other dangers. A lighthouse was recommended in as early as 1841, and possibly earlier, although some were of the opinion that a light on Baccaro Point would best serve ship traffic in the area. Finally, a decision was taken in favour of Baccaro Point and a lighthouse was erected there in 1850. The decision was much influenced by the fact that the New Brunswick government refused to share the costs of erecting a lighthouse proposed for Cape Sable.

The disastrous fate of the steamship *Hungarian*, wrecked on the sandbars of Cape Sable on February 20, 1860, and resulting in the loss of over 200 lives, called attention to the necessity of building a first-class lighthouse there. Thus on November 12, 1861, the first keeper, Hervey Doane, lit the lamps in a new lighthouse on Cape Sable.

It had an octagonal timber-frame tower, 15.25 metres high, and showed a fixed red light from 16 metres above high water. A report from 1865 states that this light, which had 19 lamps, was by far the most expensive to operate of any other on the coast, but even on a clear night the red light could not be seen over a distance of eight nautical miles. Four-sevenths of the power of the light was lost through the thick red glazing of the lantern. In 1869, the red glass was changed to clear, and ruby chimneys were used on the lamps instead. This greatly improved the range of the light, but the construction of a second lighthouse on Cape Sable

The Cape Sable station with a new concrete tower and the stub of the original lighthouse to the right of it.

CAPE SABLE	
ESTABLISHED:	1861
CCG LIGHT #:	327
POSITION:	43° 23' 24" N
	65° 37' 16.9" W
	On southernmost
	extremity
LIGHT:	Flashing white,
	once every five seconds
AHW:	29.6 metres
NOM. RANGE:	22 nautical miles
HORN:	B4, S56
DESCRIPTION:	White octagonal concrete
	tower, 30.78 metres high

was still recommended. It was also suggested that both lighthouses show a white light to distinguish the point from any other on the south shore, and that the lights be arranged to guide mariners clear of the dangerous shoals lying to the west. Finally, on July 15, 1870, the light was changed to white and a clockwork mechanism was fitted to rotate the reflectors, giving them a flashing characteristic. On July 1, 1902, a third-order Fresnel lens was installed.

In 1924, a new octagonal reinforced-concrete tower replaced the old wooden one. This beautifully proportioned tower, at 31 metres base to vane, is the tallest lighthouse in Nova Scotia. After the new lighthouse was built, the old tower was dismantled down to the top of the second storey, a new roof was put on, and the building was used as a storage barn. After the station was de-staffed on May 26, 1986, there was the threat that this historic tower would be torn down and destroyed, together with all the other station buildings. In 1991, a community group obtained salvage rights to this two-storey stub. It was taken down piece-by-piece and transported to Yarmouth, where it was expected to be re-assembled on the waterfront as part of an ongoing waterfront development project. But on May 1, 1992, it lay in a couple of tangled

heaps on Yarmouth's waterfront, and I have no idea what has become of it since then.

Today, only the lighthouse tower remains on Cape Sable. The dwelling, barn, and sheds are all gone. Sadly, the beautiful, solid old fog-alarm building has also been destroyed, and with it goes an architecturally historic structure encompassed within—from the original building of 1876 to the major addition in 1906, and all the various alterations and additions up to the time of its destruction. If ever there was an historic building, this was it, and was even recognized as such in a 1985 Federal Heritage Buildings Review Office report. Yet it was still destroyed. The lighthouse tower itself was designated a classified federal heritage building on July 28, 1989.

Follow Route 330 a short distance through the town of Clark's Harbour to a cemetery beside the road. Turn at the cemetery and proceed 2.5 kilometres to the end of the road. From here the lighthouse can be viewed at a distance of 2.6 kilometres.

047 Although not an official lighthouse, and never designed as an aid to navigation, this structure merits a place in the annals of Nova Scotia's lighthouses. Built primarily to support and display the lantern and second-order Fresnel lens that was removed from the lighthouse tower on Seal Island in 1978, it now contains other important lifesaving and navigational artifacts, including the small fourth-order Fresnel lens used in the Bon Portage lighthouse from 1946 until 1970. The white wooden octagonal tower is 10.67 metres

A close-up of the original Seal Island lantern and second-order lens, which was replaced by an aluminum lantern and 91.44-centimetre airport beacon.

high, with two broad red horizontal stripes, and topped by a 6.1-metre-high round red iron lantern—16.77 metres high, base to vane.

When word was received in 1977 that the light on Seal Island would be replaced, and that the old lantern and

Baccaro Point

lens were destined for the National Museum of Science and Technology in Ottawa, members of the communities of Barrington and Cape Sable Island protested. Their objections were heard, and on February 3, 1978, former transport minister Otto Lang gave notice that the light would be donated to the municipality of Barrington, provided they were capable of preserving it—and, indeed, they were. The Cape Sable Historical Society took the lead, and with community fundraising and volunteer workers, together with funding from the Canada Works Program, the project objectives were accomplished.

The lighthouse museum was first opened to the public on July 1, 1985, and has attracted increasing numbers of visitors every year. Stop for a visit, climb to the top of the tower for the view, or examine the complex and intricate design of the multi-prism lens. You will see why this "lighthouse" has become such a proud symbol of this seafaring community.

The museum is on Route 3 in Barrington, with convenient parking within a stone's throw of the tower.

048 After a lot of debate over the merits of a lighthouse at Baccaro Point rather than Cape Sable, a petition by Jossiah C. Pinkham and others was successful in obtaining a decision in favour of Baccaro Point on February 13, 1850.

The first lighthouse was quite extensive, being a lighthouse and dwelling combined. The building was painted white with a black ball on three sides to enhance it as a daymark and distinguish it from others in the district. Besides the lighthouse/dwelling, there was a separate storehouse, and the keeper, James S. Smith, added three additional buildings for his own use—a barn, a woodshed, and a small shop to house his shoemaking business. With a wage of just £75 per year sup-

BACCARO POINT	
ESTABLISHED:	1850
CCG LIGHT #:	336
POSITION:	43° 26′ 58.9″ N
	65° 28′ 15″ W
	East side of entrance
	to Barrington Bay
LIGHT:	Flashing white,
	F1/E1/F1/E1/F1/E5
AHW:	15.8 metres
NOM. RANGE:	16 nautical miles
HORN:	B2, S18
DESCRIPTION:	White wooden
	pepper-shaker-type tower,
	13.6 meters high

plemented by an additional fuel allowance of £20, the extra source of income was surely welcome, but it is surprising that it was allowed.

On January 16, 1934, the lighthouse was destroyed by fire, driving lightkeeper Herbert Ross and his family out of the burning building in their nightclothes. A temporary anchor light was rigged on a pole until a new lighthouse could be built later that same year—the existing square wooden tower. The record doesn't show what the light-

This lighthouse tower is all that remains at Baccaro Point—enclosed within a chain-link fence. It's probably a good idea, as this lighthouse is in quite a remote but accessible area.

keeper and his family did for accommodation, as no new dwelling was built at that time. A new keeper, W. Trueman Nickerson, was appointed in August of that year and rode a bicycle 6 kilometres from his home in Port La Tour to the lighthouse every day. A new dwelling was built near the lighthouse in 1955, providing the Nickerson family with a home on the site after 21 years of service at the light, which they continued to serve for another 10 years.

Brenton Reynolds was the last keeper at this station, transferred from Cape Roseway on McNutt Island in 1965. Although he and his wife, Annie, dearly loved McNutt Island, they were happy to come ashore after ten years, especially as they had three school-aged children. Even though Annie Reynolds was a schoolteacher, she found it difficult to teach her children through correspondence courses.

Keeping a lighthouse is very serious business, as it involves watching out

The Salvages

for folks who get themselves into trouble on the water. But there are also some good chuckles from time to time. Brenton Reynolds tells a funny story about the station's small air-horn fog alarm, which affected any rutting moose that came within earshot of its sound. It would toll them down from way up in the woods, down to the beach, right up to the lighthouse. Breton didn't say what happened when the moose realized they were being romanced by a foghorn, but it couldn't have been a pretty sight!

Brenton and Annie Reynolds retired from lightkeeping in 1984 after 28 years of service. Baccaro Point was then unmanned, and the two dwellings were sold. One was moved to Seal Point and the other was torn down in 1986. Just the lighthouse and horn remain on the site now (and perhaps the odd stray lovelorn moose).

Drive south from Route 309 at Port La Tour for about 6 kilometres and watch for the lighthouse road.

049 The Salvages is a very dangerous group of ledges and rocks on the west side of the west entrance to Negro Harbour, known locally as the Half Moons. The Salvages are a line of rocks nearly three kilometres long, with the highest parts a mere three metres above high water, and most either just uncovered at low water or concealed by very shallow water, such as Eastern Rock, which is covered by less than one metre at low spring tides. Is it any wonder, then, that when the lighthouse was constructed in 1915, it was made of concrete, with walls 41 centimetres thick to withstand the pounding and battering of the stormy North Atlantic seas. Built by day labour under contract to J. L. Colter, its initial cost was $12,058.46.

THE SALVAGES	
ESTABLISHED:	1965
CCG LIGHT #:	348
POSITION:	43° 28' 07.7" N
	65° 22' 43.4" W
	Southeast end of
	the island
LIGHT:	Flashing white,
	F0.5/E14.5
AHW:	16.8 metres
NOM. RANGE:	16 nautical miles
HORN:	B2, S3, B2, S3, B2, S48
DESCRIPTION:	White rectangular
	concrete tower,
	14.9 metres high

The station had no light in 1915—it was built to accommodate a type G diaphone air horn and the machinery necessary to operate it. Jesse Obed was the engineer appointed to operate and maintain the fog alarm at a salary of $992.50 per year. No explanation can be found as to why such a difficult and costly project could not have also included a light. When the light was finally established in 1965, Gaza Soltesz became the first lightkeeper in August of that year.

By 1978, when Jim Guptill went on the Salvages as head keeper, the station was operated by 2 two-lightkeeper teams who rotated, 28 days on, 28 days off. Jim Guptill and Stan Matthews were one team and Bill Horne and Bob

The boardwalk on Salvages Island provided access the boathouse, which is gone, and now, so is the boardwalk. It is hard to imagine that it would survive very long anyway because the island is so low lying and surrounded by open water.

Croft were the other. This system continued until the station was de-staffed on September 11, 1987. Jim Guptill recalls innumerable times when they provided fishermen and other mariners with weather reports, answered calls from yachts enquiring about distances and directions to ports, and sometimes even supplied a few gallons of gasoline to boaters who had run out and had blown ashore sideways.

Living quarters made of wood had been built onto the original fog-alarm building; a boathouse with a wooden walkway from the dwelling had also been built. It's all gone now, either dismantled purposely or blown away in a storm. But an automated light on the roof of the concrete fog-alarm building and a horn mounted on the end still provide a warning to this extremely dangerous place.

The lighthouse can be seen from Baccaro Point about nine kilometres to the east.

Cape Negro Island

Cape Negro Island is actually two islands of nearly equal size resembling a figure eight, connected by a natural, low, narrow shingle causeway about 300 metres long. Each of the island's two parts is about 200 hectares and measures about 1,800 metres long by 700 metres wide.

The first lighthouse was built by

James D. Coffin at Abbott's Point on the northeast side of the south island for $970, plus another $429.26 for lamps and the revolving apparatus. Considered a minor light, it was a square wooden building, 8.8 metres high, and surmounted by an octagonal wooden lantern. The first lightkeeper was James McKinnon, appointed at $100 per year—a post that he held for 25 years, until July 1897. Because of the small size of the lighthouse, it became necessary, two years later in 1874, to build a separate dwelling house, as well as a small store for coal and a boat landing. By 1887, the lighthouse was in such poor condition that it had to be torn down and a new one built. The new lighthouse was an octagonal wooden tower 13.4 metres high, built upon a stone foundation. A man named DeChamp did the work for the tendered price of $975. The lighting and revolving apparatus was shifted

from the old lighthouse to the new. The new tower was built at the eastern end of the dwelling and the two buildings were connected.

By 1915, it was decided that a lighthouse on the southeast end of the south island would better serve marine traffic entering Negro Harbour by either the east or west entrance as it

The lighthouse and equipment room are in exceptionally good condition in 1991, when this picture was taken. Surprising, considering that this Cape Negro Island lightstation has been de-staffed since 1966.

stood, the light was only visible to vessels approaching from the east. The octagonal reinforced-concrete tower stands today about 1,300 metres south of Abbott's Point. It was built in 1915 by contractor D. C. Mulhall, together with a wooden dwelling and combined boathouse/oil store, for the price of $11,200. By this time, according to an article in the *Yarmouth Vanguard*, there was a sizeable settlement on the island because of a large fish-packing plant there. There were numerous houses, a two-storey building used for a school and church, a grocery store, a community hall, a pool hall, and an ice-cream parlour.

CAPE NEGRO ISLAND	
ESTABLISHED:	1872
CCG LIGHT #:	349
POSITION:	43° 30′ 26.2″ N
	65° 20′ 44.2″ W
	On southeast end of
	the island
LIGHT:	Fixed white
AHW:	27.7 metres
NOM. RANGE:	16 nautical miles
HORN:	B6, S54
DESCRIPTION:	White octagonal concrete
	tower 12.8 metres high

From the 1930s to the 1960s, the island was uninhabited except for the lightkeepers and their families. Since the station was de-staffed in 1966, there have been no residents other than the few people who keep a summer camp on the north island. All that remains on the south end of the island is the light tower and fog-alarm building, and except for the foundation of the dwelling about 90 metres west of the lighthouse, there is little evidence that anyone ever lived here. There is, however, life of another sort—brightly coloured garter snakes and a large population of very curious mink that pop up and disappear again quick as a wink.

From Exit 28 on Route 103, go south on Route 309 to the hamlet of Cape Negro. Turn left and drive about nine kilometres to the tiny community of Blanche, where you should be able to see Cape Negro Island lighthouse about five kilometres to the east.

Cape Roseway

051 Shelburne, situated on the third largest natural harbour in the world, gained prominence in 1783, when the American Revolution ended and about 3,000 United Empire Loyalists from New York sailed into Shelburne Harbour to start a new life. Early settlers' names such as Bell, Harding, Holden, Irwin, Murphy, Purney, Ryder, and Van Buskirk can be found on tombstones in Shelburne's old cemeteries.

Shelburne prospered and the population swelled to over 16,000, making it one of the largest settlements in British North America. It became obvious that a lighthouse was needed to safely land vessels into the harbour, and NcNutt Island, 5.3 kilometres long by 2.6 kilometres wide, with an elevation of 39.6 metres near the centre, and situated in the centre of the Shelburne Harbour approaches, was the logical place to build it. The high white granite cliffs of Cape Roseway at the southeast point of the island provided the ideal site.

On July 18, 1786, the sum of £500 was granted for the purpose of building the lighthouse. To provide for its operation and maintenance, an act was passed shortly thereafter allowing for a duty to be collected from the ships using the harbour. For additional support, duty also had to be paid on wine, rum, and other distilled spirits, molasses, coffee, porter, beer, gunpowder, loaf sugar, and teas.

Cape Roseway, lit in 1788, became the second lighthouse in British North America—the first one was Sambro Island lighthouse at the approaches to Halifax Harbour. The first lightkeeper at Cape Roseway was Alexander Cocken, appointed at the rate of six pounds, five shillings per calendar month. Life was not easy at the station; the house that was provided for the keeper and his family consisted of just two small rooms with no kitchen or

CAPE ROSEWAY	
ESTABLISHED:	1788
CCG LIGHT #:	355
POSITION:	43° 37' 21" N
	65° 15' 52" W
	Near the southeast point
	of McNutt Island
LIGHT:	Flashing white,
	every ten seconds
AHW:	33.1 metres
NOM. RANGE:	16 nautical miles
HORN:	B3, S3, B3, S51
DESCRIPTION:	White octagonal concrete
	structure,
	14.6 metres high

cellar, nor was there a storehouse for the oil required for the lighthouse. The only landing place was at the other end of the island, 4.8 kilometres from the lighthouse over land that was impassable, even on foot. Oil and every other necessity had to be carried on men's backs. On March 23, 1795, the lightkeeper petitioned for a grant to build a kitchen, cellar, and storehouse, and £20 to make a road across the island for carts. By March 30, 1812, the lightkeeper was praying that £40 would be granted to complete the road.

The lighthouse was built of granite blocks, octagonal in shape, with walls 1.8 metres thick at the base. It was 23.5 metres tall from base to vane. Two vertical fixed white lights were shown

Cape Roseway in August 1991—probably the most complete lightstation remaining in all of Nova Scotia, with every building still in place, even the white picket fence. Wouldn't it be wonderful to have it preserved?

from the tower: one in the lantern, and the other in a bow window 11.6 metres below the lantern. An 1857 report states that the tower was enclosed in a wooden frame, boarded, shingled, and painted white with vertical black stripes on its seaward side. The additions requested in 1812 were finally built in 1835, but by this time, 22 years later, the whole station was in very bad condition. In 1858, extensive repairs were made and a new lantern was installed. In 1918, the upper light was changed from fixed white to flashing white, and the lower light was discontinued.

The lighthouse was struck by lightning and heavily damaged by fire in 1959, so a temporary light was established on the roof of the fog-alarm building until the current reinforced-concrete tower was built in 1961 and converted to electricity. Unfortunately, the old stone tower, the only one in Nova Scotia other than that at Sambro Island, was demolished—another important historic structure gone forever.

The last time I was on Cape Roseway

Sandy Point

lightstation, in 1991, five years after it was de-staffed, the buildings were getting shabby-looking, but were still in reasonably good condition. The long white picket fence still marked the north boundary of the station property, and the tower, two bungalows, fog-alarm building, barn, and two small sheds were still there. It was easy to imagine how beautiful the station had been, and obvious that keepers and their families, like the Reynoldses and Van Buskirks, had taken a lot of pride in their work. I wonder what the last ten years has wrought?

Enquire about boat trips to McNutt Island at the Shelburne Visitor Information Centre, which is about 14.5 kilometres from the marina on Dock Street. Wear comfortable hiking shoes and enjoy the hike to the lighthouse. The island abounds with wildlife such as deer, rabbits, mink, and squirrels, and you can often see seals and otters, as well as pheasants and sea birds such as coots, sea ducks, shags, and black guillemots.

052 The first lighthouse was erected by George de Champs at a cost of $725, for the purpose of guiding vessels into Shelburne Harbour and to mark the danger of Sand Point. Built on the shore at an elevation of 14.3 metres, the square wooden tower was 6 metres high with an octagonal wooden lantern, and showed a fixed red light from 20.4 metres above high water. Edward Goudock was appointed keeper in July 1873 at $200 per year. Goudock lived in his own house nearby; as recommended, a fence was erected around the lighthouse, which was surrounded by cultivated land and private property. At 10:00 P.M., February 20, 1878,

SANDY POINT	
ESTABLISHED:	1873
CCG LIGHT #:	363
POSITION:	43° 41′ 29″ N
	65° 19′ 35″ W
	East side of the entrance
	to Shelburne Harbour
LIGHT:	Fixed red
AHW:	14.3 metres
NOM. RANGE:	Unknown
HORN:	None
DESCRIPTION:	White wooden
	pepper-shaker-type tower,
	13.4 metres high

Goudock visited the lighthouse and determined that all was in good order. But at about midnight, the lighthouse was ablaze. It was totally destroyed by the fire. The cause was never determined and no one was blamed.

Plans were made to replace the lighthouse without delay. However, it was recommended that the replacement should be built on the opposite side of the harbour at Surf Point. But the Department of Marine and Fisheries became convinced that it would be more advantageous to local trade to have the lighthouse built at the end of Sand Spit. An 1880 report stated that the contract should go to George De Champs, the same man who built the first lighthouse, but at a much higher cost of $1,725. This time the cost included a pier that had to be built 1.2 metres above the low-water mark to support the lighthouse, 73 metres from the extremity of the sand spit. The pier was made from hemlock timber, nine metres square at the top and sloping out to 10.28 metres at the base. It was sunk into the sand 0.6 metres, and the top was three metres above the high-

The Sandy Point lighthouse is now under the care of a community group, which has established a lighthouse park nearby.

Gull Rock
(Lockport)

water mark. The sides were sheathed with oak plank and an iron plate was installed on the northeast corner to protect against ice. This new lighthouse, which still exists today, was put into operation on December 15, 1880, and Edward Goudock was re-appointed as its lightkeeper.

After suffering many problems with the pier, in 1903, it was decided that a new concrete foundation should be built by day labour under the direction of Amos McLellan at a cost of $ 1,562. It was built 5.18 metres high, immediately to the land side of the old pier, and the lighthouse was moved to it. It was then called the Sand Spit light.

In October 1980, when the last keeper retired, there was great concern in the community that the lighthouse itself would be removed. However, a report by the Shelburne Area Industrial Commission showed that at that time, 100 vessels used the harbour year-round and it was a major port of call for more than 20 cargo vessels. The Coast Guard decided to automate the light and continue its use.

The small community of Sandy Point is five kilometres south of Shelburne, on the east side of the harbour. A further 1.6 kilometres brings you within 250 metres of the lighthouse. There is limited off-road parking, and if the tide is low, you may be able to wade out to the lighthouse.

053 In 1851, Lockeport was known as Locke's Island Harbour, named for one of the early New England settlers, Jonathan Locke. At the entrance to the harbour there is a dangerous and extensive bank of rocks and shoals known collectively as the Ragged Islands, one of which is Gull Rock.

On March 18, 1851, the commissioners of lighthouses read a petition of shipowners and inhabitants of the county of Shelburne that pleaded for a lighthouse to warn of the outlying dangers and provide a guiding light into the safety of the harbour. In February 1852, funds were made available and the lighthouse was built on Gull Rock, which is only about 38 metres wide by

GULL ROCK	
ESTABLISHED:	1853
CCG LIGHT #:	370
POSITION:	43° 39' 18" N
	65° 05' 58" W
	At the entrance to
	Lockeport harbour
LIGHT:	Occulting white,
	F17/E5/F3/E5
AHW:	17.1 metres
NOM. RANGE:	8 nautical miles
HORN:	B3, S27
DESCRIPTION:	Square tower on
	white rectangular
	concrete building,
	13.4 metres high

100 metres long, the highest elevation being 4.6 metres above high water. It is surrounded by many dangers such as Whale Rock, Kelp Shoal, and Trinidad Rock, not to mention Chain Ledge, South Ledge, and Southeast Reef. The lighthouse also served as accommodation for the lightkeeper, Samuel Hayden, who had been appointed at a yearly salary of £80, plus a £20 fuel allowance. Samuel Hayden served for 20 years before a tragic drowning accident on October 30, 1873, killed him

and his wife as they proceeded from the island to the mainland in an open boat. He was succeeded as lightkeeper by his brother William Hayden.

In the final days of the manned operation of this lighthouse, two teams of two men alternated, 28 days on, 28 days off. Earl Flemming and Bill Ringer were one team and the other was Barry Crowell and T. D. Sidey. Gull Rock is one of only a few lighthouses in the Maritimes considered a wave-swept structure, meaning that seas can break completely over the lighthouse in stormy weather. Crew changeovers were usually accomplished in fair weather by use of the 5.5-metre station boat, or in bad weather, by helicopter, but sometimes not at all. Getting the boat on and off Gull Rock, even in fair weather, always carried some risk, and required two men with a great deal of skill, one to guide the boat and the other to operate the haul-up engine. Approaching the slipway required precise manoeuvring, especially at low tide, through a narrow channel strewn with very large boulders. The haul-up cable was hooked to the boat's bow ring to haul it up the slipway, the men negotiating a sharp turn by means of manipulating a block and tackle. Getting off Gull Rock, the slipway was greased, then both men, one on each side of the boat to steady it, pushed it along, gaining momentum to negotiate the turn near the bottom; at the last possible moment, the man who was leaving leaped aboard, started the engine as the boat hit the water, and manoeuvred it clear of the rocks before the sea smashed the boat against them.

The lighthouse was snug and built to withstand the pounding of the sea, with walls made of 30-centimetre-thick reinforced concrete. In 1986, the thickness was increased by 12.7 centimetres by spraying on athenite, which gave the building a stucco appearance. As well as

Looking down Hall Street to seaward from Lockeport, this lighthouse can easily be seen on a clear day at about 4.6 kilometres distance.

It was a tight and awkward turn to get the station boat around on Gull Rock.

the two-storey lighthouse/dwelling, there was a fog-alarm building, a workshop, and a boathouse—all connected so that it wasn't necessary to go outside in bad weather. Obtaining fresh water was always a problem so they were usually in short supply. It had to be collected from the roofs by means of an interconnected system of gutters and down-pipes, which directed the water into a huge cistern under the kitchen floor and through charcoal filters. Close attention had to be paid to the removable plugs that directed the flow of water into the cistern or bypass. Because of the mess that seagulls and other birds made on the roof, and because salt accumulated on the roof from the ocean's spray or breaking waves, whenever it rained, the water had to be dumped until it was sufficiently clean to be directed into the cistern. One careless act could contaminate the entire supply of water.

For many years, lightkeepers on Gull Rock suspected the station was home to a supernatural being or spirit of some departed soul. Strange sounds and rumblings were heard in the lighthouse, always on those dark and stormy nights associated with such things. The sounds may have had a different source, however. A submarine power cable was connected to the station on December 4, 1979, and on one occasion when divers were inspecting the cable connection, they happened to find an opening to an underwater cavern right under the lighthouse; inside it was a large round boulder. They concluded that when the sea was rough and the groundswell reached near maximum height, it was possible that the boulder rolled around inside the cavern, creating the sounds and vibrations that led to the many good stories that were told down through the years. It is possible...but maybe not!

The lighthouse was de-staffed in October 1987, and has since been stripped of all structures no longer considered necessary. The fog-alarm building, workshop, and boathouse have all been removed. The slipway and boat landing are completely gone and a couple of 13,600-litre oil tanks lie abandoned and waiting for the sea to carry them away. The concrete helicopter pad, which is securely anchored to the rocks, remain. Wonder of wonders, so does the plank walkway down to the pad.

Carter Island

Little Hope Island

054 Due to the many rocks and shoals at the entrance to Lockeport Harbour, seas break completely across it during southerly gales. Carter Island, one of the smaller of five islands within the harbour, supports the light that welcomes into the shelter and safety of the inner harbour vessels drawing less than 4.5 metres of water .

The first lighthouse on this island was a square wooden building 8.8 metres high, which showed a fixed red light from its octagonal lantern. The cost of construction by James A. Hayden was $460 plus $91.80 for the lamps and other equipment. The tower was stayed on all four sides with wire rope. A small dwelling, 5.5 metres by 8 metres, was built separate from the lighthouse for lightkeeper James Lloyd, who was appointed when the lighthouse first went into operation, at a salary of $160 per year. When the lightkeeper spoke of the great difficulty of accessing the lighthouse by sea in rough weather, he was authorized to spend up to $200 to build a landing for his four-metre station boat. In those days, if you could show that something was absolutely necessary, the best you could hope for was permission to build it yourself—and if the work were done to the satisfaction of the Department of Marine and Fisheries, you might be lucky enough to get reimbursed.

In 1930, a beautiful new combined lighthouse/dwelling was built. It was a commodious, square, two-storey dwelling surmounted by a square wooden lantern, 11.6 metres high, base to vane. A hand-operated horn was provided to answer vessels' signals. By the time automation became a serious consideration for Carter Island, it had become an attractive and efficient station consisting of the lighthouse/dwelling, a fog-alarm building, a boathouse, and an oil stores

Carter Island after all the station buildings were removed and the lighthouse was replaced by this fibreglass tower.

CARTER ISLAND	
ESTABLISHED:	1872
CCG LIGHT #:	374
POSITION:	43° 42' 19" N
	65° 06' 06.1" W
	On the south end
	of the island
LIGHT:	Flashing white,
	every 20 seconds
AHW:	14.9 metres
NOM. RANGE:	17 nautical miles
HORN:	None
DESCRIPTION:	White circular fibreglass
	tower, 9.1 metres high,
	with two red horizontal
	bands

shed. After the station was de-staffed, and after all possibilities for the community or a not-for-profit group to assume care and control of the property were exhausted, the lighthouse was replaced in 1982 by the fibreglass tower that is seen there today. Except for the fog-alarm building, all of the smaller buildings were disposed of.

Carter Island, situated as it is in the centre of the harbour and less than 1,000 metres from the wharves, can easily be seen from just about anywhere along the town's waterfront.

055 Little Hope Island, about five kilometres from the mainland, is nothing more than a pile of boulders upon a rock about one-fifth of a hectare and only 3.4 metres above high water. It is so low that it cannot be seen at all from eight kilometres away. Shoals and rocks extend out from it about 600 metres in all directions. The lighthouse, therefore, has but one purpose: to warn vessels away from this very dangerous place. Before the lighthouse was built, there were many wrecks on this isle. With little chance of surviving a wreck here, it is appropriately named Little Hope Island. The importance of a light on this islet was beyond question, especially to vessels approaching the coast from the southwest. It is much relied on by steamers and other vessels from American ports bound for Halifax. In fact, there had been a small wooden beacon on the site for 20 years—but it was rotten and about to fall down when the Committee on Navigation Securities recommended in 1864 building of a proper lighthouse on Little Hope Island.

The original lighthouse was 7.9 metres high, base to vane, and consisted of a tower rising from the centre of a dwelling, and showed a red light from a 12-sided lantern. Incredibly, there were two other buildings on this tiny heap of stones, a boathouse and an oil store—all constantly in danger of being washed away by the heavy action of the sea. The first lightkeeper was William Firth, who served until October 7, 1872, when he was transferred to Coffin Island to replace Thomas Eaton, who, unfortunately, drowned while attempting to cross from the island to the mainland. Alexander McDonald was then appointed keeper of Little Hope Island and kept the light for 20 years, through tempest and storm and the most appalling conditions imaginable.

Many times he and his family had to take refuge in the cellar, expecting the lighthouse to be washed off the island when rocks as large as 500 kilograms were washed on top of the island and up against the lighthouse itself, despite massive wooden breastworks, and sea walls of white hemlock timbers and cut stone. Although the lives of the lightkeeper and his family were in great jeopardy many times over the 82 years the light was kept, and even though the seas often broke completely over the entire island, the lighthouse survived until it was destroyed by fire in 1906.

A temporary light was quickly established and construction of the new lighthouse began almost immediately. The tower on Little Hope Island today is cylindrical reinforced concrete, 3.2 metres in diameter and 22.86 metres high from the base to the lantern platform, strengthened throughout its entire height by six vertical concrete ribs around the outside, and a concrete stairway within. Atop the tower was a beautiful classic circular iron lantern 6 metres high, bringing the lighthouse to a height of 29 metres. The lantern was

LITTLE HOPE ISLAND	
ESTABLISHED:	1865
CCG LIGHT #:	393
POSITION:	43° 48' 33.7" N
	64° 47' 21.1" W
	North end of the island
LIGHT:	Flashing white,
	every ten seconds
AHW:	30.2 metres
NOM. RANGE:	13 nautical miles
HORN:	None
DESCRIPTION:	White circular concrete
	tower, 23.5 metres high

This truncated tower on Little Hope Island was over 29 metres high before its classic, iron, first-order lantern was removed.

fitted with a second-order Fresnel lens. Steel Concrete Co. Ltd. of Montreal built the tower for $7,250. A steel-framed concrete dwelling was built for the lightkeeper at a cost of $2,860.91, with steel supplied by I. Matheson of New Glasgow, Nova Scotia, for $800.

Because of the harsh living conditions the light was made unwatched in 1948. Everything is gone from the island now except the tower, truncated with the removal of the iron lantern. The light is now produced electrically by batteries, kept charged by solar panels and projected seaward by a 300-millimetre pressed plastic lens, mounted in the open on top of the tower.

The tower, on that low-lying lump of rock, seems to rise directly out of the sea, and is visible on a clear day from St. Catherines River, a small hamlet south of Port Mouton.

056 Spectacle Island is about 900 metres long by 250 metres wide, lying 3 kilometres east of central Port Mouton. It is two islands, in fact, but the water is not very deep between them and is strewn with rocks, which makes it very dangerous, even for small vessels. The lighthouse marks the dangers, and guides vessels through the eastern and western channels into Port Mouton and good anchorage to the west of the island.

The basic station was built, as most were at that time, as cheaply as possible using materials that could be acquired locally. Built for just $1,375.25, there was a square wooden lighthouse with a wooden octagonal lantern, and a small separate dwelling measuring 4.87 metres by 6.1 metres. Lightkeepers were expected to take initiative to add whatever they could to improve their lot. Robert J. Smith was appointed the first keeper, starting on November 11, 1873, at $300 per year. The first thing he did was build a landing for the 4.6-metre station boat, and a tramway up to the lighthouse. The record shows that he also built a well and was actually paid $15.50 by the Department of Marine and Fisheries for his work. After five years on the station, he also found time to build a kitchen onto the house, which greatly improved the quality of life on this small island.

On June 16, 1882, the lighthouse was struck by lightning, shattering the lantern and splitting the south wall from top to bottom. Luckily, it didn't catch fire and burn to the ground as so often happened in those days when large quantities of oil were usually stored in the lower part of the lighthouse tower. When the lighthouse was repaired, a small separate oil store was also built.

On November 3, 1890, Robert Smith resigned and Edward MacPherson was appointed in his place. His tenure was to be short and troubled. In his first year, the wharf and landing were totally destroyed and carried away by rough seas. On June 8 of the following year, MacPherson lost his life, by drowning. His widow took over as keeper for the next six years, finally relinquishing the position to J. Oscar Campbell.

In 1922, the dwelling was destroyed by fire, but was quickly replaced. As for the light tower, the record is not clear as to what happened to it, but indications are that it was replaced in about 1937. The dwelling foundation is almost totally obscured by vegetation now, and you have to search very carefully to find any other trace of the station where families once kept the light, answering vessels' signals with a hand-operated horn.

Harvey L. Huskins, who kept this light from 1954 to 1962, told me the following story:

One night it was blowing about 15 knots easterly, which is not a good wind, and the fog was as thick as it

Today, the dwelling foundation is the only evidence that a family once lived on Spectacle Island as keepers of this Port Mouton lighthouse.

could be. So thick, it had stems on it, and wet. All of a sudden I could hear this engine, a heavy diesel engine, and I heard a horn blow, so I didn't stop, even to put anything on. I ran out to the lighthouse, grabbed the hand-operated horn, got out behind the lighthouse and started to blow it. It was about 10:30 P.M. and I could hear the horn and engine about northeast of me, maybe northerly, in around Summerville Beach. By the sound and location, I was sure a ship had come ashore. I sat there and blew the hand horn until about 1:30 A.M., when I said, that's enough of that. He ain't coming no closer and if he is ashore, I can't help him, so I quit. The next morning, I found out what it was. This was when they had first put diesel trains on the line, and this train was going across Summerville when he blew an engine and was waiting for the wrecker to come take him back to Halifax. I blew the horn for three hours for a train! Imagine that, I was just doing my job.

PORT MOUTON

ESTABLISHED:	1873
CCG LIGHT #:	396
POSITION:	43° 55' 05.5" N
	64° 48' 14.2" W
	On the northeast point
	of Spectacle Island
LIGHT:	Flashing white, F2/E10
AHW:	16.8 metres
NOM. RANGE:	7 nautical miles
HORN:	None
DESCRIPTION:	White wooden
	pepper-shaker-type tower,
	5.5 metres high

Western Head

Coffin Island

057 Western Head lighthouse is on the western side of the approaches to Liverpool Bay, opposite Coffin Island lighthouse, which is 5.5 kilometres to the northeast. The middle ground between these two lights leads into the narrower confines of the mouth of the bay. At this point, the width is 2.4 kilometres, with Moose Point on the western side, and Eastern Head.

Although the lighthouse was not established until 1962, a foghorn was established in 1924 to warn off vessels. It was a powerful compressed-air diaphone. "So powerful," says Lemuel Moreau, the last man to keep the light at Western Head, "that it shook and rattled dishes in the cupboards of houses in the area." It gave two blasts of 2.5 seconds separated by a 5-second interval every minute of every hour of every day—sometimes for days on end during the foggy spring and early summer months. An electronically operated horn of considerably less power replaced the diaphone in 1971. A radio beacon was also established in 1936.

The station grew to be an impressive establishment that included three dwellings, one for the head keeper and one each for the two assistants and their families, a fog-alarm building, a garage, and oil stores, together with the lighthouse tower and radio beacon tower.

De-staffed in January 1988, the light and horn continues to operate automatically and remains an important aid to navigation. A fuel supply and 12-metre-square concrete pad provide a refuelling base for Coast Guard helicopters. Data is recorded at this site as part of the weather-gathering network that provides us with current conditions and forecasts.

From Liverpool, drive south on the west side of the harbour about 6 kilometres to Western Head. Watch for signs. This is a very popular place for locals and visitors alike, who come to enjoy the sea, the lighthouse, and the scenic vista. Coffin Island lighthouse can be seen across the bay.

Western Head is not only the site of an important lightstation, but a fuelling station for Coast Guard helicopters. Just don't expect anyone to come running up with an offer to "fill-'er-up"—there is no one there.

WESTERN HEAD	
ESTABLISHED:	1962
CCG LIGHT #:	405
POSITION:	43° 59' 21" N 64° 39' 44.5" W West side of entrance to Liverpool Bay
LIGHT:	Flashing white, F0.6/E14.4
AHW:	19.5 metres
NOM. RANGE:	17 nautical miles
HORN:	B6, S54
DESCRIPTION:	White octagonal concrete tower, 15.2 metres high

058 Coffin Island conjures up ominous thoughts as to how the island got its name. But there's no other reason than the fact that the island was owned by one of the grantees of Liverpool, Nova Scotia, Peleg Coffin. From the time it was established in 1812 until about 1888, it was known as the Liverpool light. From 1888 until 1911, it was officially called Coffin's Island lighthouse, and then just Coffin Island. It is one of the very early lights—the fifth to be built in Nova Scotia. In 1812, the cost so far was £560, 5 shillings, and 6 pence, and another £500 was granted for a lantern, gallery railing, and to complete construction. In 1814, the accounts showed that over £908 had been expended and not yet paid. The lighthouse commissioners stated that the wages paid to the mechanics and labourers seemed exorbitant.

An early description of the station states that the lighthouse was a large wooden octagonal tower 15 metres high, and painted red and white in eight alternate horizontal stripes. The station had a dwelling house for the keeper close to the lighthouse, as well as a barn, a woodshed, and an oil store. From another store and boathouse at the landing place about 1.2 kilometres from the lighthouse, supplies were received and were carried to the lightstation at the best opportunity. A 4.88-metre boat was also supplied for the station. It is not known who the first lightkeeper was, but James McLeod had the position from 1815 to 1817.

On September 4, 1870, the entire boat slip and wharf was carried away in a gale. Not an unusual event on this or any other island station, exposed as they were to the wind and the sea. Wharves, slipways, and boats could always be replaced, and this was usually done as quickly as possible. Real tragedies occurred when there was a

How do you paint a lighthouse? This is how it was done on Coffin Island in 1991.

loss of life, and this was all too common. Just a year later, on October 7, 1871, lightkeeper Thomas Eaton drowned while crossing from the island to the mainland.

In 1872, extensive erosion of the bank was noticeable on the seaward side of the lighthouse, so breastworks over 30 metres long and no less than 1.5 metres high had to be built. In 1878, a completely new floor and foundation had to be built for the tower, leaks had to be stopped at the top, and the tower had to be shingled and re-nailed with galvanized nails.

The lighthouse was destroyed by fire in 1913. A temporary fixed white light was used while D. C. Mulhall of Liverpool built the new octagonal reinforced-concrete tower for $12,080. It was put to use on October 1, 1914.

In 1962, electricity came to Coffin Island, the lighthouse was automated, and Wallace Brenton Wentzell came ashore, thus ending 150 years of lighthouse keeping on Coffin Island. The

lighthouse is all that remains of this lightstation today. Two foundations mark the places where the dwelling and another building once stood. Extensive breastworks of wooden cribbing filled with stone have collapsed. In 1991, the bank had eroded to just two metres from the lighthouse foundation. By 1998, the foundation of the lighthouse had been undermined on the seaward side, and it was feared that if something weren't done soon, it would topple into the sea. The Coast Guard was planning to discontinue the light in the lighthouse in favour of a lighted buoy offshore, and once the tower was declared surplus, it would be disposed of economically. But then a group of concerned citizens under the leadership of Ken Wilkinson got together and founded the Coffin Island Lighthouse Heritage Society, which was able to convince the Coast Guard that the lighthouse was worth saving. Two options were considered for saving the tower, one was to move it and

COFFIN ISLAND	
ESTABLISHED:	1812
CCG LIGHT #:	407
POSITION:	Position 44° 02′ 0.5″ N 64° 37′ 44.5″ W South point of the island.
LIGHT:	Flashing white, F0.5/E3.5
AHW:	18.3 metres
NOM. RANGE:	12 nautical miles
HORN:	None
DESCRIPTION:	Octagonal white concrete tower, 16.5 metres high

the other was to shore it up again. After studying the feasibility and costs, the society decided to place about 75 metres of armour rock along the shoreline on each side of the lighthouse, and a massive wall of granite boulders in front at a cost of $70,000. By August 1999, the work was done and the lighthouse had been saved—at least for the time being. It will take quite a bit

longer to raise the money to pay for it, however. The society hopes to give regular tours to Coffin Island and the lighthouse.

Check with the Visitor Information Centre in Liverpool regarding tours to the island. Otherwise, Coffin Island lighthouse can only be seen from a distance, either from Fort Point lighthouse in Liverpool or from Western Head lighthouse, six kilometres south of Liverpool.

Fort Point

059 Inner Liverpool Bay is dangerous, especially at Fort Point where the ledge extends into the harbour almost 200 metres beyond the point in a northeast direction. It was logical to build a lighthouse in this place to guide vessels into the harbour and provide a reference marking the dangers within. So in 1855, a grant of £230, 3 shillings, 9 pence was made for the purpose of building the lighthouse. The first lightkeeper, Samuel Sellon, was appointed at £50 per year and received an additional £10 fuel allowance.

The lighthouse first consisted of just the small square front portion of the building seen on the site today. What with the lantern and the lower part of the lighthouse being used for oil stores, there was scarce room for the keeper to sleep. Sellon, who kept the light for 32 years until he retired on September 25, 1887, lived in his own house a short distance from the light. An addition was made to the lighthouse in 1878, but it is not known whether Sellon ever lived in it. It is known, however, that because the lighthouse was so close to town, and very public, a board fence was built around it to protect the women who tended the light from time to time. They were likely the keeper's wife and daughters because in those days there was no provision for hiring an assistant; family members were expected to share the responsibility of keeping the light.

Long since automated and de-staffed, the future of this lighthouse was very much in doubt until the town of Liverpool negotiated its immediate future as a landmark building. It shared the responsibility of its care for several years, until 1970, when the lighthouse and a small parcel of land were conveyed to the town by the Crown for the purpose of developing a park.

The lighthouse was officially discontinued in January 1989, and in

The Fort Point lighthouse in Liverpool is restored and open for business. Wonderfully outfitted, the lighthouse contains a presentation that tells the story of Liverpool.

FORT POINT	
ESTABLISHED:	1855
CCG LIGHT #:	411
POSITION:	44° 02' 38" N
	64° 42' 30" W
	On the point within the town of Liverpool
LIGHT:	Discontinued
AHW:	Unknown
NOM. RANGE:	Unknown
HORN:	None
DESCRIPTION:	White wooden dwelling with tower attached, 8.5 metres high

September 1997, the lighthouse and park were officially open to the public. The beautiful shady picnic park is on the site claimed to be where deMonts and Samuel de Champlain first landed in 1604, and where the Privateer's Fort once stood. Two cannons have been mounted there, one on each side of a memorial cairn, and two plaques have been erected by the Historic Sites and Monuments Board of Canada. One reads, "In memory of Samuel de Champlain who sailed from France to make the first real attempt at colonization in Acadia. They made their first landing in Liverpool Harbour on 12 May 1604." The other states, "Liverpool Privateers. Licensed by the Lieutenant Governor, armed vessels, owned and fitted out by Liverpool merchants and manned by Liverpool crews, waged war on Great Britain's enemies on the high seas. During the American and revolutionary wars and the Napoleonic wars, Liverpool privateers protected their own shores and trade and harassed shipping on the Spanish Main. Their prizes, often with rich cargos, were sold in Nova Scotia under order of the Vice Admiralty Court and enriched the owners and seamen of such active craft as the Enterprise, the Rover, and the Liverpool Packet." Settlers from Cape Cod who founded Liverpool in 1759 fought for their survival here—in the streets and on the high seas. Thus many colourful accounts have been written, and ballads sung extolling the Liverpool privateers' adventurous escapades.

Situated at the end of Main Street in the town of Liverpool, the park and lighthouse can be visited at any time, and in the summer months, visitors can go inside the lighthouse, view the displays, and climb to the lantern at the top.

Medway Head

060   This lighthouse was called Port Medway light until a second light was established within the Port Medway Harbour in 1899. The new one became the Port Medway light and this light's name was changed to Medway Head. In the early days, the lumber trade was a thriving business here, and many vessels loaded the product at this port. A lighthouse, therefore, was of great importance to the navigation of the entrance and the many dangers in the vicinity.

The first lighthouse was described as a small square lighthouse/dwelling combined, painted white with a black square on the seaward side providing a conspicuous daymark. The light shone from a three-sided window that projected from the top of the dwelling. The station had an oil store building, a boathouse, and woodshed, and was provided with a 4-metre boat. The first lightkeeper, appointed in 1851, was I. K. Perry, followed in 1853 by Elson Perry, whose starting rate of pay was £50 per year plus a £15 fuel allowance. He kept the light for 39 years, until 1892, when his annual pay was $260.

In 1927, a new dwelling was built, with a 3.66-metre-high octagonal iron lantern on top. The dwelling was 7.62 metres square, two storeys high, and contained seven rooms. The structure was 11.58 metres high, base to vane.

The last lightkeeper, Douglas R. Smiley, was appointed in 1959, and found the combined dwelling/lighthouse was lacking in many ways, considering the times. Aside from the fact that the building was leaking in several places, there was no inside plumbing and no central heating. Although the building was completely renovated and made comfortable in 1963, three years later, a decision was made to replace the light itself. A concrete pad was poured and a new maintenance-free, 9.1-metre-tall round fibreglass

This lighthouse was built on Medway Head in 1983. The fog-alarm building at the right of the picture is now gone and the bungalow in the background was sold to private interests.

MEDWAY HEAD	
ESTABLISHED:	1851
CCG LIGHT #:	415
POSITION:	44° 06' 10.3" N
	64° 32' 25.6" W
	West side of the entrance
	to Port Medway
LIGHT:	White flashing, F4/E8
AHW:	24.2 metres
NOM. RANGE:	8 nautical miles
HORN:	Discontinued
	permanently on
	June 6, 1989.
DESCRIPTION:	White wooden
	pepper-shaker-type tower,
	8.7 metres high

tower was eased into position and bolted to the pad. It was painted white with a red band around the top and another red band near the centre. A new four-bedroom bungalow was built for the lightkeeper. Five years later, in 1971, records show that the fibreglass tower had developed some structural faults and was in need of repairs. In addition to the repairs, an automatic fog detector was installed, and the station was equipped for semi-automatic operation.

In 1980, the old two-storey dwelling/lighthouse was declared sur-

plus and sold to Alden Wambolt, who, under the terms of the sale, was required to remove the building from the lightstation site. It was moved, but not very far away. It can be seen just up the hill, where it has been thoroughly renovated. An attractive observatory replaces the old lantern, providing a wonderful panoramic view of the surrounding area.

In anticipation of total automation and de-staffing, on April 19, 1983, the fibreglass tower was replaced by the combined lighthouse and equipment room currently in use. Automation arrived on October 15, 1986, when Doug Smiley, the last keeper of this light, went into retirement after 35 years, 28 of those years at Medway Head. Sadly, Smiley's retirement didn't last long, as he passed away on November 18, 1988, at the young age of 64. Gone but not forgotten, because area resident Alden Wambolt has mounted a plaque on the lighthouse in memory of Smiley and all those who kept this light before him.

Port Medway

The bungalow and property were declared surplus in October 1987, and were sold to private interests in November 1989. All that remains now is the lighthouse itself.

From Exit 17A on Route 103, drive south about eight kilometres to Port Medway, turn right on Long Cove Road and proceed about four kilometres to the lighthouse.

061 The channel into Medway Harbour lies roughly in a north by west direction about 3.2 kilometres from Neil Point, where it opens into a large, shallow basin strewn with numerous rocks and shoals. The lighthouse is situated on the seaward side of

The Port Medway lighthouse was de-staffed way back in 1959 and more or less abandoned. A community group has been formed and things are looking much better for this lighthouse.

a large fish plant at the eastern (outer) end of a 172-metre breakwater. It is visible to the mariner from the channel, north of Neil Point. A safe course to the harbour wharf can be determined by bearings taken on the lighthouse. Only those familiar with the basin should venture further without help.

The lighthouse, put into operation on April 1, 1899, is the same one that exists today. The first lightkeeper was Samuel T. Foster, appointed on February 17, 1899, at $100 per year.

The last keeper, George McConnell, retired October 7, 1959. Cecil Dolliver was appointed caretaker at $40 per year, until January 1967, when a new policy was introduced whereby the lights were maintained and operated under contract as required.

In 1979, the tower was clad in vinyl siding, which hasn't weathered very

PORT MEDWAY	
ESTABLISHED:	1899
CCG Light #:	416
POSITION:	44° 07′ 58″ N
	64° 34′ 33″ W
	On the east end
	of the breakwater
LIGHT:	Fixed green
AHW:	11 metres
NOM. RANGE:	6 nautical miles
HORN:	None
DESCRIPTION:	White wooden
	pepper-shaker-type tower,
	10.1 metres high

well, and because the tower has been left open for some time, it has fallen into a state of disrepair and neglect that has threatened its removal. However, members of the Medway Area Communities Association are determined to restore it and a plan is underway to develop this valuable historic property for the benefit of the community and enjoyment of visitors to the area. Residents of this small village, who have traditionally earned their living by fishing, and ever mindful of the dangers of the sea, have built a reputation for hosting a colourful annual seafaring event—the blessing of the fleet—on the first day of August.

From Exit 17A on Route 103, turn south, continue about eight kilometres to Port Medway, then turn left at the main intersection to the harbour and the lighthouse.

Mosher Island

062 Extending about seven kilometres south of the mainland in the mouth of the La Have River, there is a group of islets connected to each other and the main shore by a series of shallow banks, the largest being Cape La Have Island. The most

This is the new fibreglass tower on Mosher Island, installed in March 1989 together with a new equipment room.

eastern island of this group is Mosher Island; its northeast point marks the west entrance to the La Have River. This river is of extreme importance to this part of the province: with a rise of 1.8 metres at ordinary tide, the river is navigable by small vessels as far as Bridgewater, the largest town in Lunenburg County, 22 kilometres above the northeast point of Mosher Island. Thus the point was the most logical place to build a lighthouse, which was what happened in 1868. The lighthouse also serves a good purpose in guiding vessels into the fine harbour lying to the west, where many vessels can find shelter in stormy weather.

The original lighthouse was described as a square wooden dwelling with an octagonal iron lantern on the roof. Henry Mosher was appointed first keeper at a wage of $450 per year. The dwelling was described as spartan, with nothing to separate the living space

from the lighthouse. Improvements were made in 1872, with the addition of two bedrooms and a storeroom for lantern supplies. The station was also supplied with a 4.7-metre boat.

A letter to lightkeeper Edward M. Mosher from the Department of

MOSHER ISLAND	
ESTABLISHED:	1868
CCG Light #:	423
POSITION:	44° 14' 14" N
	64° 19' 01" W
	On the island, west side of entrance to La Have River
LIGHT:	Fixed white
AHW:	23.3 metres
NOM. RANGE:	11 nautical miles
HORN:	B2, S18
DESCRIPTION:	White circular fibreglass tower, 11.4 metres high

Transport in September 1950 refers to a fire in the lighthouse. The letter doesn't describe the damage in detail, but it was likely quite extensive. The light continued in operation, however, until March 16, 1953, when conditions were set out for the construction of a new lighthouse and dwelling. In September of that year, the contract was awarded to Atlantic Bridge Co. Ltd. of Lunenburg. The lighthouse was a wooden pepper-shaker-type tower, 7.9 metres high. The dwelling was a three-bedroom, one-and-a-half-storey house.

In November 1956, a new fog-alarm building was built, and in January 1962, this building, the lighthouse, and the dwelling were all wired for electricity, the power for which was supplied by diesel generators. In 1964, a second one-and-a-half-storey dwelling was built by Urban Construction at a cost of $25,348, which included $1,000 to demolish the original dwelling. Commercial power came to the lightstation from the west end of the island on August 14, 1967, a centennial gift to Ingram and Lynne Wolfe, who had transferred to Mosher Island from West Ironbound Island in June 1966, and were destined to be the last lightkeepers at this station. They spent 25 years on Mosher Island, enjoying the tranquility of the island without the rumbling roar of diesel engines 24 hours a day.

In March 1989, a new 11.37-metre-high round fibreglass tower was installed about 30 metres from the old pepper-shaker tower. But because it interfered with the visibility of the new tower, and was not considered a heritage building, the old lighthouse was disposed of on March 12, 1990—tipped over on its side and burned by Coast Guard forces.

The Wolfes left the island and their home on October 8, 1991. It was with a sad heart that they went, knowing not only that their 30 years of lightkeeping had come to an end, but that this entire way of life was ending—they being among the very last of Nova Scotia's lighthouse-keeping families.

There is no easily accessible point on the mainland from which to view this lighthouse. A boat trip through the La Have Islands group provides the best opportunity to see it as it should be seen, from seaward.

West Ironbound Island

063 The origin of the name of this lighthouse is unknown, but it probably refers to the rugged nature of the island. It is surprising that it wasn't named Wolfe Island because in 1778 the island was granted to Leonard Christopher Wolfe, and aside from Benjamin Fulker, who was appointed as its first lightkeeper, a series of Wolfes kept the light for the following 75 years: John Wolfe from 1857 to 1864, Enos Wolfe from 1864 to 1895, Howard Wolfe from 1895 to 1910, and Frederick Wolfe from 1910 to 1932. The record also shows that at the time of de-staffing in 1966, the last keeper and the one who kept this light for its last five years was Ingram N. Wolfe, who spent the next 25 years, with his wife, Lynne, keeping the light on nearby Mosher Island. West Ironbound Island is roughly 1,300 metres long by 600 metres wide, and its light on the south side serves both as a leading light to the eastern entrance to the La Have River and as a coasting light.

The first lighthouse was a simple square wooden building with an octagonal lantern at the top, serving both as a lighthouse and a dwelling. It was

WEST IRONBOUND ISLAND	
ESTABLISHED:	1855
CCG LIGHT #:	432
POSITION:	44° 13' 43.2" N
	64° 16' 30" W
	On the south side of the island at the entrance to La Have River
LIGHT:	Flashing white, F2/E10
AHW:	24.3 metres
NOM. RANGE:	8 nautical miles
HORN:	None
DESCRIPTION:	White circular fibreglass tower, 10.5 metres high, with two red bands—one at the top and the other at the middle

The fibreglass tower that was installed on West Ironbound Island in 1987.

pretty cramped and uncomfortable, the dwelling having just one room at the base of the tower with a cellar that was subject to constant flooding. In 1878, after keeping this light for 14 years under such poor living conditions, Enos Wolfe convinced the Department of Marine and Fisheries of his need for expanded facilities. So while the chimney was being rebuilt and the lantern base re-shingled, a kitchen was added to one side of the tower. This was said to have greatly added to the material comfort of the keeper and his family. A serious breach in the nearby cliff caused by the action of the sea necessitated moving the lighthouse a greater distance from the edge of the cliff in 1882. The building was given thorough repairs at that

time, but no further expansion was made.

A beautiful new commodious six-room dwelling surmounted by an octagonal iron lantern was built in 1938. There was also a boathouse and two storage barns on this station. In 1966, the iron lantern was removed from the top of the dwelling and replaced with a watertight 300-millimetre Wallace/Tiernan lantern fitted on the open deck. A six-volt flasher and lamp changer were also installed, supplied by 20 batteries and activated by a sun switch. The station was de-staffed at the same time, and the other buildings were declared surplus, to be sold and removed from the island. The boathouse was in good condition and was quickly sold, but the other two buildings were destroyed.

The lighthouse continued to serve for another 21 years, but lack of care took its toll and it was no longer cost-effective to repair or maintain the building. In 1987, it was replaced by the current fibreglass tower. Almost nothing remains to remind us of the blood, sweat, and tears that went into maintaining this important lightstation for 111 years. A couple of foundations serve as melancholy reminders of a time when keeping a lighthouse was an important and honourable vocation on which lives depended.

This lighthouse is not visible from shore.

Battery Point Breakwater

064 Lunenburg, one of the great fishing ports of North America, was settled in 1753 by families mainly from Germany and Switzerland. These farmers, who first began fishing just offshore and gradually went to Newfoundland's Grand Banks, soon rivalled the best deep-sea fishermen in the world. Lunenburg became renowned for shipbuilding, especially as the home of our famous schooner, *Bluenose*. Launched in 1921, *Bluenose* was the winner of four international schooner races and remained undefeated to the end of its days. The *Bluenose* is on a 1928 Canadian 50-cent postage stamp, which many philatelists consider to be the most beautiful postage stamp ever issued by this country. The ship has also been pictured on the back of Canadian dimes since 1937. A replica of this beautiful schooner was built and launched in 1963 by Smith and Rhuland of Lunenburg, the same company that built the original. The *Bluenose* is open to visitors when in port.

Why wasn't there a lighthouse at this important seaport until 1937? There was, in fact, a lighthouse, but on Battery Point. Built in 1864, it was a white square wooden dwelling surmounted by a 2.7-metre-high, 12-sided lantern. John A. Ernst was appointed as the first keeper in November 1864 at $240 per year.

In 1941, the Lunenburg member of parliament expressed his concern over the dilapidated condition of the lightstation. Subsequently, repairs were made and the station was cleaned up, but in 1945 plans were made to replace it with a new combined lighthouse/dwelling, even though a 1937 lighthouse and fog bell existed nearby on the end of the breakwater. In 1948, a bungalow was built near the site of the old Battery Point lighthouse, and construction of a new breakwater began

BATTERY POINT BREAKWATER	
ESTABLISHED:	1937
CCG LIGHT #:	438
POSITION:	44° 21' 36.7" N
	64° 17' 49" W
	Near the outer end
	of the breakwater
LIGHT:	Fixed red
AHW:	7.5 metres
NOM. RANGE:	8 nautical miles
HORN:	B2, S18
DESCRIPTION:	White wooden
	pepper-shaker-type tower,
	7.72 metres high

You could still get very wet tending the Battery Point Breakwater light in Lunenburg Bay.

early in 1951. It seems there was no plan to move the 1937 lighthouse because a new one was going to be built on the new breakwater. The lighthouse was completed in September 1951 and is the same one that exists there today.

The last keeper of this light was Harvey L. Huskins, who was appointed in January 1962. By then, the station consisted of a bungalow dwelling and an oil shed on Battery Point, and the lighthouse on the end of the breakwater. Coincidentally, just as Huskins reached retirement age, automation caught up with the station and on June 19, 1987, it was de-staffed. Huskins went into retirement after keeping this light for 25 years. He had been lightkeeper on Little Hope Island and Spectacle Island. "No money in it," he said, "but if I was a young man, I would go right back at it again. I loved it."

In October 1987, the six-room dwelling was declared surplus and turned over to Crown Assets for disposal. Because one of the terms of sale was that it had to be moved from the site, it sat vacant for eight years before it was finally sold, dismantled, and moved away in 1995. Nothing is left now but the automated lighthouse sitting on the end of the breakwater.

There is no public right-of-way to the lighthouse, but it can be seen from the waterfront in the town of Lunenburg.

Cross Island

065 Cross Island is about 162 hectares, located at the mouth of Lunenburg Harbour, about 11 kilometres from town. The name is thought to have come from an early beacon erected to identify the island to French traders—a large wooden cross.

As dangerous ledges near Cross Island brought more and more vessels to grief, a lighthouse was built under the direction of Rudolf & Heckman in 1832. Cross Island lighthouse became the tenth in Nova Scotia. Immediately, there was concern that it could not be distinguished from Sambro Island or the Shelburne light (Cape Roseway). So great was the concern that a second lighthouse tower was recommended to be built about 250 or 300 metres from the other at a cost of £780, with an additional annual expense of £172 to operate it. A less costly alternative was decided upon, which was to build a second tower on Sambro Island instead. A second tower was never built at either place, but a large black cross was painted on the side of the lighthouse tower on Cross Island as a distinguishing daymark.

An 1857 report states that the lighthouse was an octagonal wooden building, 16.15 metres high base to vane, and painted red, showing a flashing white light in the lantern and a fixed white light from a bow window in the side of the tower below the lantern. A dwelling house was built close to the lighthouse. The first lightkeeper, Jacob Smith, was appointed at a salary of £100 per year and given a £15 fuel allowance. It was recommended that he be supplied with a spyglass and a flag. Records do not show whether he was supplied these items, but do say that in 1874 a 4.57-metre station boat was provided, which was kept at the landing a little over 1.6 kilometres from the lighthouse.

The station experienced the usual changes in optics and fog alarms that

CROSS ISLAND	
ESTABLISHED:	1832
CCG LIGHT #:	443
POSITION:	44° 18′ 43.4″ N
	64°10′ 08.7″ W
	East point of the island
LIGHT:	Flashing white,
	once every ten seconds
AHW:	24.9 metres
NOM. RANGE:	13 nautical miles
HORN:	B3, S3, B3, S51
DESCRIPTION:	White round fibreglass
	tower with red lantern,
	11.7 metres high

Note the seats in the trailer behind the tractor. This was the Cross Island "taxi," which transported people and supplies the 1.6 kilometres between the landing and the lighthouse.

came with each advance in technology, but the greatest change came in 1960 when an oil furnace caused a fire in the adjacent engine room. The original lighthouse tower and several other buildings burned. The lighthouse was replaced with a functional but ugly aluminum skeleton tower, which was itself replaced in 1985 with the existing fibreglass tower.

George and Ethel Locke came to Cross Island as head keepers in 1981, and kept the station in top-notch condition—a showplace for visitors—until automation and de-staffing caught up to them. They left their home on Cross Island for the last time on July 10, 1989. An excellent book, *Vanishing Lights*, written by Chris Mills, describes his experience as an assistant lightkeeper to George Locke in the months leading up to the de-staffing.

Life on Cross Island revolved around the fishing industry, and it boasts one of the finest little harbours on that

coast—a long narrow indentation entering the eastern side of the island and lying in an east-west direction. Although quite narrow, the water is deep, allowing even small coastal vessels to tie up almost anywhere along its banks. It is completely sheltered and safe inside the harbour, no matter how rough the sea is outside. By the early part of the twentieth century, Cross Island was a prosperous fishing village with 16 families, a schoolhouse, and a teacher who lived on the island. Twenty fish-storage buildings lined the sides of the harbour. There was even a lobster cannery employing 30 to 40 people. As fish became scarce, boats were sold, and one by one the families moved to the mainland until, finally, only the lightkeepers remained as year-round residents. Today, there are a half a dozen or so families who keep a summer cottage on Cross Island, but for most of the year the island is deserted and the automated light from the fibreglass tower sweeps into the darkness, unseen by any island resident other than the white-tail deer that no doubt still continue to graze at night near the dark, deserted station buildings.

This lighthouse cannot be seen from the mainland.

Gunning Point Island

066 This lighthouse was built on Tanner Island under contract by A. L. Mury of West Arichat for $728. It was called Tanner Island lighthouse until a solar panel was added to supply power for the light in 1967. Then, for some unknown reason, the light became known as Gunning Point Island light. There is a Gunning Island about 1,300 metres south of Tanner

GUNNING POINT ISLAND

ESTABLISHED:	1913
CCG LIGHT #:	446
POSITION:	44 °22' 01.2" N
	64° 12' 06.6" W
	On the east end
	of Tanner Island
LIGHT:	White flashing, F0.5/E3.5
AHW:	10.9 metres
NOM. RANGE:	5 nautical miles
HORN:	None
DESCRIPTION:	White circular fibreglass tower with a red horizontal band at the top, 7.8 metres high

Island, but no lighthouse there.

The original lighthouse was described as a square wooden building with sloping sides and 8.2 metres high. The first lightkeeper was R.G Wight, appointed at $180 per year, but since the light was on average only shown from April 1 until January 1, that wage wasn't bad for the time. Harry Knickle was appointed the second and only other keeper for this light, serving from October 8, 1927, until the light was made unwatched in October 1963. There was no other building on the island, so the lightkeeper had to live on shore and tend the light each day by means of a dory supplied by the government. For 36 years, Knickle rowed out every evening to light the light and every morning to extinguish it.

The record doesn't show what happened to the original wooden tower, but I expect that after 73 years of ser-

The original lighthouse on Gunning Point Island had to be tended by a keeper who rowed a dory to and from the island twice a day. Nobody tends the light in this fibreglass tower.

vice, and with no lightkeeper to maintain it for the last 23 years, it was no longer cost-effective to carry out repairs. In November 1986, the lighthouse was replaced with a 7.8-metre fibreglass tower equipped with a 200-millimetre plastic lantern, and 12-volt lamps supplied by two 12-volt lead acid batteries, which are charged by a 10-watt solar panel.

Although they didn't get the name quite right, this little fibreglass tower still stands on an obscure little island located among innumerable ledges and shoals just east of the village of Stonehurst, which is about nine kilometres east of Lunenburg. Besides warning of these dangerous waters, its purpose is to mark the south side of the seaward end of Tanner Pass, which is used mainly by local small fishing craft. The area is pretty as a picture and a paradise for small boaters and sea-kayak enthusiasts who seek adventure exploring the maze of hundreds of islets and passages around the eastern point of the Lunenburg Promontory.

This lighthouse cannot be seen from the mainland.

Westhaver Island

067 Mahone Bay is known as the bay with 365 islands. One of them is Westhaver Island at the south side of the entrance to Mahone Harbour, 400 metres from shore at Eisenhauer's Point. The original lighthouse, oil store, and boathouse were built under contract by James Smith of Lunenburg at a cost of $1,325, and put into operation on October 10, 1882. The lighthouse consisted of a tower 11.58 metres high with a dwelling attached. J. Peter Strum was appointed as its first keeper. On June 28, 1887, a fire resulted in the total destruction of the lighthouse and its contents, though the oil store and boathouse were saved. The fire was thought to be the work of an incendiary, but the inspector was unable to arrive at a satisfactory conclusion. A temporary pole light was erected pending the construction of a new permanent light. In 1888, the temporary light was thought to be providing satisfactory service, so it was erected on a permanent mast. The old lighthouse cellar was filled in with stone and earth, and the oil store was converted into a comfortable house for the keeper—though the record doesn't show in whose opinion it made a good home—and the boathouse was used to store supplies. The new keeper, James Alfred Strum, was appointed on September 25, 1888.

On January 15, 1896, a new tower was completed on the summit of the island about nine metres above high water. It was a square wooden building, painted white, and topped by a hexagonal iron lantern painted red. Attached to its northwest side was a small white wooden dwelling.

The light was replaced by a reliable acetylene system in 1921, and made unwatched. The lighthouse itself remained in service until 1948, when it was replaced by a skeleton steel tower. In January 1985, a Coast Guard heli-

WESTHAVER ISLAND	
ESTABLISHED:	1882
CCG LIGHT #:	451
POSITION:	44° 26′ 09.5″ N
	64° 20′ 17″ W
	Mahone Harbour
	entrance
LIGHT:	Flashing white, F0.5/E3.5
AHW:	9.6 metres
NOM. RANGE:	7 nautical miles
HORN:	None
DESCRIPTION:	White circular fibreglass
	tower with red horizontal
	band at top,
	6.7 metres high

Note the foundation of the 1896 lighthouse at the summit of this tiny island.

copter lifted a 1,360-kilogram fibreglass tower into place on the prepared site. Technicians mounted a solar-powered 300-millimetre plastic lens on top to serve as the light—not a lighthouse in the true sense.

Mahone Bay is a small picturesque town with narrow streets lined with craft shops, art studios, and galleries, among other things. A town proud of its marine heritage, its beautiful waterfront, with three mid-nineteenth-cen-

tury wooden churches, is one of the most photographed in the province. If you should happen to be in Mahone Bay on any June 27, and the conditions are right, you just might see a flaming ship disappear into the waters of the bay. That would be the apparition of the *Young Teaser*, an American privateer that was chased into the bay on June 27, 1813, by a British man-of-war. On board the *Teaser* was a British deserter who realized that capture meant death, so he threw a torch into the powder magazine, blowing up the ship and sending it down in flames to the ocean's depths. Legend has it that on the event's anniversary, the ship can still be seen.

Drive about 2.4 kilometres southeast of Mahone Bay on Route 3, turn onto Herman's Island Road and continue about 1,200 metres to Westhaver Beach, from which you can see the light.

Kaulbach Island Range

Quaker Island

068 Range lights serve the purpose of precisely directing vessels into a safe channel—the mariner simply lines up the lights. In daylight, the rear tower is lined up over the front by the vertical red stripes, and at night by the lights. These lights lead vessels into the Martin River anchorage, which is safe and roomy enough, but contains many islands, ledges, and shoals that make it dangerous for anyone unfamiliar with the area.

James W. Heisler, owner of Kaulbach Island, operated a small farm there, and after the lighthouses had been erected, he was offered and accepted the job of lightkeeper at $228.29 per year. The lighthouse towers were erected under contract by N. J. Robinson of Chester, Nova Scotia, at a cost of $975 plus $477.65 for an inspection and installing the optics. Set on concrete corner posts, each tower was 6.7 metres high, base to vane. James Heisler faithfully kept the lights until 1940, when his son Reuben C. Heisler assumed the duties. In 1960, these lights were changed to ones that were battery operated, coinciding with Heisler's retirement. The lights were then considered automated, but to ensure continued reliable service, the Nova Scotia District Marine Agent recommended a caretaker be hired at $100 a year, to keep an eye on things and do minor maintenance. Since Reuben Heisler was the only resident on the island, he was offered the job and accepted. A new policy in 1966 required that all work for the Department of Transport had to be contracted out, so Heisler's services were terminated. As a tribute to Reuban and James Heisler's unfailing attention to duty from 1914 to 1968, Paul Hellyer, former minister of transport and housing, sent a letter of appreciation.

In 1969, commercial power was brought to the island by submarine

The range lights on Kaulbach Island lead vessels into the Martin River anchorage.

KAULBACH ISLAND RANGE

ESTABLISHED:	1914
CCG LIGHT #:	453 & 454
POSITION:	
Front tower:	44° 28' 11" N, 64° 16' 56" W
Rear tower:	111 metres from the front On the northeast end of the island
LIGHT:	Fixed white
AHW:	Front, 11 metres; rear, 20.7
NOM. RANGE:	Unknown
HORN:	None
DESCRIPTION:	Identical white wooden pepper-shaker-type towers with vertical red stripe on seaward side

cable, and on December 15 the range lights were connected. The power of the lights was increased considerably when they were changed to 100-watt mercury-vapour lamps, as they remain today.

Kaulbach Island is a pretty, partially wooded island about 23 hectares in size, located about 1.5 kilometres from Indian Point, the nearest point of land. The lights, however, cannot be seen from the mainland.

069 Quaker Island is only one of many good-sized islands scattered about Mahone Bay, distinct from others by the light tower that graces its summit, marking the west entrance to Chester Harbour two kilometres to the north. The island is about 15 hectares, very steep from the summit to the sea on the south side, with a long gradual grassy slope to the north, which ends at a sandy beach.

Chester has been a tourist destination for over 150 years, a favourite recreational port for yachting and sailing enthusiasts, and the location of many summer homes. Island picnics are popular among local folk and visitors alike, and Quaker Island seems to be a favourite spot.

Around the light tower are the ruins of what was once a lightstation—the old stone foundation of the original lighthouse. The square tower with a

This little fibreglass tower sits on the summit of 24.6-metre-high Quaker Island in Mahone Bay.

QUAKER ISLAND	
ESTABLISHED:	1883
CCG LIGHT #:	456
POSITION:	44° 30' 53.3" N
	64° 13' 59.5" W
	Off Chester Harbour
LIGHT:	Flashing red, F0.5/E3.5
AHW:	30.8 metres
NOM. RANGE:	5 nautical miles
HORN:	None
DESCRIPTION:	White circular fibreglass
	tower with red horizontal
	band at the top,
	6.2 metres high

dwelling attached was built under contract in 1883 by Thomas O'Neill of Guysborough, for the sum of $1,400. It was 10.66 metres high, base to vane, and painted white. An outhouse and boathouse with slipway completed the station that was first kept by William Whalen, appointed on February 15, 1884, at $300 per year. In 1912, an oil store was built by G. C. Webber at a cost of $149.94, which was sold in 1943 for $10 just as the station was starting to be dismantled. The records are not clear as to what happened at this station, but it appears that in 1939, a skeleton steel tower was constructed and the light was made unwatched. The characteristic was changed from red to flashing white and was operated by battery. With a sun switch to turn the light off during daylight hours, the life of the battery cells was extended to 250 days.

The existing tower was erected on December 11, 1981, and is still battery powered, though the battery is now kept charged by means of a solar panel. A little shed nearby was no doubt used to store batteries from the time when a greater number of batteries were required to provide power over a longer period of time.

About 4.2 kilometres to the west of Quaker Island is one of Nova Scotia's more famous islands, Oak Island. Evidence of a buried treasure thought to be Captain Kidd's was found there in 1795 and has confounded treasure hunters to this day. Millions of dollars have been spent, and lives have been lost, in the quest to find the treasure, but to no avail. Numerous books have been written and a film has been made about the treasure of Oak Island, and so the legend continues. Detailed information on the mystery is available locally.

Quaker Island and its light tower can be plainly seen from the waterfront in Chester.

070 This light is of great service to vessels that trade in Chester, St. Margaret's Bay, and Mahone Bay, and of benefit to fishermen generally. The island lies 2.4 kilometres south from the extremity of Aspotogan Peninsula, and is at an elevation of 32 metres; the island is 1.6 kilometres long by 800 metres wide, and 130 hectares. The island was named after the iron-grey stone, and was also known as Chester Ironbound Island until the early 1940s. Today, it is known to most locals simply as Ironbound Island.

On January 3, 1870, just three years after the lighthouse was built, it was destroyed by fire. The lightkeeper, Edward Young, stated that he had just come down the stairs after trimming the lights, smoking his pipe, when he saw a bright light through the window. He ran upstairs and found the top in a blaze, the flames running along the floor. He took up three buckets of water, which he threw on the fire, but had to make a quick escape. The keeper thought the house must have been struck by lightning, as the accident occurred during a violent storm. It is not improbable that the wind broke the glass of the lantern, overturning the lamps and setting the oil on fire, thus causing the flames that were seen through the window. The entire building was destroyed in just a few minutes. The superintendent concluded that the fire was entirely the result of an accident.

No light was shown from the time of the loss of the lighthouse until it was rebuilt. No time was lost, however, and a light was shown from the new lighthouse on January 5, 1871. The contract for building was awarded to Hopps and Brown of Lunenburg, for the sum of $1,200. By the time the new iron lantern and lighting apparatus were installed, the total cost was $1,811.24.

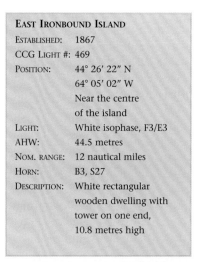

The lighthouse is described as a rectangular one-and-a-half-storey wooden dwelling with a square tower rising from the roof at one end. Besides the combined lighthouse/dwelling, the station had an oil-store building, an 8.5-metre boat, and a 400-metre road from the lighthouse to the landing.

On October 12, 1872, the lighthouse was loosened from its foundation by a terrific gale, making it necessary to secure the building with four wire-rope stays, fastened to two sides of the tower, and to eyebolts in the rock. At a later date, four more wire-rope stays were added to secure the building firmly to the ground—two stays from each of the four sides at the top of the tower, just below the lantern.

I visited the station in September 1990, while it was still manned by 45-year-old Paul C. Finck. Paul thought I might like to talk to his father, Charles H. Finck, who had kept the light for 25 years—from 1955 to 1980. Charles's father had kept the lighthouse before him, from April 1930 to 1955, and Charles had built a new home just a stone's throw from the lighthouse in which he had lived as a boy with his parents and five other siblings. He recalled that before a school was built on East Ironbound, he and his siblings had to travel to Big Tancook Island, about six kilometres away, to attend a one-room schoolhouse. There were nine families on East Ironbound at that time and almost every family had a team of oxen to haul their boats up on the skidway. This was the only way they could keep their boats safe because the island had no protected harbour. In about 1943, Charles's father, Edward, became too crippled to carry the oil for the lamps up the four flights of narrow steps to the top of the tower. His wife Violet took over the lightkeeping duties for 12 years, until Charles officially took over the job.

Four members of the Young family kept this light for the first 55 years, 1867 to 1922. Alan M. Langille was the lightkeeper for the next six years, from 1922 to 1928. For one year, 1929, it was unwatched, after which three generations of the Finck family kept the light for 60 years, 1930 to 1990. Violet Finck celebrated her 108 birthday on January 8, 2002, undoubtedly the oldest living lighthouse keeper in Nova Scotia and possibly all of Canada.

In 1966, electric power was brought to East Ironbound Island by means of a 5,486-metre submarine cable laid

There were several lighthouses of this design built at about the same time as this one was on East Ironbound Island. Church-like in appearance, it is the only operational lighthouse like it in Nova Scotia. One hopes that someone will realize the benefit of preserving it for generations to come.

EAST IRONBOUND ISLAND	
ESTABLISHED:	1867
CCG LIGHT #:	469
POSITION:	44° 26' 22" N
	64° 05' 02" W
	Near the centre
	of the island
LIGHT:	White isophase, F3/E3
AHW:	44.5 metres
NOM. RANGE:	12 nautical miles
HORN:	B3, S27
DESCRIPTION:	White rectangular
	wooden dwelling with
	tower on one end,
	10.8 metres high

from Blandford, and life became a whole lot easier for the population of about 40 people. For several years previously, limited power had been supplied to the community by a big old caterpillar diesel-electric unit; after electricity, it was kept on standby for emergency power in the event of a commercial failure on shore.

Most of the year-round residents have now left the island, and the lighthouse is showing signs of neglect. It has never been declared a national historic site, nor is it on the provincial list of protected historic buildings. The Coast Guard's policy is not to demolish old structures without first consulting the Federal Heritage Buildings Review Office in Ottawa, but the local community needs to get involved and take some responsibility for the care and preservation of this historic building. It would be a shame if the beautiful little lighthouse were lost through neglect. It is one of a kind and best exemplifies the lifestyle of the folks who kept our lighthouses in a bygone era.

The lighthouse cannot be viewed from the mainland.

Note: Violet Mae Fink crossed the bar on December 18, 2002, just 21 days short of her 109th birthday.

Notice the eight wire rope stays securing the tower against north Atlantic gales.

Pearl Island

071 Pearl Island is located about 9.7 kilometres to the south of Aspotogan Peninsula, which is the nearest mainland and separates St. Margaret's Bay and Mahone Bay. The light on this bleak little speck of an islet is one of the most isolated in Nova Scotia. Originally named Green Island, and called Isle Verte on a 1636 chart, it was changed to Pearl Island in 1914 to avoid confustion with other islands along this coast named Green Island. It was named after the Pearl family, which had kept the light since 1873.

Alex Sinclair built the original lighthouse, including an oil shed, for $2,950.29. Expensive for the time, but understandable because of the difficulty in getting materials, supplies, and workers on and off the island. The lighthouse was a white, square, wooden tower with a dwelling attached, and topped by a 3-metre-high, 12-sided wooden lantern—a very common plan at the time. The first keeper was Albert Pearl, appointed on December 29, 1873, at an annual salary of $500. In view of the open and isolated situation, the Department of Marine and Fisheries provided a good 5.5-metre boat and an allowance of $100 to aid in building a boathouse and slip. Lightkeeper Pearl also suggested early on that the lighthouse secured to the rocks by two stays because of the high winds in this exposed place.

As an indication of the beating this little island took, the lighthouse had to be replaced in 1929. The new lighthouse was a 7.7-metre-square, two-storey wooden dwelling surmounted by a red iron lantern, 11.58 metres high base to vane. The third and last member of the Pearl family to keep the light was Albert Pearl, grandson of first keeper and son of the second keeper, Mather B. Pearl, who served from 1908 until 1941. Even with a sturdy and fast boat, life on Pearl Island wasn't easy.

Since there was no sheltered harbour or any way to protect the landing, it was very often damaged by storms and the boat was wrecked several times. With no way to get off the island, there were several recorded instances of the keeper and family running out of food and water. Upkeep of the station was also an ongoing problem because of the difficulty in landing stores and materials.

An inspection in January 1962 revealed that the general condition of the lighthouse was poor. The boathouse was old and rotten and the old lighthouse building adjacent to the present lighthouse, which was being used as a work shed, was in very unsat-

PEARL ISLAND	
ESTABLISHED:	1874
CCG LIGHT #:	471
POSITION:	44° 22' 56.8" N
	64° 02' 56.3" W
	Off St. Margaret's Bay
	and Mahone Bay
LIGHT:	White flashing, F0.5/E9.5
AHW:	19 metres
NOM. RANGE:	13 nautical miles
HORN:	None
DESCRIPTION:	White square aluminum
	tower, 11.6 metres high

isfactory condition. So bad were the living conditions that the keeper's family had long since refused to live on the island, leaving Albert Pearl at the station all alone. It was recommended that the light be automated as soon as possible.

On January 21, 1962, Violet Finck, retired lightkeeper on East Ironbound Island, 6.9 kilometres to the north, told her son Charles, the current keeper, that she didn't see a light on Pearl Island and that he should go see why it wasn't lit. Charles and a couple of others went to investigate. Albert Pearl's partly eaten meal was still on the table, but Albert was gone without a trace. His body was never found and his disappearance remains a mystery to this day.

Temporary keepers kept the light for the next few months, but in October of the same year, a severe storm wrecked the station. The horn was discontinued

Almost 10 kilometres from the nearest mainland, few people get to see Pearl Island light nor would they likely care to. On a clear night from Peggy's Point, the light can be seen about 16 kilometres to the southwest.

Indian Harbour

and an acetylene light was installed. The station became unwatched in November 1963. In February 1973, the buildings were declared surplus and J. L. Nichols Contracting of Bedford was hired to demolish all the abandoned structures and build a new lighthouse—the third and existing tower. It is an ugly, square, flat-topped steel-framed building with aluminum siding, 3.4 metres square, and 9.29 metres high. A solar-powered, battery-operated light is on the open top.

It seems sad that there is nothing here to remind us of those who served in this barren, inhospitable, and inaccessible place. But perhaps it's not totally uninhabited. Some people say the ghost of Albert Pearl still occupies the island, especially on dark and stormy nights.

This light cannot be seen from the mainland.

072 This lighthouse is known locally as Paddy Head light because of its location rather than for the harbour it is intended to mark. It was established as a guide into Indian Harbour for small vessels seeking an entrance through the narrow channel between Paddy's Head Island and Wreck Island.

Situated 29 metres back from the point, it was erected by day labour under the supervision of Amos McLennan at a cost of $728.24. The first keeper was Henry Boutilier, appointed on June 6, 1901, at $100 per year.

A notice to mariners dated February 23, 1945, stated that the lighthouse was going to be connected to commercial power and made unwatched. In 1955, a caretaker, George Richardson, was hired at $50 a year. Caretaker duties for minor lights included renewing the lamp as required, periodically cleaning the glass in lantern, changing batteries when required, making minor repairs, observing proper functioning, discouraging vandalism, and to report any difficulties. Richardson continued in this position until 1967, when maintenance of the light was taken over by the Department of Transport forces.

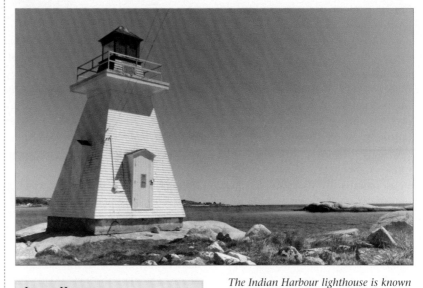

The Indian Harbour lighthouse is known locally as the Paddy Head light.

INDIAN HARBOUR

ESTABLISHED:	1901
CCG LIGHT #:	482
POSITION:	44° 31′ 20″ N
	63° 56′ 48″ W
	On the southeast
	extremity of Paddy
	Head Island
LIGHT:	Fixed white
AHW:	11 metres
NOM. RANGE:	11 nautical miles
HORN:	None
DESCRIPTION:	White wooden pepper-shaker-type tower, 7.5 metres high

To get to the lighthouse, travel 4.6 kilometres west of the Peggy's Cove intersection at Route 333 to Paddy's Head Road. Continue about 1.4 kilometres to a dead end. From here, permission is required to walk across about 200 metres of private property to the lighthouse. A picturesque view of the lighthouse can also be had across the small harbour from Route 333.

Peggy's Point

073 This lighthouse is undoubtedly the best known in Nova Scotia, and one of the most photographed places in Canada, and yet, most people mistakenly refer to it as Peggy's Cove lighthouse, when, in fact, it is Peggy's Point lighthouse. The village of nearby Peggy's Cove boasts a year-round population of about 50 people, who try to maintain a lifestyle established by previous generations despite the great numbers of tourists attracted to the cove in the summer months. Picturesque is the best way to describe the little harbour, with trim houses, weatherworn wharves, and brightly coloured fishing boats—a favourite place of photographers and artists. The landscape is remarkable in itself for the huge granite boulders scattered across the entire area, some seemingly balanced precariously atop the highest points of the barren hills, deposited there 10,000 years ago by the retreating glaciers. Down by the lighthouse and along the shore as far as you can see, there is a great expanse of granite worn smooth by the sea, a wondrous sight to behold and exactly the kind of place you would expect to see a lighthouse.

The first lighthouse built here in 1868 was a lighthouse/dwelling combined. It was made of wood, 7.7 metres square, and surmounted by a lantern—making it 8 metres high base to vane. Four years after the lighthouse was built, two bedrooms and a storeroom were partitioned off and finished in the upper part of the building, adding much to the comfort of Edward Horn, who was appointed its first keeper at $350 per year.

On April 15, 1881, during a gale from the southeast, a heavy sea broke completely over the point, doing considerable damage to the foundation and other parts of the main building, and completely sweeping away the oil store

About the only time you can get to see Peggy's Point lighthouse when there aren't crowds of people swarming over the granite rocks is in the winter time. Even on miserable stormy days, folks like to visit the lighthouse to observe the power of the sea as it crashes ashore sending sheets of water and spray over the top of the tower.

with all its contents. Extensive repairs were carried out and a new oil store was built, costing $545.

In 1915, a new lighthouse, the existing reinforced-concrete tower, was built 18 metres west of the old lighthouse, and first showed a light on August 1, 1915. Standard Construction Co. of Halifax constructed the tower at cost of $2,457. Provision and installation of the 2.44-metre lantern and optic cost an additional $1,954.92. In the 1940s, the light source changed several times: from an Aladdin oil lamp and petroleum vapour to a duplex flat-wick lamp, an electric-powered light, then back to oil again. Finally, in 1949, the light was changed back to commercial electric power.

The old one-and-a-half-storey lighthouse/dwelling contained eight rooms and was used from time to time by the

PEGGY'S POINT	
ESTABLISHED:	1868
CCG LIGHT #:	487
POSITION:	44° 29' 30" N
	63° 55' 09" W
	East side of entrance to
	St. Margaret's Bay
LIGHT:	Fixed green.
AHW:	20.4 metres
NOM. RANGE:	Unknown
HORN:	None
DESCRIPTION:	White octagonal
	reinforced-concrete tower
	with red aluminum
	octagonal lantern,
	15.2 metres high

Department of National Defence during the war years. Unoccupied after the war, and no longer fit for human habitation, the lighthouse was declared surplus and offered for sale. On March 16, 1955, there being no interest in the building, Lester E. Hubley of Seaforth, Nova Scotia, was contracted to demolish it, which he did the very next day.

In March 1958, R. R. Manuel, who had been the lightkeeper since July 9, 1934, and then the caretaker, declared that he was no longer interested in the job, so the light was fitted with a time switch and declared unwatched.

Betty Island

One of the largest pepper-shaker type lighthouses in the province, the Betty Island tower is able to have all its equipment installed within, eliminating the need of a separate equipment building.

However, because of continuing power problems, York Manuel, the son of the former lightkeeper, was hired as caretaker on April 9, 1958, at $100 per year. This he did until November 1966 when his service was discontinued.

No one seems to know whose idea it was to put a post office in Peggy's Point lighthouse, but from June 1 to September 30, 1978, the post office was temporarily set up for the tourist season. Response was beyond all expectations, so it became permanent. This is the only lighthouse/post office in Canada, and it even has its own cancellation stamp, a likeness of the lighthouse. Overlooking the lighthouse,

Note the square green glazed box fitted over the light, an uncommon and innovative means of providing the green light characteristic.

there is the Sou'Wester, a large restaurant featuring fresh seafood dinners, and a two-storey souvenirs and Nova Scotia handicrafts shop.

From the intersection of Route 103 and 333 West, travel 36 kilometres to Peggy's Cove. It's about 800 metres from the turnoff to the lighthouse, which is well marked and easy to find.

074 Betty Island is 2.5 kilometres southeast of the village of Prospect. It has an elevation of 28 metres, and is about 1.6 kilometres long with an average width of about 600 metres. The lighthouse on Betty Island plays an extremely important role in guiding vessels into Prospect Bay through a bank extending over 1.6 kilometres westward, with shallow depths and numerous rocks and shoals above and below water.

According to an article by John Gilhen, this island was named after the first child born on the island. Late in the eighteenth century, the first settler, Samuel White, is thought to have landed in a cove near Prospect with his pregnant wife, a young son, and all they

BETTY ISLAND	
ESTABLISHED:	1875
CCG LIGHT #:	495
POSITION:	44° 26' 19.4" N
	63° 46' 02.8" W
	On Brig Point
LIGHT:	Flashing white, F3/E27
AHW:	19.2 metres
NOM. RANGE:	18 nautical miles
HORN:	B6, S54
DESCRIPTION:	White wooden
	pepper-shaker-type tower,
	12.8 metres high

possessed. They pulled the boat as high on shore as possible, turned it over, and built a lean-to around it to use as a shelter while a cabin was built. Before the cabin was finished, Joanne gave birth to a baby girl under the boat. They named her Elizabeth, Betty for short, and the island was named for her. The cove they landed at was on the east side of the island, now called Gallon's Cove, but in the past it has also been called Galleon Cove, and in some early reports, Gallant's Cove and Gallantry Cove.

There have been three lighthouses on Betty Island. The first was built on Brig Point at the southern end of the

island. The building consisted of a tower painted white with two horizontal red bands, to which was attached a dwelling. In the rear there was a shed covering a brick cistern. The landing at Gallon's Cove was 500 metres from the lightstation, so it was necessary to build a store for oil and supplies that could be moved to the station afterward. The contract was awarded to a man named Baker for $2,750. By June 1875, the sum of $5,000 was expended, and a further $1,153.31 was spent during the ensuing fiscal year, bringing the total cost of this lighthouse to $6,153.31. The first lightkeeper, Patrick Christian, was appointed on September 27, 1875, at an annual salary of $500. The Christian family kept the light through three generations, until 1921, when J. W. Clancey was appointed lightkeeper. He continued to live in the same dwelling until a new lighthouse was built in 1939, about 30 metres west of the old lighthouse. Clancey enjoyed his new home for the remaining two years of his service. The combined dwelling/light tower was 7.62 metres square, two storeys high, and topped by a square wooden lantern.

Joseph Victor Kiley was appointed keeper on October 1, 1953, and although the dwelling was in excellent condition, he chose to live there alone most of the year, his wife and children living on shore during the school year. Life was not easy on remote island

Terence Bay

stations, especially where school-age children were concerned. Some were educated by correspondence, while others were boarded ashore with friends or family during the school year. Some keepers elected to transport their children back and forth by boat every school day, which was never easy and at times very dangerous.

Island lightstations suffer a lot of damage during severe weather, especially to the slipways and boathouses, which always took the brunt of it. Even in modern times, dangerous situations are bound to occur, as noted in a message from Betty Island to the Coast Guard on December 22, 1981: "Outboard motor will not work. Winch to haul up the boat will not work and tractor will not operate in reverse. There is a storm coming. Please send help."

This combined square wooden lighthouse and equipment building was built by Blunden Construction Ltd. of Halifax, and completed on November 30, 1981. In August 1982, in view of the run-down condition of the dwelling and the cost of replacing it, the decision was made to automate the station. It was de-staffed the week of June 27 and automated on July 11, 1983. All the old buildings were declared write-offs and destroyed. The old lighthouse, built in 1939, had outlived its usefulness and on December 19, 1986, was burned to the ground. The lighthouse is now the only building remaining on Brig Point. An oil tank and fog alarm stand nearby, but the emergency diesel generator set, batteries for the emergency light, and the fog-detector equipment are all housed in the base of the tower. The main power source is by submarine cable from ashore.

This lighthouse cannot be seen from the mainland. However, weather permitting, you can see its flashing white light southeast of Peggy's Point, about 13 kilometres away.

075 In 1885, a pole light was erected on Shipley Head near Tennant Point, which forms the western head of the entrance to Terence Bay, to guide coastal traffic and fishermen seeking harbour. The light was displayed from a small dioptric lantern hoisted on a mast 7.62 metres high, and had a white wooden shed at its base. Terence Bay light was built by Patrick A. Fahey for $175. The first keeper, Peter Jollymore, was appointed on September 1, 1884, at $83.33 per year.

It wasn't until 1903 that the mast was replaced by the square wooden tower that stands there today. The lighthouse was erected by day labour at a cost of $471. The last keeper, Hezron Jollymore, was appointed on February 18, 1942, and was no doubt pleased to have the light electrified on December 18, 1952. Unfortunately, commercial power, which made his job so much easier, would end up costing him his job, as the light was made unwatched on April 1, 1957. He was offered a job as caretaker of the light at a reduced rate of $40 per year, which he took. He lost this job in 1967 when the

TERENCE BAY

ESTABLISHED:	1885
CCG LIGHT #:	498
POSITION:	44° 27' 36" N
	63° 42' 24" W
	On Tennant Point
LIGHT:	Fixed red
AHW:	14.6 metres
NOM. RANGE:	6 nautical miles
HORN:	None
DESCRIPTION:	White wooden pepper-shaker-type tower, 7.9 metres high

Department of Transport decided to hire on a contract basis. A sun switch turned the light on at dusk and off at dawn.

In about 1980, the top of the tower was in very bad condition, so it was removed down to the top of the windowsills, decked over, and a watertight light was mounted on the open deck. The light had to be replaced a couple of times because of severe damage by gunshot.

Get off Route 333 at the intersection for Terence Bay and Lower Prospect. After about 7.6 kilometres of scenic paved road, there's an intersection for Sandy Cove to the left. Take this road 1.5 kilometres to a dead end and turning circle. You will see the light from this picturesque part of the shore. There is a right-of-way across private property for Coast Guard technicians— not to be construed as a public lane. The light can be reached by walking from a small beach at the end of the road along the rocky shore, but private property must be respected.

Terence Bay shore is pretty as a picture, though spoiled by the loss of the lighthouse lantern.

Halifax Metro

Halifax ● ● Dartmouth
● 081
080 ●
● 082
077 ●
● 079
076 ●
● 078

Halifax
Dartmouth

076   Pennant Harbour 70
077   Sambro Harbour 70
078   Sambro Island 71
079   Chebucto Head 75
080   Maugher Beach 76
081   Georges Island 78
082   Devils Island 79

Pennant Harbour

Sambro Harbour

076 This small harbour light is intended for the benefit of local fishermen and small boaters. The original lighthouse was built by day labour under foreman William H. Whebby at a cost of $384, and was put into operation on July 7, 1903. It was a typical harbour light of the period, a

By 1990, the 87-year-old tower was showing serious signs of deterioration, and because it was no longer economically feasible to keep it in repair, the existing circular fibreglass tower was installed. It was lit on May 30, 1991, and the old wooden tower was removed from the site.

077 Sambro is a sheltered harbour lying at the head of the bay formed between Pennant Point on the west and Cape Sambro on the east, but the dangers within are so numerous that only smaller vessels and those with knowledge of the harbour should enter. For this reason, the lighthouse estab-

SAMBRO HARBOUR	
ESTABLISHED:	1899
CCG LIGHT #:	505
POSITION:	44° 28' 30.1" N
	63° 35' 45.4" W
	On the extremity
	of Bull Point
LIGHT:	Fixed green
AHW:	10.4 metres
NOM. RANGE:	8 nautical miles
Horn:	None
DESCRIPTION:	White wooden
	pepper-shaker-type tower,
	9.7 metres high

Unlike the old tower, this fibreglass model has no lantern and no glass to clean.

wooden pepper-shaker type, 10.05 metres high. It was built on a concrete foundation 9.14 metres from the high-water mark on an elevation of three metres, showing a light only on its southwest side. The first keeper was Peter Angus Gray, who was appointed on June 30, 1903, at a yearly salary of $100. He kept the light until 1920, when J. C. Gray assumed the duties. On January 1, 1965, the light was connected to commercial power and made unwatched. At that time Lillian I. Gray had been keeper of the light for 24 years. She was offered the job of caretaker at $115 per year, one-fifth of her lightkeeper's salary, which she accepted. Gray continued in this capacity until a change of policy in 1967 discontinued the use of caretakers, by this time she and her family had kept the light at Pennant Harbour for 62 years.

PENNANT HARBOUR	
ESTABLISHED:	1903
CCG LIGHT #:	501
POSITION:	44° 28' 15.5" N
	63° 38' 03.6" W
	North side of entrance
	to Pennant Cove
LIGHT:	Fixed green
AHW:	10.4 metres
NOM. RANGE:	7 nautical miles
HORN:	None
DESCRIPTION:	White circular fibreglass
	tower, 8.1 metres high

Drive west on Route 349 about three kilometres past the village of Sambro; the light tower can be seen from the road.

lished on Bull Point was useful. The lighthouse was built by the Department of Marine and Fisheries with the supervision of foreman McLellan at a cost of $676.04. It was built 9 metres from the high-water mark and is the same tower that exists today, except that when it was built it had a square wooden lantern on top, making the tower 10.05 metres high base to vane. The first keeper was John H. Finlay, appointed on December 7, 1899.

On December 18, 1947, the lighthouse was converted to electrical power. When lightkeeper Albert Gilkie, who had been keeping the light since November 1929, advised the department of his intention to retire when he turned 65 in July 1961, the light was connected to a photo-electric sun switch that would turn the light on at dusk and off at dawn.

Interestingly, the government removed all of the old equipment and cancelled the station's inventory, which

Sambro
Island

Another truncated lighthouse in Sambro Harbour, also known locally as the Bull Point light.

typically consisted of 2 duplex oil lamps, 6 duplex chimneys, 2 bars of soap, 2 pounds of rags, 1 extension ladder 20 feet long, 1 broom, 1 mop, 3 pounds of putty, 6 light bulbs, 10 pads of stationery, 24 envelopes, 4 lightkeeper's logbooks, 9 loose forms, 3 bottles of ink, 3 pen holders, 3 pens, 4 pen nibs, 2 gallons of white paint, and 1 gallon of red paint.

Some time in 1971, due to the badly deteriorated upper part of the lantern, it was stripped away to the windowsills, a deck was built over it, and a watertight lantern was mounted on the open deck. Thus the "lighthouse" became a "light."

Sambro Harbour is home to a Canadian Coast Guard Primary Search and Rescue Unit—a group of brave and dedicated people who regularly put themselves in danger to help others in distress. On average, they respond to about 76 calls a year.

The lighthouse is very near the Coast Guard base, and can be viewed from there. Otherwise, drive into the village of Sambro, continue east on Bull Point Road until you reach the end, then walk a short distance to the light. Please respect private property.

078 At the same time that the first lighthouse in Canada—built by the French at Louisbourg in 1734—was being pounded to ruin by the British during the siege of 1758, an act for erecting a lighthouse at the entrance to Halifax Harbour was passed.

An earlier attempt had been made in 1752 to raise funds for building the lighthouse by means of a lottery. However, that failed, and subscribers were refunded their money. This time, £1,000 was appropriated from the duties paid on spirits to help with the plan. Captain Rous, owner of Sambro Island, signed a deed to the island and work was begun.

By November 3, 1758, the masonry of the lighthouse was finished and work on the lantern was started. The structure is situated at the highest ele-

The Sambro Island lighthouse after the lantern was changed to the new aluminum one. The building at the water's edge below the lighthouse is the gas house, where acetylene gas was manufactured for use as the illuminant for the light in 1906.

vation of Sambro Island, a 10-hectare heap of granite at the entrance to Halifax Harbour. The tower was octagonal, and built of granite blocks and rubblestone 1.68 metres thick at the base and 13.41 metres high, with a lantern of unknown height. The tower is 6.1 metres in diameter at the base and tapers toward the top, but the diameter inside is a constant 2.66 metres. A spiral staircase leads to the top, which is built around a solid octagonal post, 46 centimetres thick. The outside ends of the steps are carried on stringers supported by 20-cen-

CHEBUCTO HEAD	
ESTABLISHED:	1758
CCG LIGHT #:	507
POSITION:	44° 26' 12" N
	63° 33' 48" W
	Centre of island
LIGHT:	White flashing, F0.5/E4.5
AHW:	42.7 metres
NOM. RANGE:	24 nautical miles
HORN:	B2, S3, B2, S3, B2, S48
DESCRIPTION:	White octagonal stone tower, 25 metres high, with three horizontal red bands

timetre-square corbels.

On April 25, 1759, Joseph Rous, brother to Captain Rous, was commissioned as the first keeper of this lighthouse. All did not go well in the early years, especially because the cheapest materials, such as common fish oil, were used to provide illumination, but weren't very reliable and the light often went out. When that happened, the keeper would not bother to relight it if there were no ships in sight or expected. This oft-times lack of a light so angered ship masters, who were required to pay a tax for the use of the port and to support the cost of providing the light, that they sometimes fired shots at the lighthouse to make the keeper show a light.

Joseph Rous died on May 3, 1769, and although the record is not clear, it seems Joseph Woodmass was appointed lightkeeper until April 1771, when the sloop *Granby* of Boston was lost on the Sambro ledges. According to Commodore Gambier, the commander in chief, the fatal accident happened because no light had been showing in the lighthouse. An inquiry into the accident recommended that the government take over the operation of the lighthouse, but nothing seemed to come of this because in 1772, Matthew Pennell was appointed lightkeeper.

In 1834, the lantern was described as having eight large wooden posts, nearly 30 centimetres square, as uprights, which together with the wooden sashes for the 128 small panes of glass greatly obstructed the light. Strangely, serious consideration was given to lowering the height of the tower by 4.6 to 6 metres because mariners often said that in the summer months the lantern was frequently enveloped in haze (fog) and totally obscured, while the island and lower part of the tower could be plainly seen.

Sambro Island at that time was

equipped with a cannon, used to answer ships' signals as mariners felt their way through the haze, and thought themselves to be near the lighthouse. Records show that there was an artillery guard at the station for the purpose of firing the fog cannon. One of the artillerymen, so the story goes, was a Scot named Alexander Alexander. Minnie Smith, a lightkeeper's daughter, spent a great deal of time on Sambro Island hearing the stories passed down from her grandfather William Gilkie through other members of the Gilkie family, who kept Sambro Island light for almost a hundred years. Minnie recalls a story about Alexander:

"One day Double Alex, as he had become known, was sent ashore with an escort to Halifax to pick up the payroll and supplies, but fell in with bad company on the mainland, and when he returned to Sambro Island several days later without the payroll and supplies, he was, understandably, in a lot of trouble. Remorseful and sick, he asked the captain for a drink and upon being refused, staggered off to a nearby building and hanged himself. When they found him hanging,

Sambro Island lighthouse as it appeared from 1864 to 1906.

The emergency kerosene lamp—equipped with six double flat-wick burners—from Sambro Island lighthouse.

they cut him down and he was still warm. My grandfather said to the English captain, 'he's not dead, draw blood on him and his heart will start pumping,' but the captain refused, saying that in the English Army, when somebody does that [commits suicide] they let him go."

Double Alex has been known to haunt Sambro Island to this day. Different lightkeepers have related stories of his presence on the island and the things he would do—nothing serious or harmful, just annoying noises in the night, sounds of walking across the ceiling, knocking, doors opening and closing by themselves, lights turning on and off, and the toilet flushing. One keeper and his wife, Johnny and Marge Fairservice, said that they had put up with this for 24 years, but there had never been any harm done.

Although many complaints were heard regarding the poor service the light provided, the lighthouse commissioner's report of 1834 stated that nothing more could be done to improve the light until a new iron lantern could be installed. It was not until 1864 that the improvement was undertaken. In October of that year, the top of the lighthouse was stripped, thoroughly repaired, painted, and supplied with a new 12-sided iron lantern, 2.89 metres in diameter and 4.87 metres high. The tower, wood sheathed on the outside, shingled and painted white, then stood 18.3 metres high, base to vane.

The next big change in the appearance of the lighthouse occurred in 1906. An octagonal reinforced-concrete section, 6.7 metres high, was added to the top of the stone walls of the tower and surmounted by a new first-order circular iron lantern. Inside the lantern, a curved iron ladder with eight steps led to a narrow gallery at the bottom of the glazing, which extended outside about 46 centimetres. The glazing of the lantern was divided by 12 vertical mullions; within each pair there were three pieces of curved glass set vertically. The cupola was copper with riveted gores, all topped by a large ventilator ball and a weathervane. Roy Gilkie said that when he was a young man in the 1920s, he enjoyed standing on top of the ventilator ball while greasing the weathervane, which was 25 metres above the ground and 43 metres above high water. "It gave the sensation of floating in space," he said, "because you couldn't see the lighthouse below you, just the top of the ball and the lantern roof."

The work on the tower was completed by day labour under the supervision of J. A. Legere in November 1906 at a cost of $2,934. It was then 25 metres high, base to vane, painted white with a bright red lantern, and had a first-order Fresnel lens installed. Made in France by the firm Barbier Benard and Turenne Ltd, the lens was 1.84 metres

in diameter and 2.74 metres high, and had a focal length of 92 centimetres. It had four panels (faces) giving four flashes every revolution. The 1,814-kilogram lens turned smoothly in a trough containing over 400 kilograms of mercury.

In 1908, it was decided that seven lighthouses in Nova Scotia would be repainted white with red horizontal bands to make them more conspicuous when snow was on the ground. The bands on the Sambro Island lighthouse were alternately red and white, each 2.44 metres in width.

In January 1950, lightkeeper W.A. Will Smith observed that the lighthouse was swaying noticeably, and it was found to be 20 centimetres out of plumb. In May, the base of the tower was excavated in eight places to a depth of about 50 centimetres, which revealed that the mortar was cracked

This first-order Fresnel lens, displayed at the Maritime Museum of the Atlantic, projected the light from the Sambro Island lighthouse from 1906 until 1966. It is 2.74 metres high, 1.84 metres in diameter, weighs 2 tonnes, and floated in a trough of 408 kilograms of mercury. Each of the prisms is geometrically cut at a different angle to efficiently gather 83 percent of the light from a central lamp and project it in a horizontal plane.

and several stones were loose. In October, in order to haul equipment and supplies to the work site, a wooden ramp was built from the shore near the gas house to the base of the lighthouse. Grouting pipes were fitted throughout the existing masonry of the supporting base through which concrete grout was pressure pumped. This solidified the existing base, but then a new reinforced-concrete wall was poured to form a collar 90 centimetres thick and approximately 2 metres high around the base of the lighthouse.

On November 17, 1966, a 91-centimetre rotating airport beacon was installed to replace the Fresnel lens, which was removed from the lighthouse and put into storage until the following June. At that point it was given to the Maritime Museum on permanent loan to be displayed in the new Maritime Museum of the Atlantic. In May 1968, the first-order iron lantern was taken down and returned to base stores aboard CCGS *Edward Cornwallis*. A new 3.88-metre-high aluminum lantern was installed, reducing the overall height of the lighthouse to 24 metres, base to vane.

John Fairservice, his wife Marjorie, and their daughter Kelly were the last keepers of this lighthouse. John was an assistant from 1964, then head keeper until the station was de-staffed on March 28, 1988. When the family came ashore that final day, it was the first time in 230 years that there was no human presence on Sambro Island. At the time, Rob Matthews, an editor with the *Halifax Herald*, aptly described it as "A light without a heart."

Sambro Island lighthouse is the oldest operating lighthouse in North America—already 109 years old at the time of Canada's Confederation. It is difficult to imagine the history it has witnessed, but in 1758, the year this lighthouse was built, the legendary Captain James Cook was a 30-year-old petty officer in the Royal Navy. Four years later, in 1762, he made reference to Sambro Island lighthouse in his directions for entering Halifax Harbour. It is also intriguing that the lighthouse could very well have been the last Halifax landmark that General Wolfe saw in May of 1759, when he sailed away to his destiny on the Plains of Abraham at Quebec City. And it may have been the first Halifax landmark seen by some of the 12,000 Loyalists who landed here in 1783.

Sambro was very definitely the last of North America that Captain Joshua Slocum saw as he set off on the first leg of his epic voyage to be the first to sail around the world. As he noted in his log on the evening of July 3, 1895, "Sambro, the Rock of Lamentations, a noble light. I watched light after light sink astern as I sailed into the unbounded sea, till Sambro, the last of them all, was below the horizon."

Consider also that hundreds of thousands of refugees no doubt viewed Sambro Island lighthouse in much the same way that others like them looked upon the Statue of Liberty, as they anticipated the start of a new way of life in a new country. And the lighthouse was likely the last thing that many Canadian men and women ever saw of their country as they went off to war, never to return. But it no doubt gladdened the hearts of those who saw it on their return, the first positive visual indicator that they were home again.

The last Canadian warship to be sunk by enemy action, the Bangor-class minesweeper HMCS *Esquimalt*, was torpedoed by German submarine *U-190* on April 16, 1945, just 5 nautical miles from Chebucto Head, and almost the same distance from Sambro Island, resulting in the loss of 44 of a crew of 83.

Incredibly, as recently as 1993, this 235-year-old lighthouse was not listed on the National Register of Historic Buildings. Three separate surveys had been carried out in 1965, 1974, and 1986, presumably for the purpose of submitting the lighthouse for consideration as an historic building, but nothing came of them. In 1994, the Nova Scotia Lighthouse Preservation Society began lobbying for heritage status for Sambro Island lighthouse and the gas house, which was built in about 1911 and is an integral part of the station. In 1995, the Coast Guard followed through with another survey and this time it was submitted to the Federal Heritage Building Review Office. On August 22, 1996, Sambro Island lighthouse was designated a "classified building," the highest possible heritage designation bestowed by the Ministry of the Environment. The gas house, although not nearly so highly rated, was nevertheless designated a "recognized building," the second highest heritage designation.

Between September and November 1994, volunteer members of the Nova Scotia Lighthouse Preservation Society carried out extensive repairs to the gas house, particularly to the roof, which was totally replaced—including the rafters, sheathing, cedar shingles, and fascia boards—and the chimney. The gas house was then closed up to minimize further damage and deterioration of the building. By May 1995, large chunks of concrete were falling away from the gallery deck of the lighthouse tower and there was clear evidence of deterioration of the wooden sheathing and shingled exterior of the tower. On August 26, 1998, Cureggio General Contractors carried out further restoration for $193,000. Using 22,680 kilograms of steel scaffolding, all the shingles, sheathing, and strapping were removed. It was the first time since 1957 that the tower had been stripped down to bare granite, providing a wonderful opportunity to inspect the original structure. Almost four months later, on December 21, 1998, the work was complete and the workers left the island for the last time. The final bill came to $250,000 and Sambro Island lighthouse probably looked better than it has since 1906.

But there is more to a lighthouse than sheathing, shingles, and paint. The inside was still dank, with decades of yellowed whitewash hanging in strips from the granite walls. The gas house is deteriorating at a frightening rate, and two dwellings sit severely damaged by vandals and are succumbing to the ravages of the elements. It is imperative that we do everything in our power to preserve this historic structure for the benefit of generations to come. Sambro Island lighthouse embodies the maritime history of Canada, and as the oldest operating lighthouse in North America, its preservation should be a national issue.

Drive about 1.5 kilometres past Ketch Harbour on Route 349, turn left, and continue about 1.3 kilometres to Sandy Cove. Sambro Island lighthouse can be seen across the water from Sandy Cove, a little more than 3 kilometres away.

Chebucto Head

079 Chebucto Head rises 32.3 metres above high water at the southern extremity of the western shore of Halifax Harbour, one of the finest and safest harbours in the world, with water deep enough for even the largest vessels. "Chebucto" comes from the Mi'kmaq name given to Halifax — Chebookt—which means "a chief harbour."

The first lighthouse was constructed by Joseph Bowser for $2,375, with an additional $1,435.69 spent on the optics. It was first lit on August 21, 1872, by lightkeeper Edward Johnson, hired at a yearly salary of $400. The light tower and dwelling were in the

CHEBUCTO HEAD	
ESTABLISHED:	1872
CCG LIGHT #:	513
POSITION:	44° 30′ 26″ N
	63° 31′ 24″ W
	On the summit
LIGHT:	Flashing white,
	F0.5/E19.5
AHW:	49.4 metres
NOM. RANGE:	16 nautical miles
HORN:	B3, S3, B3, S51
DESCRIPTION:	White octagonal
	reinforced-concrete tower,
	13.8 metres high

same building, a white square wooden structure with a 12-sided wooden lantern that showed a white flashing light once every minute from 40.2 metres above high water. An oil store and boathouse were built down on the shore well below the lighthouse, 137 metres away, thus requiring a roadway. In 1890, it was decided that the station was admirably located for a fog alarm, which would enable a vessel approaching from any direction to establish its position in time to make a good course up the harbour. The fog-alarm building was built near the water below the lighthouse. A tramway was built to transport

Chebucto Head lighthouse remains in reasonably good condition considering how easy it is to access the site. There are vandals about, but they don't get to do their work when good folks are around.

coal from the landing to the coal room, a large reservoir to provide water for the steam fog-alarm boilers was also built.

In 1940, a new lighthouse was built 628 metres away, 240 degrees from the old lighthouse. It was a white wooden dwelling, 7.62 metres square, and topped by a 2.44-metre-high red octagonal iron lantern that showed a light from 50 metres above high water. The lighthouse was 10.97 metres high, base to vane. The fog-alarm building was now almost 800 metres away from the lighthouse and hazardous to get to, especially in the winter months. Even so, it wasn't until 1951 that a new fog-alarm building was completed about 60 metres from the lighthouse. Having no further use for the old brick, slate-roofed fog-alarm building and with no offers to purchase it, it was given to the military at Fort Chebucto to remove as a demolition exercise. Thus ended all physical evidence of the existence of the old lightstation.

In 1949, a one-and-a-half-storey dwelling had been built for an assistant keeper at the new station. In 1967, another new lighthouse was built. This one is the existing reinforced-concrete octagonal tower built just 20 metres from the last lighthouse, now missing its 3-metre-high aluminum lantern, which was removed and installed atop the new lighthouse. Shortly afterward, a new dwelling was built for the head keeper, and in 1969, a radar remote-control station was built together with assorted towers for Halifax Harbour Control. The lightstation was also

Maugher Beach

undergoing technological changes: it became semi-automated in preparation for total automation.

On December 31, 1980, the last lightkeeper, Stanley Flemming, retired after over 30 years at the station, and the light was automated. In 1983, one of the dwellings was sold and removed from the site in accordance with the terms of sale, and in 1984, another dwelling was sold and removed. The remaining two-storey dwelling, which was the previous lighthouse, was used for a period of time by other government agencies but transferred back to the Coast Guard in 1985 and staffed by a caretaker, Sydney Malone, a former lightkeeper. On September 1, 1989, Jim Guptill, another former lightkeeper, and his wife Dale, took over the caretaker job; they continue to live in the old lighthouse building. With the establishment of the Regional Advisory Council on Lighthouse Alternative Use in 1997, the possiblity exists for an interested community group or organization to restore and preserve Chebucto Head lighthouse as an historic building.

Just north of Ketch Harbour, there is a turn-off onto a paved road to Duncan Cove and a sign for Chebucto Head. Drive 2.1 kilometres to the lighthouse and a parking area that provides a breathtaking view of the approaches to Halifax Harbour. It's a popular place to view ships of all nations and descriptions entering and leaving. Whales can often be seen in this area, and at about 9 kilometres to the northeast, you can see Devil's Island and the lighthouse that marks the east side of the harbour entrance.

080 McNab's Island was formerly known as Cornwallis Island. In 1783, Peter McNab bought it for £1,000 and it is by his name that it has been known on maps since 1818. Joshua Maugher was a merchant and trader who came to Halifax from Louisbourg when the fortress was restored to France in 1749. He was involved in several enterprises in and around Halifax, and certainly was not without influence in the area. Among other things, he operated a fish plant on a beach that he owned and to which he gave his name. It is also known as Hangman's Beach, although no one is known to have actually been hanged there. In his book *Hangman's Beach*, Thomas Raddall describes how during the Napoleonic wars, the Royal Navy used the beach to display bodies of exe-

MAUGHER BEACH	
ESTABLISHED:	1815
CCG LIGHT #:	527
POSITION:	44° 36' 08.2" N
	63° 32' 01" W
	Near the west end of the beach at the southwest end of McNabs Island
LIGHT:	Flashing yellow, Fl/E29
AHW:	17.4 metres
NOM. RANGE:	8 nautical miles
HORN:	B2, S18
DESCRIPTION:	White octagonal reinforced-concrete tower, 16.5 metres high

cuted sailors as a warning to those foolish enough to disobey the laws of His Majesty's Naval Service. After the sailors were executed, usually by hanging from the yardarm of their ship, the bodies were tarred to keep crows and gulls from picking their flesh, so that they might be preserved as long as possible to serve their grizzly purpose. Then they were chained to a gibbet by their wrists and ankles, a rusty iron col-

The existing Maugher Beach lighthouse, built in 1941, witnessed huge convoys of ships slip past in secrecy during the Second World War as they started their perilous voyage across the North Atlantic.

lar was put around their necks, and they were left there for as long as nature allowed. At one time, six gibbets dangled skeletons with blackened shreds of skin and sinews clinging to the bones—mutineers from HMS *Columbine*.

Every vessel in and out of the port of Halifax passes within close range of this beach, which extends nearly a full kilometre out into the harbour entrance. Thus a lighthouse was considered essential for their safe passage. In the late 1790s, serious attention was paid to fortifying the port of Halifax

This is the Sherbrooke Tower, the first Maugher Beach lighthouse, which showed a light on April 1, 1828. This picture shows the lantern after it was raised three metres in 1906.

because the French were in Louisbourg. In 1814, building began on a Martello tower, known as Sherbrooke Tower, at Maugher Beach, but lack of funding delayed its completion until 1828. Although a small light was exhibited from the top of the tower from as early as 1815, it was only lit when naval vessels were expected. In 1826, an appropriation of £1,500 was paid by the legislature to place a light on top of the tower. This light was actually shown for the first time on April 1, 1828, and its first known keeper was J. Bolser. The tower was 15.25 metres in diameter at the base, tapering slightly to 14.78 metres at the top. It was 9.9 metres high from the base to the top of the stone tower, with a roof and lantern extending upward another 4.7 metres. The walls were 2.29 metres thick at the base, and the light was shown from 17.68 metres above high water a distance of 10 nautical miles.

In 1846, Doctor Abraham Gesner, a Nova Scotian physician more interested in geology than practicing medicine, discovered a means of distilling kerosene from coal. It was here at Maugher Beach that he got permission to carry out the experiments that proved kerosene was superior to other fuels because it gave a safer, cleaner, brighter flame, not to mention that it was much cheaper. His discovery ushered in the dawn of the age of petroleum as an illuminant.

Because the tower was constructed on such an exposed site, it suffered a lot of damage from the sea with every storm, and, eventually, it was abandoned as a fort, and support by the Imperial government for its upkeep was discontinued. In 1867, responsibility was transferred to the Dominion government, but by this time several of the outside stones were loose and had to be fastened in place with wood wedges. Temporary breastworks of timber were erected that year, and a sleeping apartment was built for the accommodation of the keeper during stormy weather. The rest of the time, David George, who had kept the light since 1846, lived in a dwelling separate from the tower but connected by a bridge. During the autumn and winter months, the violence of the winds and waves would often completely wash over the house, threatening to completely destroy it.

In 1875, an elaborate breakwater almost 200 metres long was constructed and credited on several occasions with saving the beach and the dwelling from certain destruction. The breakwater, however, had to be rebuilt time and time again.

In 1906, the height of the lantern tower on top of the Martello tower was increased by 3 metres and a new larger iron lantern was fitted. The lantern and two sloping roofs of the circular tower were painted red, and the vertical parts of the Martello tower and superstructure were painted white, giving the effect of red and white horizontal bands. In 1913, a new double dwelling and a boathouse for the station boat were built.

A terrific storm in 1931 nearly destroyed the seemingly indestructible Martello tower, smashing away the entire outer wall on the south side and a great deal of the stone contained between the outer and inner walls. It was rebuilt, but the continuing high costs of repairs and restoration meant the tower's end was near.

The existing lighthouse was built in 1941. At the same time, workers began to tear down the Sherbrooke Tower, though it wasn't until June 1944 that it was finally demolished.

The last lightkeeper, Hector G. Lowe, served at this station from 1970 until it was de-staffed in 1983. The heavy damage so often inflicted upon this station was finally resolved in 1987, when the breakwater was rebuilt with massive granite boulders. Ironically, now that there was no longer any risk to human life in keeping the light, the government arranged for most of the station buildings to be burned to the ground in February 1988. But by this time, they had become an eyesore and a liability, with no hope of any kind of restoration and preservation program. Nothing is left now but the lighthouse tower, which is an important landmark that can be seen from most parts of the city's waterfront, and still serves as a seamark to thousands of pleasure boats and ships of all descriptions from around the world. Interestingly, a 13-cent Canadian postage stamp was issued in 1938 depicting Halifax Harbour, including the Martello tower lighthouse.

McNab's Island is being developed into a 400-hectare wilderness park and is visited by thousands of residents and tourists every summer. Ferry service operates from Cable Wharf on the Halifax waterfront from June to Labour Day.

Georges Island

081 This lighthouse is actually the front light of a range called Halifax Harbour Inner Range. The rear light was established in 1903, on a skeleton tower with a red vertical stripe, located on shore in Dartmouth, 2,735 metres from the front light. For the purpose of this account, only the tower on Georges Island will be described.

The contract for building the first lighthouse was given to Thomas Hallowell for the sum of $1,300. The lighthouse was completed and first lit on January 15, 1876. It is described as a drab square wooden building displaying two vertical fixed white lights 6 metres apart. The total cost of the lighthouse, including the lighting apparatus, was $1,746.01. Robert Ross, a sapper in the Royal Engineers, was appointed keeper on January 18, 1876, at an annual salary of $150. His duties also included keeping a fog bell.

Early in 1903, the lighthouse was replaced by a square wooden tower adjoining the western side of a dwelling, surmounted by a polygonal iron lantern. It was built by day labour at a cost of $2,813.08, which included the installation of the light. The lighthouse was painted white with a black diamond on the seaward south side just below the lantern, which was painted red. This lighthouse was 10.6 metres high, base to vane. Unfortunately, it was totally destroyed by fire in 1916. A temporary light was put in place immediately and plans were made to replace the lighthouse as soon as possible. However, it wasn't until January 1919 when the existing lighthouse was put into service.

In 1963, the island that had been named George Island in honour of King George II was renamed Georges Island. The reason is not clear, and there has always been some confusion as to its actual name.

GEORGES ISLAND	
ESTABLISHED:	1876
CCG LIGHT #:	538
POSITION:	44° 38' 26.3" N
	63° 33' 37.2" W
	On the west side of
	Georges Island
LIGHT:	Fixed white
AHW:	17.1 metres
NOM. RANGE:	Unknown
HORN:	B3, S27
DESCRIPTION:	White octagonal
	reinforced-concrete tower,
	15.8 metres high, with a
	fluorescent red vertical
	stripe to seaward

In 1970, commercial electric power came to the island and with it came semi-automation. Two years later, David and Jean Barkhouse, the last family to keep the light on Georges Island, became victims of the new age of automated lighthouses and the light was made unwatched. A 61-centimetre-wide fluorescent red vertical stripe was painted down the south side of the tower in 1973.

Georges Island, situated in the middle of Halifax Harbour a mere 325 metres from shore, can hardly be

Georges Island lighthouse in Halifax Harbour can be seen daily by more people than any other lighthouse in the Maritimes, but few take notice.

missed, especially by a lighthouse enthusiast, as it can be seen from just about any part of the city with a view of the harbour. And yet this island is, without a doubt, one of the best-kept secrets in the city of Halifax, especially considering that it was an integral part of the harbour defence system. Georges Island is one of four sites that made up an elaborate fortification unequalled by any other city in Canada. In 1965, it was declared a National Historic Site, but restoration and a plan to open the island to the public seem to be going painfully slow. Structures from every military period for over 240 years survive on Georges Island: from the earth and wooden fortifications of 1757 and a Martello tower from about 1812 to Fort Charlotte, built over 10 years from the late 1860s until 1872. A wonderful place to visit if it should ever be opened to the public.

The lighthouse can be viewed from the waterfront boardwalk, with the best view from Pier 21.

Devils Island

082 According to *The Sea Road to Halifax*, a book by Admiral Hugh Pullen, the island was originally known as Rous Island, named for Captain John Rous, to whom it had been granted in 1752. Later on it was called Wood Island, until a fire destroyed all the trees. The name was then changed to Devils Island, apparently because mariners and fishermen claim to have seen ghosts there. A more likely explanation was provided by the *Dartmouth Patriot* on July 6, 1901, in which it says that at one time the

on which the lighthouse was built. Besides the lighthouse tower, all that remains is the keeper's dwelling, which is in a derelict state, a couple of small sheds (also in ruin) and the collapsed ruins of a couple of other buildings.

There was a day beacon on Devils Island in as early as 1837. A Commissioners of Lighthouses report suggested that if it were fitted with a distinguishing light, it would provide security for the increasing number of trade vessels at sea, as several valuable ships had been lost in the vicinity. On

DEVILS ISLAND	
ESTABLISHED:	1852
CCG LIGHT #:	545
POSITION:	44° 34′ 51.4″ N
	63° 27′ 30.5″ W
	Southeast end of
	the island
LIGHT:	Flashing white,
	once every 10 seconds
AHW:	15.8 metres
NOM. RANGE:	13 nautical miles
HORN:	None
DESCRIPTION:	White octagonal wooden
	tower, 11.9 metres high,
	and no lantern

What a sin to have removed the lantern from this beautiful timber-frame octagonal lighthouse on Devils Island with no thought of replacing it. There are only two of this type left in Nova Scotia.

island was owned by a man named Deval or Devol, and his name was corrupted to Devil.

Situated at the eastern approach to Halifax Harbour, this 13-hectare treeless island lies about 800 metres southsouthwest of Hartlen Point. A 1951 topographical map shows 17 buildings on the island, including a school and post office. Sadly, the island is now uninhabited. It is privately owned by Bill Mont, except for the plot of ground

April 2, 1851, a lighthouse for Devils Island was approved. The fact that the *Southampton* had recently been fatally wrecked, no doubt played a big part in the decision.

The lighthouse was built in 1852 on the southwest side of the island. It had an octagonal wooden tower 13.7 metres high, and was painted dark brown with a white lantern showing a fixed red light 15.8 metres above high water. Because the lighthouse was built with every intention of using gas as the illuminant, another small building was built near the lighthouse to contain a furnace and two retorts to manufacture the gas. This occupied the greater part of the main floor, so the keeper's apart-

ment had to be made in a very small room over it. As was often the case, the well-being of the lightkeeper was the least concern. The first lightkeeper, Edward Bowen, who had been appointed at £60 per year with a £15 fuel allowance, lived entirely alone on the station. With only one small room in which to cook, eat, and sleep, it was not a fit place for a family, so they resided in Eastern Passage, 4 or 5 kilometres away. Sometimes Bowen didn't see his family for weeks at a time, and with his small salary, he wasn't able to hire anyone to help him at the lighthouse. It wasn't until seven years later, in 1859, that a house was built for the lightkeeper and his family.

It became clear that the low power of the red light at this station made it unsuitable for navigation, but because of the characteristics of the lights to the east and west of Devils Island, the light couldn't be changed. It was, therefore, recommended that a second lighthouse be erected about 182 metres from the present tower, which would show two powerful fixed white lights. This idea had its advantages. One keeper could attend both lights, and by bringing the two lights into alignment, vessels could clear the Thrum Cap shoals. On October 15, 1877, the second lighthouse was complete, 160 metres east of the old light, and two white lights were exhibited for the first time. A bridge crossing the gulch between the towers was also built. The whole cost of the improvements was $4,770.07, and the incumbent lightkeeper, Benjamin Fulker, saw his salary increased to $500 a year because of the extra duties entailed.

In 1890, a new dwelling was built for the keeper, the oil store was moved to a new location, a boathouse and slip were constructed at the landing, the old light tower was re-shingled, and its upper room was lined with matched lumber. The buildings were painted and the bridge across the gulch was renewed. All of this work was done by a man named Lund under contract for $1,115.

By 1950, flashing lights had become more practical and easier to install. Thus it was decided that the southwest point light would be discontinued and the characteristic of the newer east light would flash three times every 36 seconds—white flash, eclipse 6 seconds, amber flash, eclipse 6 seconds, white flash, eclipse 24 seconds—which made it different from any other light in the area. By 1958, lightkeeper Charles MacDonald wrote that extensive work and repairs were needed at the station, including a new breakwater and slipway, at an estimated cost of over $9,000. Over several years, families had been moving off the island until finally, the lightkeeper and his family were the only ones left. At this point, considering the costs involved in providing facilities for the lightstation, thought was given to converting it to automatic operation. In 1967, the light was made unwatched, and the following year all the buildings except the lighthouse tower were declared sur-

plus and sold to private interests.

In 1978, when the iron lantern was pushed off the top of the tower and smashed to pieces on the granite rocks below, it was no longer a lighthouse in the strictest sense, but simply a light. Despite its truncated state, this structure is one of the few octagonal, wooden, timber-frame towers remaining in the Maritime Provinces. Inside it there are three floors and a gallery deck, each slightly more than 3 metres high, with conventional wooden stairs going from floor to floor in the centre of the tower. One can also still see the 45.7-centimetre-square shaft in which the weights that turned the lens descended the full height of the tower. In this particular light tower, the weights had to be wound back to the top every eight hours.

There is no human presence on Devils Island now, and people seldom visit, not even to bear witness to the continued existence of the ghost of Henry Henneberry, a fisherman who was drowned near the shore in view of his daughter in 1917. According to his daughter and two granddaughters, he has haunted the island from that day onward.

The closest vantage point is from Hartlen Point. Drive south from Dartmouth on Route 322 past Eastern Passage.

Marine Drive

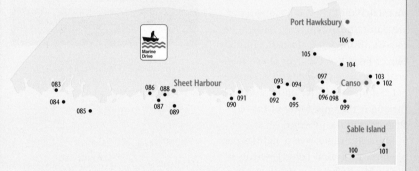

Marine Drive

083	Musquodoboit Harbour Range	.82
084	Jeddore Rock	.83
085	Egg Island	.84
086	Spry Bay	.85
087	Sheet Rock	.86
088	Sheet Harbour Passage Range	.87
089	Beaver Island	.87
090	Liscomb Island	.89
091	Redman Head	.90
092	Port Bickerton	.91
093	Fisherman's Harbour	.92
094	Isaac's Harbour	.93
095	Country Island	.94
096	Berry Head	.95
097	Charlos Harbour Range	.96
098	Hog Island	.97
099	White Head Island	.98
100	Sable Island West	.101
101	Sable Island East	.102
102	Cranberry Island	.103
103	Canso Range	.105
104	Queensport	.106
105	Guysborough	.107
106	Eddy Point	.108

Musquodoboit Harbour Range

083 These light towers were built by day labour under the supervision of Halifax Marine and Fisheries officers for the purpose of guiding vessels into safe anchorage inside of Steering Beach. The rear tower was built on a small knoll, but when the front tower was built on Shag Ledge, the only place it could be, it was found that the lights didn't range properly and the rear tower had to be moved off the knoll. To maintain the proper height of the light above high water, a straight-sided 3.66-metre extension had to be built under it, making it the only tower of this configuration in the province.

Strangely, there was a lightkeeper appointed for each light. Jeremiah H. Kent was appointed on April 29, 1904, to keep the front light, and John Kent was appointed on the same day to keep the rear light. Because the front light had to be tended by boat, that keeper was paid $125 per year, $25 more than the keeper of the rear lighthouse. But never mind, it was all in the family, and so it remains to this very day. For three generations, the Kent family kept these lights: from Jeremiah and John, to Fred and Archibald, then Ivan R. Kent, the grandson of the first keeper, who was still caretaker of the light in 2002.

Both lights became automatic in 1951. A 1960 report shows that the front light used battery power and the rear was on commercial power.

In 1972, extensive repairs were made to the front light, and the pier it sat on. A fluorescent vertical red stripe was painted on the seaward side of both towers at that time.

In 1985 and again in 1987, notice was given that the lights were going to be discontinued. But both times, the community rallied together under the leadership of Ivan R. Kent to voice their objections—the first time with a petition signed by 62 people who wanted

MUSQUODOBOIT HARBOUR RANGE	
ESTABLISHED:	1904
CCG LIGHT #:	Front, 568; rear, 569
POSITION:	
Front:	44° 41′ 41.4″ N, 63° 04′ 43.9″ W, On a pier on Shag Ledge.
Rear light:	1,219 metres from the front on French Point
LIGHT:	Front is quick flashing, F0.2/E0.8 Rear is fixed red
AHW:	Front is 6.4 metres; rear is 14.6 metres
NOM. RANGE:	Unknown
HORN:	None
DESCRIPTION:	Front is a white square wooden tower, 3.7 metres high, with sloping sides and red horizontal band at top; rear is white square wooden tower with sloping sides near the top, 11 metres high

at least the rear tower to remain. It was successful: the order to discontinue the light was cancelled, much to the relief of Kent, whose family has watched over it for so many years, and on whose property it sits.

With the introduction of the Alternate Use Program by the Coast Guard in 1997, it is hoped that the lighthouse will be transferred to Ivan and Mildred Kent, who operate the

[LEFT] The two range lights in Musquodoboit Harbour. Notice that the vertical red stripe is gone from the rear tower, as its use had been discontinued by this time.

[BELOW] A vertical extension was added to the bottom of the rear tower of the Musquodoboit Harbour range so that it would range properly with the front light.

Seaview Fisherman's Home bed and breakfast on French Point, just a stone's throw from the lighthouse.

From Route 7, east of Musquodoboit Harbour, turn south at Ostrea Lake/Pleasant Point Road; drive about 13 kilometres to Kent Road and the lighthouse.

Jeddore Rock

084 Jeddore Rock is about 35 kilometres east of Halifax, lying in the approaches to Jeddore Harbour, 2.9 kilometres, 108 degrees from Jeddore Cape. The passage is clear except for a rocky ledge that extends some 275 metres west of Jeddore Rock, which itself is only 370 metres long and, at the outmost, 100 metres wide. It is formed of slate and there's no vegetation other than a thin covering of soil and grass on the upper portion of the rock. The summit is 15.2 metres above high water.

In May 1881, tenders were invited for the construction on Jeddore Rock of a lighthouse with a dwelling, a barn, an oil store, and an outhouse, The contract was subsequently awarded to Jacob Bowser of Halifax for the sum of $3,362. The first keeper, Albert Warnell, was appointed on September 27, 1881, and the fixed red light was lit for the first time on December 15. The lighthouse with dwelling attached was painted white with two horizontal red bands painted on all sides.

Warnell, apparently not overjoyed with the isolation and constant danger in the face of North Atlantic gales, resigned his position after only one year. He was relieved by John W. Mitchel, who apparently didn't mind this kind of life, or so it would seem, as he faithfully kept the light through good times and bad for over 39 years until 1921.

In 1884, the landing slip was totally destroyed by heavy gales, so instead of another slip, a substantial landing platform was built at 5.5 metres above sea level. To this was added a stout derrick and winch to raise the station boat to a safe location. Even so, some damage did occur from time to time. The buildings regularly suffered the brunt of storms and deteriorated at a much faster rate than similar buildings ashore. By 1943, "the rock" was in need

JEDDORE ROCK

ESTABLISHED:	1881
CCG LIGHT #:	570
POSITION:	44° 39' 46.8" N
	63° 00' 39.6" W
	On summit of rock
LIGHT:	White flashing, F2/E10
AHW:	29.3 metres
NOM. RANGE:	8 nautical miles
HORN:	None
DESCRIPTION:	Skeleton tower with
	enclosed stairway,
	14.6 metres high

of a new lighthouse and dwelling. It turned out to be a 7.62-metre-square, two-storey wooden dwelling surmounted by a lantern—15.24 metres high, base to vane. A hand-operated horn was supplied for the keeper to answer vessels' signals.

Because of mounting costs and the difficulty of keeping the family supplied and the station in good repair, in 1955 it was recommended that the light be made unwatched. Despite local citizens' protests, and the fact that 35 fishing boats used this port and oil tankers made 10 trips a year here, two banks of 10 batteries were installed to operate a 12-volt lamp, all switched on and off by a sun switch. On November 26, 1958, the last lightkeeper, Albert Arnold, left Jeddore Rock and the station was officially listed as unwatched.

There never was a lantern on the Jeddore Rock skeleton light tower. The lantern roof seen in the foreground came from the previous lighthouse, which was torn down in 1977.

The new caretaker was Captain F. A. Germain, who was only required to go on the island if there was some sign of a problem with the light. When he died in 1961, his wife became caretaker. When a helicopter landing pad was constructed on the island in 1963, her only responsibility was to report if the light had failed to come on.

With the old dwelling leaking badly and showing signs of severe neglect after eight years of inattention, a skeleton tower on Cranberry Island was dismantled and transferred to Jeddore Rock, where it was rebuilt and lit on November 4, 1977. The old buildings were then demolished, and a new helicopter pad was built over the concrete foundation of the old lighthouse.

Today, nothing much remains but the skeleton tower, the helicopter landing pad, and the top of the octagonal iron lantern, lying where it fell when the lighthouse was demolished, looking very much like a child's giant spinning top, cast aside and forgotten. Next to it is a small heap of broken iron, the remainder of the lantern.

At least one person is absolutely certain that English pirates buried treasure here in 1668. Apparently, the treasure is located by rocks in the formation of the eagle constellation, which early navigators sailed by. My source says that as long as he can get his licence renewed under the Treasure Trove Act, he will continue his search.

There is no close vantage point from the mainland.

Egg Island

085 The light at this station is a leading light for adjacent harbours, but it's more important as a coast light for the many vessels on trans-Atlantic routes on their approach to Halifax about 72 kilometres to the west. Egg Island is the outermost of a group of islands on this part of the coast. A barren lump of rock less than a hectare in size, its highest point is 13.7 metres above high water. About 457 metres south of the island, although always above water, there are very dangerous ledges.

The original lighthouse tower was octagonal and made of wood. It was 13.7 metres high, base to vane, and painted with black and white vertical stripes on the seaward side to make a

EGG ISLAND	
ESTABLISHED:	1865
CCG LIGHT #:	580
POSITION:	44° 39′ 53″ N
	62° 51′ 48″ W
	Centre of island
LIGHT:	White flashing, F1/E19
AHW:	25.6 metres
NOM. RANGE:	10 nautical miles
HORN:	None
DESCRIPTION:	Skeleton tower with
	enclosed stairway,
	16.5 metres high

more visible and distinctive daymark. Separate from the tower, the station had a dwelling, a storage barn, and a boathouse. Lightkeepers were supplied with a 5.48-metre station boat and a hand-operated foghorn to answer vessels' signals. A landing place was constructed on the most sheltered part of the island for landing stores and hauling up boats, but on such a small exposed island, there was really no safe place, and the sea constantly damaged the landing. On September 3, 1870, a severe storm inflicted heavy damage to the station. The sea rolled up the

The Coast Guard erected two light towers only about 12 kilometres apart that appear identical by day. Even the two islands on which they stand are similar in appearance. But if you look closely, you will see differences between this tower on Egg Island and that on Jeddore Rock.

island, making a clean sweep over it and striking the southwest end of the dwelling house, carrying away the foundation wall and filling the basement with water. The keeper and his family immediately escaped to the lighthouse tower, praying it would withstand the force of the storm. No sooner were they inside when the next wave carried the house 46 metres down the slope, destroying the foundation, chimney, and everything within it. The house crashed into both the stores buildings, which were completely wrecked. The freshwater tank was destroyed, and about 30 metres of the landing disappeared. The light tower, was severely damaged, and the boats, fences, and buildings were all swept away. The foundation had to be entirely renewed and iron stays in solid rock were bolted to four of the lighthouse faces. Small temporary apartments were built into the lower part of the tower for the lightkeeper and his assistant until the house could be rebuilt. Marine and Fisheries subsequently sup-

plied the station with three life preservers for which William Condon, the first keeper of the station, must have been truly grateful.

The old dwelling was placed on a new foundation and thoroughly repaired the following year, but it took over two years to repair all the damage from the storm. A new 50-metre-long slip and landing was built, even with the knowledge that a year wouldn't go by when major repairs were not required. During the 10-year period 1892 to 1902, there was major storm damage no less than six times. To facilitate easier and quicker access to the light, a foot bridge was built between the dwelling and the lighthouse in 1886.

A major change came about in 1918 with the installation of a third-order lens and the associated apparatus at a cost of $7,856.58. Finally, a light worthy of the importance of the station. It gave two very bright flashes every 15 seconds out to a range of 15 nautical miles. In 1924, a new five-room dwelling was built. The old house had been used for 59 years, an amazing length of time considering all it had gone through.

In May 1962, the existing skeleton steel tower was constructed 11.27 metres from the old light tower with an aluminum lantern on the top deck.

Spry Bay

The bottom of the old tower was converted into an engine room and storeroom, and the station began generating electric power, significantly changing the living conditions and providing electricity for a 91-centimetre rotating airport beacon with a 1,000-watt lamp, which replaced the 55-millimetre oil-vapour lamp. This advancement raised the notion of automation.

On April 11, 1970, the lantern was removed from the tower, together with the airport beacon, which was replaced with an acetylene gas light. Two weeks later, the light was automated and the last lightkeeper on Egg Island, Ernest Roache, went ashore.

In November 1972, two sheds were torn down and burned, but I can find no record of what happened to the old tower or dwelling. However, on April 6, 1988, the records say there would be controlled burning on Egg Island, following which all that remained was the skeleton tower and a helicopter landing pad amid foundation ruins. Today, the tower has six landings within a 2.28-metre-square enclosed stairwell, leading to a 3.65-metre-square open gallery deck on which is mounted a small marine lantern and a solar panel to keep the batteries charged.

There is no close vantage point from the mainland.

086 Originally, there was a pair of range lights erected on Tomlees Head to guide small coasting and fishing vessels into the harbour and a safe protected anchorage. They were built by Standard Construction Co. Ltd. of Halifax for $2,556.96, which included acquisition of the site, the two towers, a shelter shed, and the installation of the lighting apparatus. The rear tower, which was 285 metres from the front one, was a black steel skeleton tower with white wooden slats on the upper portion of the side used for alignment, with a vertical red stripe painted down the centre. Its light was a Sunhinge 3 large locomotive headlight lantern. A. N. Leslie was appointed keeper at $165 per year. By 1958, electric power was running these lights.

SPRY BAY	
ESTABLISHED:	1916
CCG LIGHT #:	591
POSITION:	44° 49′ 21.5″ N
	62° 35′ 54.3″ W
	On Tomlees Head
LIGHT:	Sector light, fixed white, red, and green
AHW:	23.4 metres
NOM. RANGE:	10 nautical miles
HORN:	None
DESCRIPTION:	White wooden pepper-shaker-type light, 7.5 metres high

In 1970, the front tower was completely overhauled. The rear tower was torn down and replaced by an aluminum skeleton mast, its bottom portion enclosed and coloured red. It was topped by a watertight Wallace/Tiernan lantern with a 20-centimetre lens.

In February 1987, the rear light was discontinued and the front was changed to a sector light. That is, it had three coloured lenses: a red, a white, and a green. The white indicated the preferred channel and the other two colours indicated the change in course necessary to get into the channel. A helicopter landing pad is near the light tower, used to service the light.

Spry Harbour is a typical small Eastern Shore fishing community, with a beautiful provincial park nearby at Taylor Head. To get to the lighthouse, look for a gravel road about 1,300 metres east of Spry Bay, and follow this to the end, about 1,200 metres. Park here and follow the power line on foot about 1,400 metres to Tomlees Head, where you will see the little pepper-shaker lighthouse and get a great view.

There's no road, only a foot path, to Spry Bay lighthouse, and no boat landing either. The helicopter pad in the foreground was built to provide Coast Guard access.

Sheet Rock

The broken and abandoned lantern from the 1936 lighthouse on Sheet Rock lies amongst the rubble within the foundation where it fell when the lighthouse was burned by the Coast Guard in 1980.

087 Sheet Rock is a small islet at the entrance to the Sheet Harbour. It is about 200 metres long by 100 metres wide and rises steeply from all sides to a height of 13.7 metres. The length of the island lies in an east/west direction, extending more to the west where a very dangerous rock lies about 90 metres from the end of Sheet Rock, waiting to wreck the ships of careless mariners. Both ends are bare slate. The north side is green with grassy vegetation, but there's not a tree or shrub of any kind. The south side has a steep cliff that from a distance resembles a suspended sheet, hence the island's name. Sheet Harbour, one of the finest harbours on this coast, is nearly midway between Halifax and Country Harbour.

In 1878, parliament appropriated

SHEET ROCK	
ESTABLISHED:	1879
CCG LIGHT #:	594
POSITION:	44° 49′ 50″ N
	62° 29′ 34″ W
	Entrance to
	Sheet Harbour
LIGHT:	White flashing, F0.5/E3.5
AHW:	23.5 metres
NOM. RANGE:	9 nautical miles
HORN:	None
DESCRIPTION:	White circular fibreglass
	tower with two red
	horizontal bands,
	9.1 metres high

$2,000 for the erection of a lighthouse here. The contract was awarded to R. Rutledge and D. Drake of Sheet Harbour for $2,150. On December 17, 1878, John Perry of Sheet Harbour was appointed the first keeper at a yearly salary of $500. Although the lighthouse was not quite finished, it was put into operation in February 1879. Made of wood, the building consisted of a square tower 12.49 metres high with the keeper's dwelling attached. Because there was no decent place for a landing, it must have been very difficult for the keeper to get on and off the island on any but the calmest days. No record can be found of a slipway until an 1884 report, which states that a boathouse had been built on the north side. Like on all island stations on Nova Scotia's Atlantic coast, it was almost impossible to keep a slipway intact for any length of time, and Sheet Rock was no exception. Annual reports are filled with notices of building and rebuilding the landing slip at Sheet Rock, and of losing a couple of station boats as a result of wild winter storms.

The lighthouse/dwelling foundation was made of stone, and on a couple of occasions it was badly damaged and had to be rebuilt. The building was used for 57 year, but was finally replaced in 1936 by a building of popular design in those years—a two-storey, 7.62-metre-square wooden dwelling with a red iron octagonal lantern on top.

In December 1964, the slipway and landing was totally destroyed in a storm yet again, but this time it was not rebuilt. Modernization and automation were on their way. In early 1966, a new building was constructed for a 4.5-kilowatt generator, and the lighthouse became semi-automated. On September 6, 1968, the light became unwatched. The last lightkeeper, Albert Arnold, and his wife were transferred to Liscomb Island, which no doubt seemed like a whole continent compared to Sheet Rock, the tiny islet they had called home for 10 years. The light was changed to a 12-volt system supplied by a bank of 20 batteries. A sun switch was installed to turn the light on at dusk and off at dawn. In 1969, two storage buildings and the boathouse were declared surplus, but with no interested buyers, the buildings were burned down. The new generator building was purchased in 1972 and removed from the island in accordance with the terms of sale.

In December 1980, a concrete pad was poured 18 metres from the old light and the existing white circular fibreglass tower was bolted into place. It was battery-operated and charged by solar energy.

The old lighthouse/dwelling was also burned down, leaving only the foundation as evidence of its existence, with the rusted remains of the iron lantern and the clockwork mechanism for the light lying nearby. The stone foundation from the original lighthouse and pieces of the slipway and landing are also still evident—all remnants of the 120-year history of the lighthouse and the people who kept its light.

Not visible from the mainland.

Sheet Harbour Passage Range

Beaver Island

088 Sheet Harbour was settled in 1784 by United Empire Loyalists and British veterans of the American Revolution, and became a prosperous centre of the lumber industry. The range lights are used to mark the eastern end of the passage to Sheet Harbour and to guide small vessels to the government wharf.

In 1887, a red fixed light was displayed 12.8 metres above high water from a window in the dwelling of James Wambolt, for the benefit of small vessels navigating the passage. This light was never mentioned in the records after that year, and it wasn't

SHEET HARBOUR PASSAGE RANGE	
ESTABLISHED:	1915
CCG LIGHT #:	598 and 599
POSITION:	44° 51' 30" N
	62° 26' 56" W
	Rear tower 278.3 metres from the front
	East of Kirby River
LIGHT:	Fixed white lights having
AHW:	Front light 15.8 metres; rear light 19.8 metres
NOM. RANGE:	Unknown
HORN:	None
DESCRIPTION:	Both are white wooden pepper-shaker-type towers with a red vertical stripe on the seaward side; front tower is 8.2 metres high; rear tower is 8.9 metres high

until 1915 that a proper pair of range lights was built. These were constructed by A. Balcon of Halifax at a cost of $1,792, plus an inspection fee of $303.75, and $70.74 for the cost of searching titles and purchasing the site.

The Wambolt family—George, Arthur, and William—kept the lights at different times in the early years, but the job was eventually taken over by a caretaker at much less cost to the gov-

The front tower of the Sheet Harbour Passage range sits near the water's edge.

ernment. Laurie A. Spears was hired as the caretaker in 1956 at $75 per year, and the lights continued to be tended by a caretaker until 1967, when a new policy determined that the job would be contracted out.

From Route 7, just east of Sheet Harbour, turn onto Sober Island Road, drive 6.3 kilometres to the intersection to Sober Island, then bear left toward Sheet Harbour Passage for another 1.8 kilometres. You should see the range lights here, one on each side of the road. Respect private property.

The rear tower of the Sheet Harbour Passage range is quite high up the hill, 278.3 metres from the front tower.

089 In as early as 1840, the advantages of having a lighthouse in this area were well recognized, and were detailed in a report to the Admiralty by Captain Boxer of HMS *Pique*. Captain Owen, a naval surveyor, emphatically agreed. In his report to Vice Admiral Sir Charles Adam dated October 9, 1843, he stated: "It appears very extraordinary indeed that in the whole distance from Cape Sambro to Cranberry Island, a distance of about fifty five leagues [265 kilometres] of coast, studded with ledges and dangers, there is not now one intervening lighthouse, and the frequent occurrence of wrecks bears sufficient testimony of their need. If our poverty prevents their erection, it is deplorable, if our negligence, it is reprehensible."

In 1840, the house voted to put £400 toward that undertaking, but in each succeeding year it postponed the work because the fund was deficient. After much debate as to where a lighthouse should be built to the best advantage, the decision was made in favour of Beaver Island. In 1846, the lighthouse, so long desired, became a reality.

The lighthouse/dwelling combined was painted white with two black balls on the seaward side, and was described by the government as quite commodious. It is not known whether the first lightkeeper, Simon Fraser, would have described it that way, but there is no record of him making any complaint in that regard. Having to store oil in the cellar could not have been desirable; however, about 1,364 litres of it was burned annually.

In 1874, it was recommended that a small oil store be built near the lighthouse. At the same time, the station was supplied with a 5.79-metre whale boat and a flat boat. In 1876, a new lantern and revolving lighting apparatus with new lamps and reflectors was installed, which gave a bright flash

After 139 years, a fully automated lightstation replaces the manned station on Beaver Island in 1985.

every two minutes. Masters of vessels praised the much increased brilliance of the light, but just 10 months later, the apparatus and the glazing on all 12 sides of the lantern were destroyed by fire. Fortunately, a new apparatus designated for Scatarie Island was on hand and was used at Beaver Island.

In 1908, the lighthouse took on a different look. It was decided that some lighthouses would be more easily seen as daymarks if they were painted with red stripes, especially in winter, so seven of Nova Scotia's more important lighthouses, including Beaver Island, were painted with red horizontal bands.

After 108 years in service, it was time for a new lighthouse. Built in 1954, it was a square wooden tower with a red vertical stripe on each side, 10.67 metres high, and topped by an octagonal aluminum lantern. In 1958, Blair Cameron was appointed head keeper, and in 1961, Bert Fleet became the station's assistant keeper. From that time until the station was de-staffed in June 1987, the story of Beaver Island is also their story. With almost 30 years service on Beaver Island, Cameron was the longest-serving light-

keeper in the history of this lightstation, and Fleet served beside him for over 26 of those years. Neither man had a bad word to say about the other. Between them they had the skills to solve almost any problem or challenge that the day-to-day operation of the lightstation might present. In 1964, the station got electricity and was to become a marine radio beacon station. A new fog-alarm building was built, as was a third dwelling for a second assistant lightkeeper, Earl E. Wentzell.

By the summer of 1965, Beaver Island was an up-to-date, well-appointed, three family lightstation manned by the head keeper and two assistants.

BEAVER ISLAND	
ESTABLISHED:	1846
CCG LIGHT #:	602
POSITION:	44° 49' 34" N
	62° 20' 38" W
	Eastern end of the island
LIGHT:	Flashing white,
	Fl/E2/Fl/E2/Fl/E13
AHW:	19.9 metres
NOM. RANGE:	13 nautical miles
HORN:	B6, S54
DESCRIPTION:	White circular fibreglass
	tower with red octagonal
	lantern, 11.5 metres high

Central to the whole operation was the 10.67-metre, square wooden light tower with sloping sides and a red vertical stripe on the face of each of the four sides. There was an electrical generating plant, fog-alarm building, a boathouse and 6.7-metre station boat, an oil store, and a tractor. Then, in 1968, just when the marine radio beacon was put into operation and everything was going smoothly, the auditor general observed that too much money was being spent on the operation of lighthouses. Shortly after, the automation of lighthouses began in earnest. On February 7, 1972, the diaphone foghorn was replaced with an electronic horn, so there was no need for diesel engines, compressors, and air tanks for the horn. The station was reclassified as semi-automated, so the second assistant keeper was no longer required. His dwelling became surplus, and in 1977, it was placed on the open market. As there were no takers, it was destroyed and the site was cleared. Commercial power came to the island in 1981 by means of a submarine cable; with the incessant roar of the diesel generators was gone, a new kind of peace and quiet settled on the island.

In keeping with the goal of creating a low-maintenance, fully automated station, a new fibreglass tower was installed approximately 500 metres southwest of the old light tower in 1985. The old lantern was disassembled and stored, and the old tower was cut into sections, transported to the beach, and burned. On June 17, this lightstation was de-staffed, and a short time later, the remaining two dwellings were declared surplus and offered for sale to the public—again, there was no interest. The Coast Guard subsequently arranged for the dwellings to be removed.

The lightstation is not visible from the mainland.

Liscomb Island

090 Just short of 4 kilometres long and about 1,300 metres wide at its widest point, Liscomb Island covers the approaches to Liscomb Harbour and protects the entrance from easterly gales that frequently play havoc with less protected harbours all along Nova Scotia's Atlantic coast. The lighthouse is well positioned to guide vessels into this sheltered harbour.

In his report for the year ending June 30, 1869, Thomas P. Jost, superintendent of lighthouses, recommended that a lighthouse be built at or near Liscomb, but it wasn't until August 10, 1872, that a light was first exhibited there. It was described at the time as a very superior light, built by D. S. Ferguson on the west side of Liscomb Island at the east side of the entrance to Liscomb Harbour. It was a combined lighthouse/dwelling, had a square tower 8.53 metres high, and was painted white with a red roof. The lighting apparatus was contained within a 12-sided iron lantern. There was also an oil store building, and a 4.26-metre station boat kept at a landing about 400 metres from the station. A boathouse and store at the landing were considered an absolute necessity.

Seth Crooks was appointed the first keeper at a yearly salary of $350. It didn't take him long to realize that the living accommodation was much too small, but, as was usually the case, it took a long time, in this case 12 years, to get an addition built—two small rooms for which the keeper was no doubt grateful to have for the remaining 10 years of his 23-year tenure. Demas Crooks, who became keeper in August 1894, wasted no time in getting extensive repairs made to the station. Three sills in the tower and two in the dwelling and part of one corner post were repaired. The old clapboard siding was stripped off and replaced with shingles. The building got two new

window frames, a sash, two door frames, a new porch, railing, and steps at the front entrance. Two doors to the cellar were also replaced. Inside, the walls of the hall were sheathed with pine, and two rooms were sheathed with tongue-and-groove boards.

The next major change came in 1921, when a new boathouse and slipway were built, and a contract was taken by G. Y. Grant and Sons to build the existing octagonal reinforced-concrete lighthouse tower, which is 13.7 metres high base to vane. The lantern from the old tower was dismantled and erected on top of the new tower complete with lighting apparatus.

LISCOMB ISLAND	
ESTABLISHED:	1872
CCG LIGHT #:	615
POSITION:	44° 59′ 15.8″ N
	61° 57′ 58.4″ W
	On the west side of island
	near Cranberry Point
LIGHT:	Flashing white,
	once every 10 seconds
AHW:	21.9 metres
NOM. RANGE:	20 nautical miles
HORN:	B3, S27
DESCRIPTION:	White octagonal
	reinforced-concrete tower,
	13.7 metres high

In 1977, at the age of 80, L. C. Grant visited Liscomb Island to look over the lighthouse tower that he had helped build—he was one of the sons of the contractor G. Y. Grant. He says that in 1921, a team of heavy horses had to be transported by scow out to the island to haul gravel and sand from the inner end of the island to the construction site. All other supplies, including building materials, feed for the horses, a blacksmith's forge, and tools, were shipped by sailing vessel—loaded at Guysborough and landed at the light during fine weather. Grant recalls that

The Liscomb Island light tower has been fitted with a metal security door, as have many other Nova Scotia lighthouses, so it is reasonably safe for the time being.

they had purchased a double-dory from Lunenburg in which to store a supply of water close to the work. Using a dry aggregate of six parts gravel to two parts sand to one part cement, two strong men mixed every bit of the cement by hand on a mixing board. Some 56 years later, Grant wasn't at all surprised that the lighthouse was still in good condition. He met up with Charles Misner, the lightkeeper on this station from 1930 to 1964. Misner informed him that in 1921 he was a boy of 15 years, and that they had employed him to carry water from a

Redman Head

small spring to a nearby truck wagon to be hauled to the works.

In 1954, a diaphone horn was established here, requiring an assistant keeper and a new dwelling for his occupancy. In 1960, a new 30-metre slipway and 20-metre breakwater were built two kilometres from the lighthouse, and there were plans to build a new boathouse. In 1968, a new four-bedroom, one-and-a-half-storey dwelling was ready for occupancy—then came automation. Five years later, the station received commercial power by means of a submarine power cable and one lightkeeper position was eliminated. In 1977, the surplus dwelling was sold and removed from the site. On November 14, 1979, the station was classified as automated, although it wasn't until July 2, 1986, that it was de-staffed. In December, the station was brought to the point of no return when two dwellings, a garage, and a boathouse were all declared surplus and offered for sale to the general public. By August 1989, there had been no offers to purchase, and the authorization was given for the Coast Guard to dispose of the buildings.

Not visible from the mainland.

091 Redman Head is a steep wooded bluff about 30 metres high with dangerous waters to the east, which leaves a safe channel of only about 365 metres wide on that side. With about 600 metres between the head and the dangerous water east of Hog Island, vessels must keep about 180 metres to the west of Redman Head, which leads into a passage between Hemloe Island and the mainland, then into the harbour at the small village of Little Liscomb.

A lighthouse was erected on Redman Head in 1909 as a reference point for mariners navigating these dangerous waters. At that time, it was called Little Liscomb Harbour light. It was built by James Hemloe, Jr. of Liscomb at a cost

REDMAN HEAD	
ESTABLISHED:	1909
CCG LIGHT #:	618
POSITION:	45° 00' 45" N
	61° 57' 33" W
	On the southwest
	end of head
LIGHT:	Flashing white, F0.5/E3.5
AHW:	10.7 metres
NOM. RANGE:	6 nautical miles
HORN:	None
DESCRIPTION:	White wooden
	pepper-shaker-type tower,
	6.4 metres high

of $525. John Croft was appointed keeper of the light on September 10, 1909, at $240 per year.

In about 1963, the light was electrified and made unwatched. In 1965, a hurricane drove a World War Two liberty ship, the Liberian freighter *Fury*, onto the rocks about 5 kilometres to the east of Redman Head. No evidence was found that the unmanned Redman Head lighthouse played any part in the wreck, but whether it was lit at the time or not is unknown. In 1991, the ship was still sitting bolt upright on the

Vandals had their way with this pretty little lighthouse on Redman Head until it was no longer cost-effective to keep it in repair. It is now, unfortunately, gone forever—replaced by daymarks.

rocks, badly beaten by the sea—just a rusting hulk with holes through the sides big enough for a small boat to pass through with ease.

On October 24, 1988, the light was permanently discontinued, and within weeks, a red glow in the sky was observed by many local residents—the final light from Redman Head lighthouse as it burned to the ground. The government had decided to dispose of the lighthouse after it had suffered extensive damaged by vandals and had become a danger to the public. As a result of a petition taken up by local fishermen, who had depended on the light, the Coast Guard agreed to provide a daymark at the site, which was established by May 1989.

Port Bickerton

092 A small harbour light was put into operation at Port Bickerton on October 10, 1901. The entire square wooden tower with sloping sides was painted white. The 7-metre-high tower, with a square wooden lantern on top, showed a light from 13.1 metres above high water, and guided vessels through a 365-metre-wide channel between Barachois Head and Bickerton Island, thus providing safe passage over 6 fathoms of water into a snug little harbour. The lighthouse was built by Emery Taylor of Stillwater, Nova Scotia, at a contract price of $500. The first lightkeeper was Theodore O'Hara, appointed on January 26, 1901, at $150 per year.

The Department of Marine and Fisheries may not have gotten much of a bargain, because the lighthouse was not very well built and in 1930 it became necessary to build a new one. This lighthouse was a square, two-storey dwelling topped by a white square wooden lantern. The station was equipped with a hand-operated foghorn to answer vessels' signals. This part of the coast gets an average of 1,549 hours of fog annually. In 1948, a powerful diaphone foghorn was established and because of the added responsibility, an assistant keeper was required. In 1959, a new dwelling was built by Quemar Co. Ltd. of Bedford at a cost of $21,825—this bungalow still exists. At the same time, the lighthouse/dwelling had all new plumbing installed. As late as 1960, there was still a big problem with the road to the station, which was quite often flooded at high tides and washed out in places during stormy weather. The station boat could be used, weather permitting, but for the keeper's three school-age children, a decent road was more desirable. However, as often happened in such cases, there ensued a denial of responsibility by various levels of

PORT BICKERTON	
ESTABLISHED:	1901
CCG LIGHT #:	629
POSITION:	45° 05′ 24″ N
	61° 42′ 01.5″ W
	Near the west extremity
	of Barachois Head
LIGHT:	Isophase white flashing,
	F4/E4
AHW:	20.4 metres
NOM. RANGE:	12 nautical miles
HORN:	B3, S3, B3, S51
DESCRIPTION:	Square concrete tower on
	corner of square concrete
	fog-alarm building,
	10 metres high

bureaucracy and government agencies. Although this was a land station, there were times when the lightkeepers here must have felt very isolated from the community.

On March 28, 1962, the assistant keeper was removing paint from the floor of the fog-alarm building with a blow torch, when the oil-soaked boards caught on fire. Because of the lack of proper fire fighting equipment, the fog-alarm building was destroyed. Only the quick thinking of the assistant's wife saved the station from a

Two lighthouses at Port Bickerton? The one on the right, deactivated in 1963, was restored and opened on June 28, 1997, as a Nova Scotia lighthouse interpretive centre.

greater loss. She rushed into Bickerton and brought back several men and a small pump.

Commercial power was extended to the lightstation in 1962, and the following year, the existing combined lighthouse/fog-alarm building was built. The head keeper lived in the bungalow, and the assistant used the old two-storey dwelling/lighthouse, which at this time had no lantern, and the rafters had been spliced and extended up to the peak.

When the diaphone horn was replaced with an electronic horn in April 1972, there was considerably less work, so when head keeper Lamont Lovett retired in 1982, the assistant, Edgar Schrader, was promoted to head keeper and the assistant's job was declared redundant. In 1983, it was decided that the old lighthouse would be stripped of all useful materials and offered for sale or otherwise disposed of. However, the deputy minister of fisheries intervened and requested the

Fisherman's Harbour

use of the old building as accommodation for biological research field officers involved in research of hatchery-reared juvenile lobsters released in an area near Bickerton Island. Thankfully, the request was granted and the disposal of the building was put off indefinitely, even after the lightstation was de-staffed on May 16, 1988, and the last keeper, Hector Lowe, retired. The Port Bickerton and Area Planning Association subsequently entered into an agreement with the Coast Guard for an alternate use of the property. The old lighthouse was restored to its original splendour and opened as an interpretation centre for Nova Scotia lighthouses on June 28, 1997. The grand opening attracted over 500 people to this community of about 300 souls, and a parade of 14 vessels sailed past with sirens and horns blasting, as fireworks were fired to mark the occasion. The association is also developing nature trails in the area, and has plans to restore the head keeper's dwelling. Great community spirit at work here practically ensures the success of the project.

Accessible by car and easy to get to. From the village of Port Bickerton, find Lighthouse Road and follow it about 1 kilometre to the end of the paved road. Proceed another 2.3 kilometres on a good gravel road along the water's edge to the lightstation.

This is the "other" lighthouse at Port Bickerton. The active lighthouse was built to replace the old lighthouse in 1963.

093 Inside Fisherman's Harbour, sheltered by a long narrow shingle beach, lies Neverfail Cove, which provides safe anchorage for small vessels. Within this snug cove there is a 47-metre-long government wharf. Not only does this lighthouse mark the entrance to the cove, but it provides a reference for determining the location of a dangerous rock that lies at the harbour entrance with at least 3 metres of water covering it.

John McMillan of Isaac Harbour built this lighthouse at the contract price of $539. Theodore Beiswanger was appointed its first keeper on December 8, 1905, at an annual salary of $150.

At one time, the area surrounding this lighthouse was heavily populated by Arctic terns. Although the population has been greatly diminished, these birds are slowly regaining in number.

A short distance east of Port Bickerton on Route 211 you will find an intersection and sign for Fisherman's Harbour. The road is a dead end near a small cemetery. The lighthouse can be easily viewed across the cove from the government wharf. For a closer look, find the footpath at the cemetery and follow about 300 metres to the shore end of the shingle spit and out to the lighthouse.

The long narrow shingle beach makes an attractive setting for this little lighthouse at Fisherman's Harbour.

FISHERMAN'S HARBOUR	
ESTABLISHED:	1905
CCG LIGHT #:	634
POSITION:	45° 06' 41" N
	61° 40' 41" W
	On the west extremity
	of a shingle beach
LIGHT:	Fixed green
AHW:	7.6 metres
NOM. RANGE:	6 nautical miles
HORN:	None
DESCRIPTION:	White wooden
	pepper-shaker-type tower,
	7 metres high

Isaac's Harbour

094 Isaac's Harbour is the easternmost of two long narrow harbours separated by a large point of land. The harbour runs in a northerly direction for a distance of about 4.8 kilometres, with a maximum width of 371 metres for three quarters of its length. The harbour is well sheltered with depths varying from 3 to 4.6 metres and is open year round.

First put into operation on November 9, 1874, the lighthouse was built for the purpose of guiding vessels into Isaac's Harbour. J. T. Sinclair built the square wooden dwelling, which had an octagonal wooden lantern with an iron floor, for the contract price of $870. The first lightkeeper was C. W. Bigsby, who was appointed November 9, 1874, at a salary of $200 per year. He lived nearby in his own house.

Because of many complaints that the light could not be seen at a sufficient distance from the coast, it was changed in 1876 to two vertical lights 6 metres apart. The upper light remained the same physically, but changed from fixed red to white. The lower light was accommodated in a projecting window built into the seaward side of the lower floor, occupying about one third of the lower floor space. Beyond a thin board partition, were the stairs, and on the same floor, the oil and tanks were kept. The only room for the keeper to live in measured 3.65 metres square and was placed between the two lanterns. The heat and smell of burning oil would have been oppressive, and the situation was dangerous in the case of fire. There is no mention in the records as to whether the keeper's family lived in this house, but it seems the keeper lived under those conditions because he had been provided with a hand-operated horn to answer ships' signals and had to be available without notice. He was eventually authorized to build an oil store separate from the light-

ISAAC'S HARBOUR

ESTABLISHED:	1874
CCG LIGHT #:	637
POSITION:	45° 09′ 53″ N
	61° 39′ 16″ W
	On the west side
	of the harbour entrance
LIGHT:	Fixed white
AHW:	25 metres
NOM. RANGE:	12 nautical miles
HORN:	None
DESCRIPTION:	White square wooden
	two-storey dwelling
	surmounted by a red
	lantern; 12.8 metres high

house, and an addition to the dwelling was built the following year.

Because oil barrels and other supplies had to be hauled up a steep rocky hill, which caused them to leak, it was determined that a road had to be built to the harbour some distance away. The keeper was then authorized to remove, by blasting, some large rocks that were obstructing the landing. A landing was built, but it was often too rough to land the stores, in fact the landing had to be replaced several times after stormy weather during the 20 years that the keeper served there.

In 1929, the existing lighthouse was built. It is 7.62 metres square, two storeys high, and has an octagonal iron lantern—all built solidly on a concrete foundation. On September 14, 1954, commercial electric power was brought

The 1929 octagonal iron lantern on Isaac's Harbour lighthouse was replaced with the aluminum lantern seen here. The building appears to be in good repair, probably the result of being protected as a designated federal heritage building.

to the station and living conditions improved.

The last lightkeeper, Ernest B. Davidson, retired on May 11, 1966, after 28 years. On the same day, the light was listed as unwatched and the horn was discontinued. Davidson did, however, accept a job as caretaker at $100 per year. His only duties were to observe proper functioning of the light, replace burned out bulbs, watch for vandalism, and report any serious difficulties. He wasn't even required to turn the light on and off because a time clock had been installed to do that.

In January 1990, the lighthouse was declared surplus. The plan was to replace it with a fibreglass tower, but the Coast Guard asked for the Federal Heritage Buildings Review Office to evaluate the lighthouse. The resulting score of 54 was enough to get the building "recognized" as a federal heritage building; as such, it is protected.

On Route 316, from Isaac's Harbour North crossroad, turn south and travel 3 kilometres along the west side of the harbour on a paved road, which gives way to gravel for about 300 metres before there's a gate across the road. You must obtain permission to proceed beyond this gate and walk the 600 metres to the lighthouse. The lighthouse can be viewed at a distance from a couple of places on Route 316 on the east side of the harbour.

Country Island

095 At the time that the lighthouse was established in 1873, this island at the entrance to Country Harbour, Guysborough County, was known as Green Island. But probably because of the confusion caused by the existence of another Green Island, with a lightstation established just eight years earlier and no more than 70 kilometres away to the northeast, near Isle Madame, this one became known as Country Harbour lighthouse. However, it wasn't until the 1930s that it was listed as Country Island in the official list of lights, and even then the list of lightkeepers called it Country Harbour lightstation. It is unclear when everyone came to know it as Country Island.

This is an important coastal light that also serves to guide vessels into Country Harbour and Fisherman's Harbour. The contract for building the lighthouse was taken by James McDonald and should have been in operation by July 1872 when the first lightkeeper, William Foster, reported for duty. He was paid an annual salary of $400, but spent most of his first year waiting for the lantern to be installed. It had been severely damaged in a shipment from Montreal and had to be returned for repairs, which took until May 1, 1873. The dwelling and lighthouse were in one building that was entirely too small for a family to live in comfortably. Families were expected to make do and adapt to this kind of life, which was so different from living in a community on the mainland. There were two other buildings on this station, an oil house and a storage barn at the landing, which was 800 metres from the lighthouse. The bulk of the oil and other supplies were kept there until the wintertime, when they were more easily conveyed to the station. Because of the exposed location, the buildings frequently suffered damage

during stormy weather. Even after the lighthouse tower had been stayed with wire rope, the lightkeeper reported that the building "rocks a good deal" during high winds. In 1878, a September gale beat right through the sides of the tower and dwelling, damaging the foundation, and also destroying the station boat. In 1884, the stone foundation was taken down and rebuilt with cement mortar. An addition was made to the dwelling for the accommodation of the keeper and his family, and the entire building was re-shingled. Even with the addition, the

Not as much taper to the Country Island lighthouse, making it a bit more identifiable than some.

dwelling was apparently still not big enough, for a further addition was made to the kitchen a few years later.

In 1927, after 55 years of hard conditions, the old lighthouse was replaced. The new lighthouse, typical of the times, was a two-storey square wooden dwelling surmounted by a lantern. It was 11.28 metres high, with two horizontal red bands on its sides to provide a distinctive daymark.

By 1961, an inspection report stated that the lighthouse/dwelling had badly deteriorated and recommended it be replaced and that Country Island become a three-man station. The esti-

mated cost for bringing the station back up to standard was $125,000 for three new dwellings at $25,000 each; a new reinforced-concrete tower and fog-alarm building costing $25,000; foghorn equipment costing $20,000; and a new landing, ramps, and the cost of removing the old building for $5,000. A complete makeover of the station began on November 10, 1963, and was completed in 1965. Keith Guptill, who had been appointed to the station on September 17, 1960, was promoted to head keeper with two assistants.

Here we had the ultimate, completely new, fully manned, fully operational coastal lightstation. It had an octagonal reinforced-concrete light tower showing a flashing white light from a 25.4-centimetre rotating airport beacon, two bungalows, a one-and-a-half-storey dwelling, a storage shed, an oil store shed, a boathouse and a 4.87-metre station boat, and a fog-alarm building with a type F diaphone horn.

Berry Head

There were also two diesel engines with compressors to keep two large tanks filled with compressed air for the horn, together with two diesel generator sets to provide power for the station. However, the new era of austerity was upon us. Automation began at the station on December 15, 1971, when the diaphone air horn was replaced with a 400-watt electronic horn. With the diaphone horn went the associated engines and compressors, allowing the station to revert to a two-man operation. One seven-year-old dwelling was now vacant, and in 1977 it was

COUNTRY ISLAND	
ESTABLISHED:	1873
CCG LIGHT #:	639
POSITION:	45° 05' 59.8" N
	61° 32' 31.9" W
	On the south side
	of the island
LIGHT:	White flashing, Fl/E19
AHW:	16.5 metres
NOM. RANGE:	16 nautical miles
HORN:	B6, S54
DESCRIPTION:	White octagonal
	reinforced-concrete tower,
	13.7 metres high

declared surplus and offered for sale. By December 1979, there were no offers, and the building was slated for disposal by the Coast Guard.

Commercial power had been brought to Country Island in 1982 by submarine cable and there seemed to be no reason not to go ahead with total automation and de-staffing. In 1986, the necessary alterations were made to the lighthouse tower—the diesel generators and fog detector were moved inside the tower, and everything was boarded up. On September 29, 1986, the last lightkeeper, Clyde M. Lahey, came ashore, and for the first time in 113 years there was no human presence on Country Island.

In 1996, the Canadian Wildlife Service expressed an interest in acquiring the island for the purpose of preserving the nesting habitat of roseate terns, a threatened species. In the late 1990s, the Department of Natural Resources was given permission to use the island and one of the dwellings for two years to study the terns. Other interest has been expressed in managing the island's resources, but the Coast Guard has not been willing to commit to any long-range plans until a definite position has been taken on their alternate-use program.

Not visible from the mainland.

096 Berry Head is a low rocky point at the eastern extremity of a peninsula roughly 3 kilometres long, east to west, by 1,300 metres wide, and connected to the mainland by a very narrow spit, about 150 metres wide, on which there is a range of sandhills. The peninsula guards the western side of Tor Bay wherein lie the communities of Larry's River and Charlos Cove. This lighthouse has pretty much always been called the Tor Bay light, but has been officially listed as the Berry Head light ever since the new lighthouse was built in 1985.

At the 1874 session of parliament, the decision was made to build a light-

BERRY HEAD	
ESTABLISHED:	1876
CCG LIGHT #:	646
POSITION:	45° 11' 28.8" N
	61° 18' 39.9" W
	On the east point of
	Berry Head, west side of
	the entrance to Tor Bay
LIGHT:	Fixed white
AHW:	12.5 metres
NOM. RANGE:	Unknown
HORN:	B2, S3, B2, S3, B2, S48
DESCRIPTION:	White rectangular
	wooden building with
	white square wooden
	tower on the roof;
	5.8 metres high

house at Tor Bay Point. The contract was awarded to James McDonald, who completed construction in time for the light to be put into operation on April 10, 1876. The total cost was $1,222.15, which included the cost of building an oil store and a fence around the lighthouse property. A boat was also supplied for the first keeper, Joseph Delory, who was appointed at a yearly salary of $250.

The lighthouse tower was a square wooden building, 10.97 metres high

Charlos Harbour Range

Certainly not the standard configuration one would associate with lighthouses of Nova Scotia, however this was built on Berry Head to be functional, not pretty, although it does possess a certain charm. Everything is there, the fog sensor, the alarm, and the light, all automated.

097 Charlos Harbour is situated on the western shore of Tor Bay and has a maximum depth of only 3.7 metres. But by aligning the range lights, vessels of shallow draft can stay clear of the reefs off Forester Island.

These lighthouse towers were built by the Department of Marine and

CHARLOS HARBOUR RANGE	
ESTABLISHED:	1901
CCG LIGHT #:	649 and 650
POSITION:	Unknown
Front:	45° 14' 38" N, 61° 20' 02.5" W
Rear:	215.5 metres from the front at 285° 29' On extremity of point, west side of harbour
LIGHT:	Both fixed red
AHW:	Front is 8.2 metres; rear is 14.6 metres
NOM. RANGE:	3 nautical miles
HORN:	None
DESCRIPTION:	Both are white wooden pepper-shaker-type towers, 7.01 metres high

base to vane, with a dwelling attached. It was painted white with vertical red stripes, and the top of the lantern was painted black. A fixed red light showed to seaward while a fixed white light showed northward into the bay. There was no landing at this station because it was very exposed and the water was generally rough, so the keeper rigged a crane with a hoisting gear, until a few years later when a 4-kilometre road was built from the station to the main road.

In 1951 the station was rebuilt. The new tower was a typical pepper-shaker design with a square wooden lantern. A new three-bedroom, one-and-a-half-storey modern dwelling was also built using the best materials.

In February 1958, the slipway was totally destroyed by a storm and there was no intention at the time to rebuild it. Rather, the light was changed to a battery-operated system using three banks of large cells in parallel, and the station was made unwatched on September 11, 1959. Lightkeeper Wilfred Sangster retired and Chester Gammon was hired as caretaker at $100 per year.

A report from May 12, 1971, stated that the boathouse had partially collapsed and was hanging over the embankment, the storage shed had also partly collapsed, the dwelling's

windows were all smashed out, there were no doors, part of the main floor had collapsed, and the lighthouse tower's door was missing. On November 2, 1972, all surplus buildings were burned down. On February 18, 1975, a letter from the Department of Fisheries stated that there were upwards of 32 boats operating in the vicinity and many complaints regarding the poor light from the lighthouse, with requests for a proper foghorn. The following year, a commercial power line was extended to the lighthouse and a more powerful light was installed. In April 1978, an electronic horn was also installed.

In 1985, the current utilitarian lighthouse was built containing all the equipment you would expect to find at a larger lighthouse. It's supplied with a 400-millimetre glass drum lens with a 120-volt, 175-watt mercury-vapour lamp that provided a fixed white light, and a 1-kilowatt electronic foghorn operated by a Sperry Videograph fog detector. The old lighthouse tower and everything associated with it are gone.

Although the site is considered inaccessible to the public, it is possible to hike out to the lighthouse. It's about 3.5 kilometres from where the road ends at the community of Tor Bay.

The front tower of the Charlos Harbour range was discontinued in about 1988 and is now, unfortunately, gone.

Hog Island

Fisheries under the supervision of A. McLellan at a cost of $814.29, and first showed a light on October 10, 1901. The first keeper was Stephen C. Richard, who was appointed on November 4, 1901, at $120 per year.

At one time, there were 24 boats fishing out of this harbour, but by 1988 there were only two boats remaining,

The Charlos Harbour rear range light tower was still on site in 1998, privately owned and in excellent condition. Note that the red stripe is gone.

so the lights were permanently discontinued. After requesting a review of the lighthouses for heritage status and finding that they had no historic value, the Coast Guard removed the fittings and fixtures, declared the lighthouses surplus, and offered them for sale. A visit in May 1998 revealed that the rear tower was still there, privately owned and in very good repair, but the front tower was gone.

Just off Route 316 in the community of Charlos Cove.

098 This lighthouse was named Port Felix light after the port it served, but in November 1971, the name was officially changed to Hog Island light for the island upon which it was built. The purpose of the light has not changed, however. It guides vessels through the maze of islands, large and small, that block the entrance to Molasses Harbour at the northeast corner of Tor Bay, and warns of the shoals surrounding them. It is through these waters that mariners must find the way to little Port Felix Harbour.

The lighthouse was built by the Department of Marine and Fisheries,

HOG ISLAND	
ESTABLISHED:	1902
CCG LIGHT #:	654
POSITION:	45° 13' 43.6" N
	61° 13' 11" W
	On the east end
	of the island
LIGHT:	Flashing white, F2/E10
AHW:	10.6 metres
NOM. RANGE:	5 nautical miles
HORN:	B2, S18
DESCRIPTION:	White circular fibreglass
	tower with two red
	horizontal bands,
	9.1 metres high

under the supervision of James A. Hall, foreman of works, for $2,517.58. It was put into operation on Dominion Day 1902. The first lightkeeper was W. C. Boudreau, appointed at $250 per year.

The building consisted of a square wooden dwelling with a square wooden lantern rising from the middle of the cottage roof. The whole building, including the lantern, was painted white and was 11.27 metres high, base to vane. Soon after, a stores building was added as well as a boathouse and slipway for the station boat. A hand-operated horn was added in 1914 to answer vessels' signals, which added immeasurably to the keeper's responsibility. Fifty years later, in 1964, a small electronic horn was installed. It was called a "one mile horn" because of its rather feeble blast, which carried only about a mile away. It was operated by 11 large-capacity single-cell batteries producing 15 volts, sufficient to produce a 2-second blast every 10 seconds for several months of intermittent use. And if the horn could be battery operated, why not the light? So in 1966, a 6-volt lamp system was installed, including an automatic lamp changer that would rotate a new bulb into position whenever the operating bulb burned out, as well as a flasher to extend the life of the batteries. Similar to the horn, the light used 10 large single-cell batteries. A lightkeeper was then no longer required, but a caretaker was employed for about six months until January 1, 1967.

The boathouse and storage shed were declared surplus, then sold and removed from the island on March 21, 1967. On November 22, 1988, the existing fibreglass tower was bolted into place

This lighthouse served on Hog Island for 86 years. Its style was popular at the turn of the twentieth century. Photo courtesy of Captain Mel Lever—Canadian Coast Guard, Dartmouth.

White Head Island

on a concrete pad, spelling the end of the familiar old lighthouse that served the community of Port Felix for 86 years. The new light and horn, both mounted on top of the tower, are battery operated and require a 70-cell solar panel to keep the batteries charged. A 7.31-metre-square wooden helicopter landing pad was built on top of the old lighthouse foundation to provide quick and easy access, weather permitting.

As with any island lighthouse, you need a boat to get to it, but it is worth the effort to see a lighthouse as it is meant to be seen, from seaward. Otherwise, you can see this one from just a bit east of Port Felix on Route 316, at a distance of about 3 kilometres.

The new lighthouse tower on Hog Island was installed in 1988. Note the small electronic foghorn fitted at the top of the tower, just below the light, and at the base of the tower, the solar panel. The batteries are just inside the door at the base of the tower.

099 Four lighthouses were built on White Head Island from 1854 until the current structure was built in 1978. The first one was a small, white, wooden lighthouse/ dwelling out on the head, where evidence of a foundation can still be found. An early report stated that it was barely big enough for the lighthouse's revolving apparatus, let alone for use as a dwelling, especially as there were 10 people living there—the keeper, his wife, and their 8 children. It was also reported that the keeper was very industrious, having built an excellent landing wharf with a store building next to it, and had made a good road from the landing to the lighthouse. It commended his wife, who, despite insufficient and cramped quarters, kept everything remarkably clean and neat. For all this, the first keeper, Patrick Dillon, was paid £90 per year with a £20 fuel allowance. Many subsequent reports referred to the necessity of adding a couple of rooms. Ten years later, the superintendent of lights reported that the building, which was leaky and uncomfortable, needed another room and that the whole place should be painted. Sadly, Patrick Dillon died without ever seeing an addition made to the family home.

In 1867, James P. Dillon, presumably a son, continued on as keeper of this important station. He lived under the same conditions until 1875, 21 years after the lighthouse was first put into operation, when some improvements were made. The tower, which was attached to the dwelling, got an additional storey, 3 metres high and octagonal in shape, to which a new 12-sided iron lantern was erected on top. The addition was meant to improve the light and increase the range of the coastal beacon, rather than provide some comfort for the family, but they did benefit from extending their quar-

ters into the tower.

In 1914, some big changes were made; the station got a new fog-alarm building, a new oil store, and, finally, a much-needed new dwelling separate from the lighthouse. A small bridge was built over the gulch between the high ground of the station over to the lighthouse on the head. Two red vertical stripes painted on the side made a distinctive daymark.

The second lighthouse was attached to the fog-alarm building, was built in 1934. It was a 3.65-metre-square, 10.36-metre-high wooden tower with a red octagonal iron lantern. Like almost every island station, it suffered storms that invariably damaged landings and slipways on quite a regular basis. In

WHITE HEAD ISLAND	
ESTABLISHED:	1854
CCG LIGHT #:	659
POSITION:	45° 11' 49.1" N
	61° 08' 10.8" W
	Southwest side of
	the island
LIGHT:	Flashing white, F0.5/E4.5
AHW:	18.2 metres
NOM. RANGE:	16 nautical miles
HORN:	B3, S27
DESCRIPTION:	White square concrete
	tower on the corner of
	a white rectangular
	cement-block building,
	9 metres high

December 1961, the landing and slipway were totally destroyed, and in January 1963, a heavy storm did severe damage to the wharf and station dory. The 6.09-metre station boat seemed to have escaped serious consequences, as it was no doubt more securely stowed. On December 14, 1964, a storm resulted in the loss of the boathouse, 152 metres of plank walkway, and a number of barrels of oil. The dwellings were badly damaged and both oil stores

The fourth and probably the last light-house on White Head Island. The yellow object to the right of the lighthouse is a fibreglass fuel-oil tank.

were pushed off their foundations—one was completely turned around and pushed back 8 metres into the bog. All this just a year after a lot of work had been done to bring the station up to standard. Another dwelling had been built to provide living accommodations for an assistant keeper and his family, as the station now became a two-man operation. It took a full year to get the station back in shape after that storm, which included a new boathouse and slipway. Once two diesel generator sets were installed, the station also had electric power.

In 1967, with the need of a second assistant, a new one-and-a-half-storey dwelling was added to the station complex. Then in 1970, a study was done to determine the feasibility of laying a 6,100-metre submarine power cable to the island, and plans were approved for bringing a 9.14-metre fibreglass tower to the island to replace the old light-house. By late summer, the fibreglass

tower and a small prefabricated metal building to house the monitoring equipment had been brought onto the island and installed. The tower apparently wasn't very well suited for such an exposed position, as a letter from head keeper Wilfred P. Conway stated that the tower was very shaky. He said that it shook so much that the beacon sometimes made a complete revolution even when it was shut down, and the tower was considered too dangerous to climb. The Department of Transport responded by installing four guy wires to the top of the tower, but the result was less than satisfactory. In October 1972, a contract went out for a new equipment building made of concrete blocks, which was completed by December 11. The following year three new generator sets were installed inside.

The old light tower and fog-alarm building were torn down by the light-keepers in 1974. In 1978, a new light-house tower was added to the end of the generator building and was accepted from the contractor on November 1 of that year. The shaky and much-damaged fibreglass tower was then removed from the station, much to

everyone's relief. The new, existing tower, made of concrete, measures 3.04 metres square and 9 metres high, and rests on the corner of the fog-alarm building, all of which is covered with vinyl siding.

The small, old, two-storey dwelling from 1914 had been declared surplus in 1977 and was finally torn down by the lightkeepers in about 1982. The following year, an inspection report listed 101 defects at the station, many of them minor in nature, but the handwriting was on the wall. Once a commercial power submarine cable was laid from Deming Island to White Head Island in 1986, total automation and de-staffing of the station was imminent. Just over two years later it was done. Head keeper Ernie Keefe and assistant John MacQuarrie, the last lightkeepers of White Head Island, came ashore, and on June 20, 1988, the station was officially de-commissioned and de-staffed. Two dwellings, two storage sheds, and the boathouse were immediately declared surplus to Coast Guard needs and offered for sale through Crown Assets. The sheds were quickly disposed of but the two dwellings remained.

The Coast Guard has since initiated the Alternate Use Program and is looking to divest itself of these properties to worthy groups or organizations rather than purposely destroy them, as has been the case at so many other light-stations. Interest has been shown in developing White Head Island into a resort of some kind, but no hard decisions had been made as of October 1996.

The lighthouse is not visible from the mainland and the island is difficult to visit. The landing and 535 metres of boardwalk leading to the station have been destroyed and are overgrown with vegetation, which would make it a tough hike to the lighthouse even if a landing was made.

Sable Island

SABLE ISLAND is located about 240 kilometres east of Halifax and about 145 kilometres south of Cape Canso, the nearest point of the mainland. It is crescent shaped, and concave to the north, its size and shape constantly changing by the action of the sea as sand erodes from the west end and builds on the east. Charts show that in the 200 years since 1766, the island has shifted almost 14 kilometres eastward while at the same time maintaining basically the same configuration and dimensions—40 kilometres long by 2.4 kilometres wide at its widest part. The two lighthouses are 19 kilometres apart, each some distance from the actual ends of the island. Lake Wallace, named after the first commissioner of the island, is a saltwater lake that was open to the ocean in the 1700s, forming a lagoon that ships of a good size could safely enter. The shifting sands have steadily diminished its size, however, and it is now not much more than a shallow pond. The island is so low-lying and the sand dunes so light in colour that ships often get too close before noticing it—especially in the days of sail when ships needed much more room to manoeuvre. There have been over 250 recorded shipwrecks on the island, thus it has become known as "the graveyard of the Atlantic."

Ever since 1801, when Governor Wentworth tried to have cannons installed at each end of the island to answer vessels' signals, there was talk of building lighthouses on Sable Island, but it never amounted to anything more than talk. With each new government or island administration, talk concerning lighthouses was renewed, but it wasn't until after Confederation in 1867, when Canada became financially independent of Britain, that a decision was made to go ahead. In 1873, two powerful lighthouses were

built, one on each end of the island, at a total cost of $80,000. Since that date, severe and constant erosion of the west end of the island has necessitated moving the lighthouse seven times, a total distance of just under 13 kilometres from the original site. But not always the same lighthouse, as there have been six different towers. It has never been necessary to move the east light, which has had three different towers over the years.

Sable Island is known for a couple of other things. Usually, the first thing that comes to mind are the horses. These horses were thought to be descendants of a herd brought to the island in the years just before the founding of Halifax in 1749, by the Reverend Andrew Le Mercier, who claimed that he owned the island at that time. However, other records indicate that those animals died off and that it is more likely that they descended from 60 horses shipped here in about 1760 by Boston merchant and shipowner Thomas Hancock. In any case, some of the horses survived and became wild. These feral horses have been protected from all human interference since June 2, 1960, and live in peace in family groups throughout the island. The person most knowledgeable about these animals is Zoe Lucas, who has been studying them for many years and recognizes them by name. This is no small feat when one considers that there is an average of 250 horses—the number fluctuates with the conditions on the island. Sadly, some years the loss is great, usually due to an especially hard winter and the general age and condition of the herd. Lucas is also very much involved in the study of erosion and ways of preventing it.

Unknown wreck, west end Sable Island. Canadian Coast Guard Ship Edward Cornwallis *can be seen at anchor on the horizon. Shoal water prevents a closer approach. The black spots in the water are seals, curious creatures.*

Marram grass is the most natural and effective means of protecting against erosion. It looks like ordinary beach grass, but the root system extends metres below the surface, spreading out throughout the dune and sprouting grass across the surface, holding the dunes in place.

Seals are protected on Sable Island, which has, therefore, become home to the largest concentration of seals anywhere in the western North Atlantic. The large grey seals can be found here year-round and the smaller harbour seals come here to breed and have their pups.

There are major breeding colonies of great black-backed gulls and herring gulls, as well as terns, including scarce and diminishing numbers of roseate terns. But the most interesting bird to be found here is the little Ipswich sparrow; recognised as one of the world's rare birds, it breeds exclusively on Sable Island.

Sable Island West

100 A light was first exhibited from this lighthouse on November 15, 1872. It was one of the most powerful revolving white lights to be seen on the continent, with three distinct flashes at intervals of half a minute followed by a one-and-a-half-minute eclipse, and seen up to 29 kilometres away. The lighthouse was a white wooden octagonal tower 29.87 metres high. A powerful steam fog-whistle gave an 8-second blast followed by 52 seconds pf silence and could be heard from 4.8 to 24 kilometres away, depending on the conditions. William Morrison was appointed engineer and lighthouse keeper on July 9, 1872, at a salary of $600 per year, and was given two assistants. There was a dwelling sit-

SABLE ISLAND WEST	
ESTABLISHED:	Originally, 1872; in current position, 1951
CCG LIGHT #:	665
POSITION:	43° 55' 54.8" N 60° 01' 25" W At the west end of Sable Island
LIGHT:	Flashing white, once every 15 seconds
AHW:	32 metres
NOM. RANGE:	20 nautical miles
HORN:	None
DESCRIPTION:	Skeleton tower, 26 metres high, with rectangular red and white daymark slats

uated a short distance from the light-house—two commodious and comfortable houses under one roof, each complete in itself. A barn was also provided, and two cows and a horse for the lightkeeper and his assistants. There was a fog-alarm building with a large addition for fuel, a large oil store, and a blacksmith shop. By 1876, some doubts had been expressed as to whether the fog-whistle was of any use

to navigation. Because a bar of sand extended past the end of the island, it was likely that a vessel would be on it before it was close enough to hear the whistle. So on July 1, 1878, the fog-whistle was discontinued.

By 1882, the bank had washed away to only 1.5 metres from the tower buttresses and the terrified lightkeeper reported that he could feel the tower shudder from the combined forces of wind and sea. The light was quickly dismantled, and the superstructure was moved to safety just as an enormous bank of sand vanished into the ocean, taking the lighthouse foundation with it. In 1883, a new foundation was built of cement 371 metres east of the old position, and the tower rebuilt on top of it.

In 1888, due to further rapid encroachments by the sea, it was necessary to move the lightstation another 2.4 kilometres to the east. This time it became necessary to build a new tower, a 29.56-metre-high octagonal concrete tower with four equally spaced winged buttresses. It was built on top of a large dune, 6 metres above sea level, and put into operation on October 20, 1888. The dwelling was also taken down and rebuilt with a cellar and concrete cistern under one side. A new stable and oil store were also built at the new station, all under the superintendence of Henry Watt.

In the winter of 1916, the foundation

The dwelling at the west lightstation on Sable Island is used by researchers with the Department of Fisheries and Oceans and the large Quonset hut contains a garage and machine shop. Note the ATVs parked at the left of the picture—the main means of getting around the island.

of the lighthouse was once again threatened by erosion, so a new structure was built 400 metres further east on a broader part of the island. It was a black, square, steel skeleton tower, 32.6 metres base to vane, with a white watch room and red polygonal iron lantern on top. White wooden slats on the upper portion of the tower below the watch room provided a clear daymark. A red cylindrical tube enclosing the staircase extended from the base to the watch room. The island also had six relief stations connected by telephone and patrols, and three lifesaving stations.

In 1940, a new light had to be moved again a distance of 3.6 kilometres and in 1951, another 2.4 kilometres. The 1940 lighthouse was also a skeleton steel tower, but with an added section, bringing it to 31 metres high from the base to the platform deck on which the beacon was mounted. Rectangular white slatwork provided a daymark on the north and south sides. The light was provided by a Crouse Hinds 91.44-centimetre rotating airport beacon,

Sable Island
East

West tower showing red and white slats as a daymark with 91.44-cm rotating airport beacon on the open gallery deck.

which showed a 1,700,000-candlepower flash every 15 seconds and could be seen a distance of 32 kilometres.

In 1958, all the lightstation buildings were transferred to Air Services. On August 26, 1960, the light became unwatched and lightkeeper Arthur R. Dooks was transferred to Maugher's Beach lightstation. In 1970, the decision was made to replace the free-standing steel tower with a 22.86-metre mast supported by four guy wires, one on each of the four corners. An attempt to raise the mast on November 16, 1970, failed, resulting in extensive damage, and delaying construction until July 26, 1971, when it was successfully completed. The old tower was torn down a month later.

After seven towers on the west end of Sable Island, you would think this would be the end of the story, but it isn't. In 1980, the decision was made to build a tower similar to the one that was torn down in 1971. The $189,977 contract was awarded to J. L. Nichols of Bedford for the construction of the existing 26-metre aluminum skeleton tower with 9-by-3-metre red and white horizontal bands as a daymark on the north and south sides.

101 By June 1872, construction was nearly complete on a new lighthouse at Sable Island East. Built on high ground, it was also intended to be an excellent lookout for the people on watch. A light was first shown on December 2, 1872, but the first official lighting was February 14, 1873. It was a powerful fixed white light of the second order, elevated 36.57 metres above high water. In clear weather, it could be seen 28 kilometres away, although it could apparently be seen from much farther, such as from the mast of a ship 40 kilometres away. The wooden octagonal tower was 26.21 metres high, its sides were painted alternately white and dark brown, and it stood about 2.41 kilometres from the end of the island. It was a useful day beacon for ships at a distance because it enabled those on board to distinguish the island long before they could see it or come near its dangerous bars, which extended 27 kilometres past the dry spit at its end. A powerful steam fog-whistle was also put into operation at the same time.

J. Norman was appointed engineer (because of the fog-whistle) and lightkeeper on December 24, 1872. He had two assistants, and was paid $600 per year. After just six and a half months in operation, the foghorn was destroyed by fire. The machinery was taken to

Halifax for repair, but like the west fog alarm, its range was less than the distance the bar extended from the end of the island, so it was not re-established. The dwelling was similar to the one at the west light—two dwellings under one roof. There was also a barn, and two cows and a horse were kept for the use of the lightkeeper and his assistants.

In addition to their lighthouse duties, on foggy days the keeper and his assistants patrolled 14.5 kilometres up one side of the island and back down the other side.

Unlike the west end of the island, things remained quite stable at this

SABLE ISLAND EAST	
ESTABLISHED:	1873
CCG LIGHT #:	666
POSITION:	43° 57' 35.6" N
	59° 47' 29" W
	At the southwest of
	extremity of the
	northeast dry spit
LIGHT:	Flashing white,
	F0.5/E3/F0.5/E16
AHW:	36 metres
NOM. RANGE:	18 nautical miles
HORN:	None
DESCRIPTION:	White square tower,
	18.1 metres high, with
	a red vertical stripe on
	each of the four sides

East end lighthouse, Sable Island. Deep-rooted marram grass at the top of this sand dune has held it to this pyramidal shape.

Cranberry Island

The fence around the east lighthouse on Sable Island prevents the feral horses from eating the marram grass, which helps prevent erosion of the sand and the undermining of the tower. Note the very large solar panel for charging the huge banks of batteries for the light.

lightstation; however, by 1935 a new lighthouse was required. This was a black, steel skeleton tower with a red iron lantern on top, built on concrete piers. Inside the skeleton tower there was a 2.13-metre-square enclosed staircase rising from a 4.87-metre-square shed. The tower was 19.2 metres high, base to vane, and displayed a white flashing light from 29.87 metres above high water. It was 6.85 metres square at the ground, tapering to 3 metres square at the lantern deck.

The records show that John Gregoire was the lightkeeper in March 1935, but since that date, the job of keeping the light was assigned to three of the lifesaving staff. The position of lightkeeper was re-established on August 13, 1958, when James William Cleary was appointed at $3,270 a year. He resigned four months later and the job went to Ross Leonard Negus, who resigned after eight months, leaving the position to James Gordon Rhyno who served from August 14, 1959, until the light was made

unwatched on September 1, 1960.

A four-bedroom dwelling was built in 1931, which was still in good condition when a 1973 report stated that the tower was in very poor condition. The bank on which the tower sat had eroded 6 metres in the previous five years and the tower's foundation was only 3 metres from the edge of the sand bank. It was recommended that a new tower be built about 18 metres from the old. On September 10, 1974, J. L. Nichols of Bedford got the contract to build the existing tower. It is 2.4 metres square with a 2.4-metre by 3.6-metre aluminum shed at the base, all sitting on a concrete foundation. The tower is 18.1 metres high, which includes the red aluminum octagonal lantern, and has a vertical red stripe on the face of each of its four sides. The light shows from 36 metres above high water, the power for which is supplied by a bank of 92 large single-cell batteries, kept charged by a huge solar panel. The old tower has been knocked down and its wreckage left behind to catch the blowing sand and refill the damaged site. The dwelling, unoccupied since 1960, had partially collapsed and was covered with blowing sand until, by 1992, only a small portion of the rooftop could still be seen.

A beautiful and unique part of Nova Scotia, Sable Island is like being in another part of the world. We can only hope that it won't be ruined by offshore exploration.

102 Cranberry Island is a low-lying and rocky island situated at the northeast side of the entrance of the channel into Canso Harbour—about 4.2 kilometres from the front range light at the town of Canso. It's about 500 metres in length and half as wide. At about half-tide, the island is divided into two distinct parts, but can be traversed at low tide provided the sea is calm. The lighthouse marks the turning point for vessels entering or leaving the Gut of Canso, where thousands of vessels of every description continually pass. There had been a lightstation at the north end of the island, but since 1929 it has been located at the south end. In fact, there have been four lighthouses on the north end and three at the south end of Cranberry Island.

On February 27, 1808, a committee was appointed to consider the expediency of erecting a lighthouse at Cranberry Island, and £400 was appropriated for that purpose, but it wasn't actually built until 1815. The first lighthouse was a large octagonal wooden building, 18.29 metres high, and painted with red and white horizontal stripes. Two fixed white lights were shown vertically, 10.66 metres apart— one light was in the lantern, and the other light was in a bow window on the ground floor. A wooden dwelling was built nearby for the lightkeeper and his family. As early as 1834, the keeper was complaining that the lantern was rotten, and that the upper floors were badly decayed because water was getting in through the lantern. The low elevation of the island meant it suffered many an onslaught by the sea. In August 1873, the sea washed completely over the island, carrying away two boats and about 10 tons of coal, severely damaging the wall under the dwelling, tearing off the shingles, carrying doors away, and tearing up fences. It was considered better to rebuild than to try to repair the damage.

In 1880, tenders were called for the construction of a new lighthouse with a dwelling attached. The contract was awarded to Philson Kemton of Milton, Queens County, for the sum of $3,800. On October 13, 1881, with the work almost finished, a fire occurred in the new tower, which completely destroyed most of the buildings on the island, including a new lighting apparatus and lantern, the furniture, and the provisions and the supplies of the lightkeeper and his assistants. Only the new oil store and a storehouse were

CRANBERRY ISLAND	
ESTABLISHED:	1815
CCG LIGHT #:	668
POSITION:	45° 19′ 29.4″ N
	60° 55′ 40.8″ W
	South part of the island,
	off Cape Canso
LIGHT:	Flashing white, Fl/E14
AHW:	16.9 metres
NOM. RANGE:	16 nautical miles
HORN:	Two horns blast in
	unison, B3, S3, B3, S51
DESCRIPTION:	White square tower,
	14.6 metres high,
	on the corner of a
	rectangular equipment
	building

spared. On November 8, 1881, provisional lights were promptly provided by a skeleton tower 15.24 metres high, topped by a temporary wooden lantern for the upper light, and a rough lantern 6.09 metres below for the lower light.

A new lighthouse was constructed under contract by John G. Sinclair of Country Harbour for $3,690, which included an attached dwelling and shed. Reconstruction of the fog-alarm building also began, and was fitted out by Henry Wall of Dartmouth for an

additional cost of $4,942.80. The lighthouse was an octagonal wooden tower 23.77 metres high. A bow window was built into the face of the tower, below the upper light, to maintain the same light characteristic—this was completed by June 30, 1883. With an average of over 2,000 hours of fog annually, great attention was paid to the fog alarm. The fog-alarm building was rebuilt at the south end of the island in 1906, in place of the one at the north end of the island, and not long after, in 1929, another new lighthouse was built at the south end, together with a fog alarm. This lighthouse was a white wooden tower, 3.05 metres square, attached to the fog-alarm building and surmounted by a red iron lantern.

In March 1961, two diesel generator sets were installed to provide electric power to the island and two more diesel engines and compressors were installed to supply air to the diaphone horn. In 1963, a two-storey double dwelling was built, after which the old dwelling was demolished and another single dwelling was erected, thus the island became a three-family station. In addition to the lighthouse/fog-alarm building, there was an engine room, another storage building, and a

Without knowledge of the waters surrounding Cranberry Island, landing is difficult even for my Zodiac, seen here on the beach. In 1996, no decision had been made yet on the final status of this lightstation or the buildings on it.

boathouse at the station.

On September 21, 1970, it was decided the the station should be semi-automated, so contracts went out for another new lighthouse tower and monitoring building. The tower was completed on March 28, 1971—a self-supporting galvanized steel skeleton tower with an enclosed stairwell. On May 26, the powerful diaphone horn was replaced by a rather feeble electronic horn, thereby eliminating the need for the large engines and compressors—and the second assistant lightkeeper. Thus the station reverted to a two-family station. A year later, it was decided that yet another lighthouse should be built on this site, and the skeleton tower would be transferred to Jeddore Rock, where it now exists. The current lighthouse and adjoining equipment building were constructed in its place and went into service on July 5, 1978. It is a rectangular concrete building connected to a

Canso Range

square concrete block tower, which rises to 14.6 metres to support an octagonal red aluminum lantern and a 91.44-centimetre airport beacon that rotates twice a minute, flashing a white light every 15 seconds.

Even as a new boathouse and slipway were being built in the spring of 1980, total automation and de-staffing were being planned. In July 1981, the single dwelling and metal prefab building were declared surplus, and a submarine power cable was being laid from Canso to the island. In June 1985, the surplus dwelling was torn down and the following year, in August 1986, the station was de-staffed. Everything was boarded up and the station was monitored from ashore.

The double dwelling and boathouse were declared surplus in February 1989, to be removed from the site. The boathouse was quickly sold and removed, but the duplex remained. The Canso Historical Society has shown interest in preserving the station, but the Coast Guard can't exercise its options for disposing of it until they ascertain the level of service it requires.

The lighthouse can be seen from Canso, but it can only be reached by boat. Landing should only be attempted by those with knowledge of the surrounding waters, and with permission from the Coast Guard.

103 The Nova Scotia Pilot describes Canso Harbour as having considerable historical and nautical interest. It was visited by French fishermen and traders in as early as the sixteenth century, and over the next 200 years it was the frequent site of French and Indians battles against British colonists; it fell with the rest of Acadia in 1759. Grassy Island, which is actually part of George Island, is the site of historic ruins and has been developed as a national historic park made accessible to the public by a short, free boat ride. Information is available at the visitor reception centre on the town's waterfront off Union Street.

CANSO RANGE	
ESTABLISHED:	1905
CCG LIGHT #:	672 and 673
POSITION:	45° 19' 56" N
	60° 58' 48" W
	South of Lanigan Beach,
	near the south entrance
	to the harbour
LIGHT:	Fixed yellow
AHW:	Front light is 10.4 metres;
	rear is 384 metres from
	the front and 28.7 metres
	above high water
NOM. RANGE:	8 nautical miles
HORN:	None
DESCRIPTION:	Both are white wooden
	pepper-shaker-type
	towers with a red vertical
	stripe from the base to
	the gallery on the
	seaward side. The front
	tower is 8.5 metres high,
	the rear tower is
	14 metres high.

In 1905, these range light towers were built on the south side of the harbour by contract to E. F. Munro of Westville, at a contract price of $2,590. The first lightkeeper was William J.

The front tower to the Canso range is seen here at the harbour's edge.

Mathews, appointed on December 17, 1904, at $200 a year. There were no other buildings directly associated with the range lights. The keeper lived nearby in his own home.

When the lights were electrified, the lamps used ordinary 100-watt bulbs and were fully automated, fitted with time clocks to turn them on and off. There were also battery-operated emergency lights in case the main lights failed. Robert Eustace, who had been keeper of these lights since June 11, 1931, was then no longer required; he retired from this job in November 1958, at which time George McNeary was appointed caretaker. His responsibility was to observe the proper operation of the lights, change burned-out bulbs, and report any failure or acts of vandalism. This job was also discontinued on January 1, 1967, in accordance with new departmental policy.

On January 9, 1968, both lights were changed to Crouse Hinds floodlights using 400-watt mercury-vapour lamps. This changed the characteristic from fixed red to fixed yellow. The lantern on the front tower was badly rotted below the windowsills, so the upper section was removed, decked over, and the light was mounted on top of the open deck. The overall height of the tower was, therefore, reduced by about

Queensport

1.25 metres, but the light focal plane remained unchanged. The red vertical stripes were painted on the seaward side of each tower in September 1972.

In May 1988, the light apparatus was changed on both towers to hooded lanterns with 20-centimetre lenses, and the electrical system was changed to 12 volts DC by means of a transformer/rectifier. There are four lamps in a changer that automatically rotates a new bulb into operating position whenever a bulb burns out. A sun switch automatically turns the lights on at dusk and off at dawn.

The rear light tower is just above the hospital parking lot and the front tower is 384 metres away at the water's edge. Please respect private property.

The rear tower of the Canso range seen here in 1998, in good condition.

104 Although known as the Queensport lighthouse, named after the bay or the village of Queensport about 1.2 kilometres away, it is built on Rook Island and was known as the Crow Harbour lighthouse from the time it was established until about 1902. Some people also referred to it as the Chedabucto Bay light.

The first lighthouse was constructed under contract by James McDonald for the sum of $1,429. The building was painted white and consisted of a square tower 12.19 metres high from the base to the top of the lantern, with a keeper's dwelling attached. The fixed white light, first lit on November 25, 1882, was 15.24 metres above high water. There was also a boathouse for the station boat, an oil store, and an outhouse. John Ehler III was appointed first keeper at $300 per year.

The existing lighthouse was built in 1937 at the time Curtis C. Munroe was lightkeeper. The fixed white light was produced by a duplex kerosene-vapour lamp and a seventh-order lens. The fog alarm was a hand-operated horn used to answer vessels' signals. Besides the lighthouse/dwelling, there was a boathouse for the 5.5-metre station boat, and a storage shed.

A notice to mariners dated December 8, 1955, advised that the light had been changed from fixed white to flashing white, that the hand fog-horn had been discontinued, and that the light would now be unwatched. A caretaker, Colin Hendsbee, had been hired. It seems the automated light was not providing satisfactory service because the

Considerable work has been done on this Queensport lighthouse on Rook Island by a community group that wants to develop it into a park and historic site. In 1996, negotiations were ongoing and no decision was in sight.

light was once again manned from September 10, 1957, until it was automated and de-staffed again on January 30, 1967. In April 1968, the boathouse and shed were declared surplus, sold, and removed from the island within two months. In February 1979, the dwelling was declared surplus and given the price tag of $1,000. Luckily, the condition of sale was that the building had to be removed from the island, so there were no takers. Instead, a community-minded citizen, Darryl Spidell, requested that consideration be given to leaving the lighthouse on the island and restoring it to its former

Guysborough

QUEENSPORT

QUEENSPORT	
ESTABLISHED:	1882
CCG LIGHT #:	683
POSITION:	45° 20' 52" N
	61° 16' 21" W
	On Rook Island,
	Chedabucto Bay
LIGHT:	Flashing white,
	F0.5/E3.5
AHW:	16.5 metres
NOM. RANGE:	12 nautical miles
HORN:	None
DESCRIPTION:	White square wooden
	dwelling surmounted by
	a square red wooden
	lantern,
	13.41 metres high

105 Guysborough Harbour is at the head of Chedabucto Bay, from which an 11-kilometre-long inlet extends to the north. Six kilometres of it is navigable to vessels drawing up to two metres, and small craft can go almost another 5 kilometres farther to Haven Bridge, where the tide ends. The problem is the narrow and crooked channel at the entrance to Guysborough Harbour where there's a swift tidal current and two dangerous bars. The lighthouse, at the south end of the shingle beach of Peart Point, provides a reference to navigate the 73-metre-wide channel between it and Stony Patch, then into the channel to

GUYSBOROUGH	
ESTABLISHED:	1846
CCG LIGHT #:	685
POSITION:	45° 22' 32.7" N
	61° 29' 27.4" W
	On the west side of the
	Guysborough Harbour
	entrance near Peart Point
LIGHT:	Fixed white
AHW:	12.5 metres
NOM. RANGE:	10 nautical miles
HORN:	None
DESCRIPTION:	White circular fibreglass
	tower with two red
	horizontal bands,
	9.1 metres high

The old Guysborough lighthouse, a square, two-storey dwelling with a lantern on top, has been gone from this site for over 20 years, replaced by this fibreglass tower in 1981.

splendour. This created interest in the community and prompted the local municipal council to write to the Minister of Transport requesting that the lighthouse not be sold. This subsequently led to the formation of a community group, the Fisherman's Lighthouse Association, which successfully negotiated a five-year lease on the property, giving the group time to restore and develop the property into a park and historic site. Some of the restoration work has been done, and the District of Guysborough has permission to continue the work until a more permanent arrangement is achieved. Negotiations are ongoing.

Drive about 1 kilometre west of the village of Queensport on Route 16, along the shore of Chedabucto Bay. This will bring you to a small roadside parking area where there's a plaque with information about the lighthouse and the lightkeepers. At this spot you are only 600 metres from Rook Island and may enjoy a clear view of the lighthouse in this picturesque setting.

clear the inner bar. A simple beacon was established in 1846 at the expense of the county, an economical means of saving lives and the property of fishermen and others who navigate that part of the coast. Once the value of this bea-

con was realized, a petition was made in 1849 for its continuance and for it to be taken under the care and protection of the provincial authority. The building had no lantern—the light was shown through two windows. It was a white square dwelling 6.09 metres high, which was too small for its intended purpose, in fact, the lightkeeper chose to live in his own house, which, fortunately, was quite near the lighthouse. Godfrey S. Peart was the first appointed

Eddy Point

lightkeeper at £30 per year.

On September 12, 1904, disaster befell the lighthouse, as it did so many others in those years: it burned down. A temporary light was soon in place, and an anchor lantern was hoisted on a 9.14-metre mast on the site of the old lighthouse. Almost immediately construction began on a real lighthouse. The six-room, wooden-frame dwelling had a wooden lantern on top with iron corner posts for strength. It showed a fixed white light with a red sector light over Stony Patch.

On June 10, 1957, the light was electrified, and four years later, on October 25, 1961, it became automatic, at which time lightkeeper James L. Jarvis was left without a job. A caretaker was employed at $100 per year. It was a very unusual light at the time, because it had a green main light visible from all points of approach by water, and on a lower floor, it had a fixed red main light showing over Stony Patch on a bearing of 220 degrees true. The upper main light had a 200-watt bulb, and the lower light, a 100-watt bulb. Both had 12-volt standby lights of the appropriate colour, supplied by a bank of 10 large single-cell batteries. A time clock controlled the lighting and extinguishing of the lights.

By May 3, 1967, the lantern had deteriorated beyond economical repair. It was removed and replaced with a Millard skeleton mast installed on top of the lighthouse, with a 300-millimetre acrylic lantern and a 125-watt mercury-vapour lamp. By 1972, the lighthouse building itself was so badly deteriorated that it was advertised for sale "as is." There was no interest by 1981, so the old structure was demolished and a new one was erected in its place—the existing 9.1-metre fibreglass tower. It had a 300-millimetre gas lantern that was converted to electricity; it uses a 175-watt metal-halide bulb.

A sun switch turns it on and off from May to December.

Less than a kilometre south of Guysborough on Route 16, there are side roads branching off in an easterly direction. Take the lane south of Ingersol Creek, which leads to a dead end on private property a little over a kilometre away. A short walk of about 200 metres will bring you to the light. Please respect private property.

106

Low-lying Eddy Point is at the southern entrance point of the Gut of Canso. It cannot be seen from over 3.2 kilometres away in daylight, besides which, a spit extends from the point another 450 metres to the northeast. Thus the lighthouse is very important to the many vessels that pass through the Strait of Canso.

EDDY POINT	
ESTABLISHED:	1851
CCG LIGHT #:	689
POSITION:	45° 31' 18.3" N
	61° 14' 58.4" W
	On the point at the south
	entrance to the
	Strait of Canso
LIGHT:	Fixed white.
AHW:	11.8 metres
NOM. RANGE:	18 nautical miles
HORN:	Discontinued
DESCRIPTION:	Round white fibreglass
	tower, 11.8 metres high

The original lighthouse was a dwelling with three-sided dormer windows at the east and west ends of the roof, from which lights were exhibited, giving the characteristic of two horizontal fixed white lights, 7.31 metres apart at 7.62 metres above high water. The lamps with their reflectors were arranged in the windows to show two lights northward, two lights southward, one light to the east, and one light to the west. The white building had a black diamond daymark painted on its seaward side. Joseph Mundell was appointed as its first keeper at £50 per year with £20 a year for fuel.

Eventually, the two horizontal lights proved not to be very efficient. In 1894, T. M. Crowe of Truro was contracted to build a new square tower attached to the old lighthouse building, so the light could be changed to show one fixed light from the lantern on the tower. This new light was put into operation on January 1, 1895.

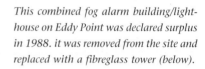

This combined fog alarm building/lighthouse on Eddy Point was declared surplus in 1988. it was removed from the site and replaced with a fibreglass tower (below).

By 2001, the shore had eroded right up to the equipment building beside the Eddy Point fibreglass tower shown here. Part of the concrete pad supporting it has been undermined, and local mariners are concerned that the station might be discontinued and removed.

In 1929, the entire station was rebuilt, including a new fog-alarm building to contain the machinery for a diaphone horn, and a new combined lighthouse and dwelling. This was changed again in 1938 to a white square wooden tower surmounted by a red iron lantern, attached to a white wooden fog-alarm building. The two-storey dwelling was a separate building nearby.

In 1970, a 500-millimetre cut-glass drum lens was installed with a 400-watt mercury-vapour lamp, and a 250-millimetre battery-operated emergency light. The following year, an electronic foghorn was installed, and the gas engines and compressors for the horn were removed from service. A diesel generator was then provided for emergency power and the station was classified as semi-automated.

Even though this was a shore station, living conditions were not always ideal. One lightkeeper's report stated, "A big storm swept away the northern beach and cut a gap through it approximately six metres wide and 1.5 metres deep. The gap extended through the road and into Mundell Pond and

widened with each high tide. The whole point was flooded to one metre deep over the whole road at high tide and the basement was flooded. It was only possible to get across with hip boots at low tide. The car was marooned at the lighthouse and the telephone line broken at the gap and all phones in the immediate area out of service. The children not able to attend school if high tide occurred in the morning and on the other hand if high tide was in the afternoon, they couldn't get home. The standby engine was out of order and if there was a power failure the fog alarm would also not be in operation." Since the causeway was completed in 1955, studies found that the tides have been about 28 centimetres higher than usual in this area. There has also been an ongoing problem with contractors removing large quantities of gravel from the bar, which no doubt contributes to the problem.

In April 1977, the station was reduced to a one-man operation, and after remote monitoring was established from the Coast Guard's Eddy Point Traffic Centre across the road from the lightstation in August 1978, the station was de-staffed in April 1979. The dwelling was declared surplus, and was removed from the site.

In 1988, a concrete slab was poured over the former dwelling foundation and a round, 11.8-metre fibreglass tower was bolted into position. Part of the contract included demolishing the old lighthouse/fog-alarm building, but because of a great deal of public controversy over the historic value of the building, it was instead declared surplus.

On January 5, 1993, the fog detector and horn were turned off permanently, but the light tower remains operational. A community group, the Eddy Point Marine Park Association, is dedicated to preserving the history of the area and developing a marine park and picnic spot.

Located 15 kilometres southeast of the town of Mulgrave on Route 344, Eddy Point is the only location within Guysborough County listed in the Nova Scotia Doers and Dreamers Guide as a land-based whale-watching destination.

Fisherman's Harbour Lighthouse marks the long shingle spit that protects the snug harbour. At left, the government wharf is piled high with lobster traps.

The sea gives Hog Island a lick. Note the helicopter landing pad, built on top of the old lighthouse foundation in front of the tower.

Cape Breton Island

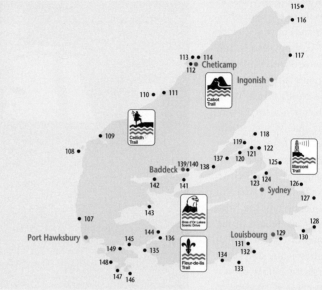

Ceilidh Trail

Cabot Trail

Fleur-de-lis Trail

Marconi Trail

Bras d'Or Lakes Scenic Drive

107	Balache Point Range 112	129	Louisbourg 140
108	Henry Island 113	130	Main-à-Dieu 142
109	Mabou Harbour 114	131	Gabarus 143
110	Margaree Island 115	132	Rouse Point 143
111	Margaree Harbour Range 116	133	Guyon Island 144
112	Chéticamp Harbour 117	134	Fourchu Head 146
113	Enragee Point 118	135	Jerome Point 147
114	Caveau Point Range 119	136	Gregory Island 148
115	St. Paul Island 120	137	McNeil Beach 149
116	Cape North 122	138	Man of War Point 150
117	Neil's Harbour 125	139	Kidston Island 151
118	Ciboux Island 126	140	Kidston Island West 152
119	Carey Point Range 127	141	Gillis Point 153
120	Great Bras d'Or Range 128	142	Little Narrows 154
121	Black Rock Point 129	143	Cameron Island 154
122	Point Aconi 130	144	Cape George 155
123	Sydney Range 131	145	Bourgeois Inlet 156
124	Sydney Bar 132	146	Green Island 157
125	Low Point 133	147	Marache Point 158
126	Glace Bay North Breakwater . . .135	148	Jerseyman Island 159
127	Flint Island 136	149	Grandique Point 161
128	Scatarie 138		

Balache Point Range

107 The Gut of Canso separates Cape Breton Island from mainland Nova Scotia and was used as the most direct route to the Gulf of St. Lawrence by thousands of vessels every year, especially coasting vessels and those from the United States. Marked by Eddy Point lighthouse at the southern entrance and the North Canso lighthouse at the north entrance, the 23-kilometre passage was quite safe, especially as the water is not less than 27 metres deep in all but a few places. The narrowest point of the gut is also the deepest, and was selected as the site on which to build a causeway connecting the Nova Scotia mainland to Cape Breton Island. With water 66 metres deep, the 823-metre-long causeway is the deepest in the world. To enable shipping to continue using this route between Chedabucto Bay and St. Georges Bay, a canal and set of locks were built at the east end of the causeway. Highway traffic is carried across a swing bridge at the south approach to the locks. The causeway was opened in 1955.

BALACHE POINT RANGE	
ESTABLISHED:	1963
CCG LIGHT #:	701 and 702
POSITION:	45° 38′ 57.5″ N
	61° 25′ 02″ W
	North end of
	the Canso locks
LIGHT:	Fixed amber range lights
AHW:	Front, 11.3 metres;
	rear, 13.8 metres
NOM. RANGE:	Unknown
HORN:	None
DESCRIPTION:	Front is a skeleton mast 6.1 metres high, the rear is a white pepper-shaker-type tower, 8.53 metres high. The rear tower is 203.9 metres from the front, both have a vertical red stripe on the seaward side.

To assist vessels approaching from the north, a set of range lights was established on Balache Point. The rear tower sits on a knoll among a few scattered tombstones in a small cemetery at the side of the canal locks near the highway. A skeleton tower in a graveyard has a certain morbid appeal, but the existing pepper-shaker tower is aesthetically pleasing, and, even considering its location, is bound to be attractive to lighthouse enthusiasts. This range was put into service in the fall of 1963. There was no lightkeeper appointed; the lock-master was the caretaker.

The 30-centimetre-wide vertical fluorescent red stripe was painted on the

A peaceful setting for a lighthouse, in a cemetery at Balache Point beside the Canso Canal locks.

seaward side of these towers in March 1973. Otherwise, very few changes have been made since they were built.

There is parking at either end of the swing bridge, where the operation of the bridge and locks might be observed as a vessel goes through. The little park beside the graveyard is a good place from which to enjoy the lighthouse.

Henry Island

At the northeast corner of the wide entrance to St. Georges Bay are two sizable islands. The larger of the two, situated about 1.6 kilometres off shore from Port Hood, Cape Breton, is Port Hood Island, and 1.6 kilometres southwest of Port Hood Island is Henry Island.

Henry Island is triangular in shape and comprises of 50 hectares of sandstone rising to a maximum height of 59.4 metres. The southern end of the island forms the base of the triangle and is 800 metres wide. The other two

sides are about 1.6 kilometres long. It is almost entirely surrounded by cliffs and landing is extremely dangerous, except at a small stretch of sandy beach on the east side, which has always been used to land personnel and supplies for the lightstation. Shallow water runs out from Fishery Point on the southeast point of the island, and this is where the Canadian warship HMCS *Sorel* came to grief. A flower-class corvette that had fought throughout the Battle of the Atlantic, the *Sorel* had been decommissioned at the end of the World War Two and was being taken up the St. Lawrence River by a skeleton crew when it struck on Henry Island. Although a total loss, none of the crew were lost or even injured. Parts of the ship can still be seen on the point.

The passage between Henry and Port Hood islands contains numerous rocky

[ABOVE] Henry Island, the pride of Bill Baker, has one of the most unusual light towers. It is constructed without a frame by stacking planks on their flat side, and interlocking each of the eight sides at the corners.

[LEFT] Inside the Henry Island Lighthouse, one can see the edges of 7.62-centimetre-thick planks stacked together and interlocking at each of the eight corners to form a frameless building with walls 25.4 centimetres thick.

shoals that are so deviously scattered that navigation should not be attempted except in a small boat during fine weather and with local knowledge. The existing lighthouse tower is the original, and was put into operation on December 1, 1902. The keeper's original two-storey dwelling is located 50 metres south of the lighthouse and measures 7.11 by 8.5 metres. It has recently been completely restored by Bertie Smith of Port Hood Island, for the owner of the island, Bill Baker, who along with his family thoroughly

enjoys living under the beam of an operational lighthouse.

The lighthouse was built under contract by Joseph McDonald for the price of $3,489. The first lightkeeper was John Angus McLennen, who was appointed on July 21, 1903, at $405 per year. The lighthouse tower is different—only one other like it is known to exist. The building doesn't have a conventional wooden frame. The walls were built by layering 7.62-centimetre-thick by 25.4-centimetre-wide planks, one on top of the other, and lapping them together at each of the eight corners from the base to the gallery deck, forming solid walls that are 25.4 centimetres thick and taper from an inside diameter of 7.16 metres at the ground floor, to 3.96 metres at the fourth floor. The windows are placed in such a way that it produces a beautiful visual effect of spiralling from the ground to the top of the tower. The pediments on each window and the door add to the overall attractiveness. The tower is topped by a polygonal red iron lantern, 3.96 metres high and 3.04 metres in diameter, and glazed on all 12 sides.

In 1962, the light illuminant was changed to acetylene gas, which meant that the light could be left unattended for extended periods of time, and so Stanley Morrison, who had kept the light for only two years, became the last lightkeeper on Henry Island. From July 1963 until January 1967, a caretaker, James R. MacDonald, was hired to observe the proper functioning of the light, watch out for vandalism, and report any major mechanical or other difficulties. After 1967, the Coast Guard, conducted regular inspections, made necessary repairs, and reporting any irregularities.

In 1985, the light was changed to battery-operated, using 12 large single-cell batteries kept charged by a 36-cell solar panel fitted to the southwest side of the gallery—turned on and off by a

Mabou Harbour

sun-switch.

The trail from the beach to the light-station is a 650-metre hike up a steady incline to an elevation of 61 metres. It's an enjoyable walk along a mossy trail through the spruce and fir trees, but it

---

HENRY ISLAND

ESTABLISHED:	1902
CCG LIGHT #:	881
POSITION:	45° 58' 37.4" N
	61° 36' 01.8" W
	West side of the island
	on the summit
LIGHT:	Flashing white, F1/E3
AHW:	73.15 metres
NOM. RANGE:	6 nautical miles
HORN:	None
DESCRIPTION:	Octagonal wooden tower
	with sloping sides,
	16.15 metres high base
	to vane. Each of the eight
	sides is painted
	alternately red and white.

---

must have been difficult for the light-keeper, who had to lug all the supplies up this same trail. He had to transport the station's oil, which was dropped overboard in 204-litre steel drums from the Canadian Coast Guard ship *Tupper*.

Henry Island and its lighthouse can be seen from Route 19 as you approach Harbourview and Port Hood Mines, but the closest you can get without a boat is 5 kilometres. The island is privately owned so permission is needed to visit.

109 Mabou Harbour is actually the mouth of a river and resembles a mountain lake. It's about 5.3 kilometres long and from about 500 metres to 1,400 metres wide, which all sounds good except that it must be entered over a bar and through a narrow dredged channel. A swift tidal current adds to the difficulty of entering at any time other than at flood tide and when the sea is smooth. For these reasons, range lights were erected in 1884 to guide vessels through the channel. Once inside, mariners are rewarded with deep water and a safe harbour, not to mention marvellous scenery along its entire length.

Calm water in a pretty little harbour in Mabou just after sunrise.

The first range lights were put into operation on July 15, 1884. They served 15 to 20 local fishing boats, as well as visitors and pleasure craft. Each light shone from a small lantern hoisted on a mast with a shed at the base—all painted white. The front one showed a fixed white light from the end of the breakwater pier on the southwest side of the dredged channel. The rear lantern showed a fixed red light 900 metres from the front one, on the shore at McFayden's Wharf. There was a lightkeeper appointed for each

lighthouse—John McDonald was keeper of the front light at $59.16 per year and Allan McLean was keeper of the rear light at $54.16 per year.

The front light had to be removed at the close of each navigation season because of the dilapidated condition of the pier, and, indeed, on November 14, 1904, it was carried away in a fierce gale. A temporary pole light was maintained until 1908, at which time both range lights were replaced with permanent towers. The front was a square wooden tower with sloping sides and a square wooden lantern—10 metres high base to vane. The rear tower is the one that exists today, which is 14.6 metres high, and 600 metres from the front one. Both were erected under contract by E. C. Embree of Port Hawkesbury at a cost of $2,450.

By June 1, 1961, due to severe erosion of the breastworks, it was increasingly difficult for the keeper, who had to resort to wearing hip waders to get to the lighthouse at all times but low tide. The light was eventually made automatic, controlled by a sun switch and powered by batteries. However, it continued to be battered by the elements and in December 1964 a storm ripped about half of one wall completely off the tower, leaving it open to the weather. It was abandoned in the spring, and

Margaree Island

in June 1965 it was demolished and replaced by a red steel skeleton tower 6 metres high. In August 1966, the rear tower was changed from an oil light to electric and made unwatched. The red vertical stripe on the seaward side was added in January 1973.

The front light was permanently discontinued on November 9, 1987, leaving the rear tower the only lighthouse in Mabou Harbour, structurally much the same and sitting in the same place it was built in 1908. However, early in 2001, this lighthouse was declared surplus by the Coast Guard and Government Services Canada was instructed to dispose of it. Let us hope that someone in the community will realize the historic significance of this lighthouse and establish a group of citizens interested in taking responsibility for its care and preservation.

At the village of Mabou, turn west at the main intersection, which takes you along the north side of the harbour. At 2.2 kilometres, bear left at a fork in the road, and proceed another 4.5 kilometres to a gravel road on the left. This will take you down about 400 metres to the lighthouse on Mabou Harbour Wharf.

110 Early and current records refer to this lighthouse as either Margaree Island (Sea Wolf) or Sea Wolf (Margaree Island). However, Margaree Island seems to be the more popular of the two in more recent times. It is an island of about 81 hectares, lying 3.9 kilometres from the west shore of mainland Cape Breton, 14 kilometres from Inverness. As you drive along the coastal road, the island is visible from just about anywhere you view the sea. Made of sandstone, the island is 2 kilometres long by about 550 metres wide, and quite high at 79 metres. The sea rolls against the island on all sides, making it hazardous to land except on the most calm summer day. In winter, when the sea is frozen solid between the island and mainland, the more adventurous might want to walk across.

In 1853, Captain Thomas Coffin, a member of the legislature, recommended the erection of a lighthouse on Margaree Island and construction began almost immediately. The light was expected to be a useful coast light, as there was no other between it and St. Paul's Island, a distance of over 100 kilometres. It would also provide a guide to the adjacent harbours. The dwelling house was built adjoining the lighthouse tower, which was 12.2 metres high, and entirely made of wood. The first keeper was Nathaniel C. McKeen, whose salary was £60 per year plus a £20 fuel allowance. The dwelling part of the building was very small and afforded little room for the family. The kitchen was in the cellar, which was wet and terribly uncomfortable. Three years after it was occupied, the lighthouse inspector remarked that it must have been wretchedly built to be in such bad condition, and he recommended that a small addition be built on the house to make life a little more comfortable. Three years later, the family was still

A shorter than usual octagonal concrete tower doesn't need to be tall as it sits at the highest point of the island at 82 metres elevation. The octagonal lantern on this lighthouse is unusual in that it is wooden.

waiting for the addition, but the keeper was resourceful, as lightkeepers had to be in those times. Over the years, he built a good road, about 450 metres long, from the landing to the lighthouse, and built three buildings of his own. He cultivated some 12 hectares of land from which he cut enough hay and grain to winter 7 head of cattle, 2 horses, and 100 sheep. Of course, this

was on Crown land and he had no right of claim. He estimated that his buildings and improvements were worth over $400, and when he left after 20 years of service, the government gave him $150 for them.

No light was shown during the three months of winter, but in the early years, the keeper was still required to man the station and was instructed to show a light whenever he could see clear water.

In 1883, a new iron lantern was installed and the entire building was given thorough repairs; it wasn't until 1910 that such extensive repairs had to be done again. In 1921, a second-order lens was installed, which showed a

Margaree Harbour Range

clear strong light at 21 nautical miles. Because of the abrupt high cliffs, it was distinctly possible the light would become obscured from view by vessels that approached the island too closely.

Extensive building was carried out at this station from 1956 to 1958, in particular, a new one-and-a-half-storey dwelling and the existing reinforced-concrete lighthouse tower were built. The last keeper was John R. MacLeod, who worked at Margaree Island from May 1968 until the station was de-staffed in October 1971. At this time, the light was produced by 12-volt bulbs supplied by a bank of 10 large single-cell batteries kept charged by a solar panel.

Shortly after de-staffing, the island came under the care and control of the Canadian Wildlife Service, which built a small building near the old landing place at the southeast corner of the island. Besides the lighthouse, there is a small barn, still in fair condition, and the dwelling, no doubt a total loss, from having been vandalized and left open to the elements.

Walking across the island one warm day, I was struck by the sweet smell of the small shrubs, and looking down, noticed that the ground was blue with blueberries. A leisurely 20-minute walk up a moderate incline beneath a canopy of overhanging trees brought me to the lightstation, where the ground is flat and opens to a beautiful panoramic view of the Cape Breton hills and coastline. As I took it all in, I was reminded of something Angus Y. MacLellan, keeper of this light from 1912 to 1946, wrote about Sea Wolf Island: "Sing this song to the happy island...where does sweet summer arrive earlier?...the thrush sing more beautifully?...the beauty and many species of birds...my eternal slumber will be tranquil if my pillow is placed in the Happy Island."

The island can be clearly seen from the mainland, but not the lighthouse.

111 Margaree Harbour is difficult and dangerous to enter: tidal currents run at 4 knots in the narrow channel that has been dredged through a sand bar that obstructs the entrance. The surf on the bar can be particularly heavy when the strong current is running against the wind and sea. Breakwaters were built on each side of the harbour entrance, and in 1885, a 6.4-metre-high square wooden tower was built on the end of the breakwater pier on the south side. It was fitted with a sector light that showed either a bright white light or a red light on each side of the channel. In 1900, the two new range lighthouses were built to replace the sector light, which was permanently discontinued on May 4, 1901, and the tower removed. The existing lighthouse towers were built by the Department of Marine and Fisheries under the supervision of foreman A. McLellan, with materials sent from Halifax. The total cost of construction was $1,062.95. When the towers were completed, the front one was 51 metres back from the high-water mark on the bank facing the channel, and the rear tower was 64.6 metres from the front. They had a nominal range of 10 nautical miles. Roderick McLellan was appointed keeper of the rear light and Nicholas Daigle, keeper of the front light, both started on June 8, 1901. Each was paid $50 a year.

Both lights were converted to electricity on June 13, 1963, and the characteristic was changed from fixed red to flashing red, flashing 30 times every minute, each flash one second in duration. It is unusual for range lights to be flashing, but this was rectified in

MARGAREE HARBOUR RANGE

ESTABLISHED:	1900
CCG LIGHT #:	872 and 873
POSITION:	46° 26' 22.8" N
	61° 06' 47.3" W
	On the west side of
	the river entrance
	Rear is 64.6 metres
	from the front
LIGHT:	Fixed red.
AHW:	Front is 22.8 metres;
	rear, 32 metres
NOM. RANGE:	Unknown
HORN:	None
DESCRIPTION:	Both are square white
	wooden pepper-shaker-
	type towers with a red
	vertical stripe on the
	seaward side;
	front is 6.4 metres high,
	rear is 10.7 metres high

October when they were changed back to fixed red. The lights were powered by five large single-cell batteries and declared automated. John L. Mackinnon, who had been the lightkeeper since October 31, 1952, was made caretaker of both lights. Soon after the lights were connected to com-

Chéticamp Harbour

[OPPOSITE] The front tower of the Margaree Harbour range in detail.

[BELOW] The rear tower of the Margaree Harbour range in a close-up for more detail. Steel-wire guys are attached to each of the four corners of the tower.

mercial power in 1970, the caretaker's services were no longer required.

From Route 219, take Margaree Harbour Shore Road, turn right for Margaree Harbour, and continue for about 800 metres to a dead end where there's a small turn-around area near the range lights. To view them in line, as mariners would see them, proceed across the Margaree River Bridge for 2 kilometres, turn left on Belle Cote Beach Road, and follow it a short distance to the end.

Note that the boat described by well-known writer Farley Mowat in his book *The Boat Who Wouldn't Float* is on display in Margaree Harbour at the junction of the Cabot Trail and Route 219.

112 This lighthouse was originally the Eastern Harbour range when it was put into operation in 1890 for the purpose of aiding vessels through a dredged channel to a well-protected harbour between Cheticamp Island and the mainland. Chéticamp Island, which is just over 5 kilometres long on its east side, is connected to the mainland at its south end by a causeway over an existing low beach of sand and shingle that got overflowed at high tide. The open northeast end of the harbour is obstructed by a sandbar located 914 metres inside the entrance. The sandbar is usually dry or covered by less than a metre of water at high tide. A channel 30 metres wide and 4.9 metres deep had to be dredged through the bar to allow vessels to reach a safe harbour and good anchorage in 6.4 metres of water.

The original lights were shown from lanterns hoisted on masts, having a small shed at their base. The front light was fixed red, 13.7 metres above high water, and the rear light was also fixed red, 27.4 metres above high water and 300 metres from the front light. The first keeper was Henry Aucoin, who served for an annual salary of $92.62.

A beautiful boardwalk promenade in Chéticamp with the lighthouse as the centrepiece.

In 1894, two new enclosed towers were constructed to replace the pole lights. The work was done under the supervision of John Chisholm, employing local labour. Both white pepper-shaker-type towers had a square red wooden lantern. The front was 7 metres high; the rear was 9.8 metres high and 256 metres from the front.

Because of the shifting sandbar, from time to time, the dredged channel had to take a slightly different direction, which, unfortunately, created the need to relocate the range lights. Once, in 1914, both towers had to be shifted, and in 1931, it was necessary to move only the rear tower. In 1950, the front

CHÉTICAMP HARBOUR	
ESTABLISHED:	1890
CCG LIGHT #:	865
POSITION:	46° 37' 55.5" N
	61° 00' 42.1" W
	On crib at the shoreline
LIGHT:	Fixed red
AHW:	7.6 metres
NOM. RANGE:	Unknown
HORN:	None
DESCRIPTION:	White wooden pepper-shaker-type tower, 7 metres high, with fluorescent red vertical stripe

Enragee Point

lighthouse was moved to a crib on the shore, and the rear was changed to a tripod skeleton mast with white slatted daymark. The front light was then 8.23 metres above high water and the rear 18.3 metres above high water, both still showing a fixed red light.

The 1980 list of lights shows that the name was changed from Eastern Harbour to Chéticamp Harbour range. These range lights were discontinued in 1986, replaced in about 1990 by an inner harbour sector light mounted atop a round white fibreglass tower 7.5 metres high, with a red horizontal band around the top, very near where the old square wooden front range-light tower once stood. When the range was discontinued, the front tower came under the care of the community.

Chéticamp is an interesting Acadian fishing village with a population of about one thousand people, situated at the entrance to the Cape Breton Highlands National Park. Extensive work has been done on the waterfront since 1995, including the construction of the Quai-du-Phare Marina board-walk, a tourist information centre, and various marine services. The centre-piece of the project is the old front lighthouse tower of the Chéticamp Harbour range, which has been moved from its original position just a few metres away.

113 Because of a principal fishing station at the southwest end of Chéticamp Island, including several buildings and fish stages, a lighthouse was established there in 1872 and was called Chéticamp light. It was actually located in a cove northeast of La Pointe, when no other lighthouses existed on this part of the coast. Patsy Lefort, lightkeeper on Enragee Point from 1968 until 1988, told me that a beautiful 38-metre-long vessel, *Kimber*, was making its way from Mulgrave to

Chéticamp with a load of flour in a snowstorm on New Year's night in 1936, when it struck Enragee Point. Since there was no radio on board, no one on shore was aware of its plight. The crew shifted the flour from side to side to try to free the vessel, but failed. The next morning, a storm struck from the westward and the *Kimber* went down, though, luckily, everyone got off safely in the lifeboat. The boilers can still be seen in the summer at low tide. The captain had made that trip three times a week every week, week after week. He usually checked the light at La Pointe, and timed himself from there to make his turn clear of the harbour, but on that night, the wind and tide conditions fooled him, and in the blinding snow he made his turn thinking he was clear. If there had been a lighthouse on Enragee Point at that time, there would have been no wreck.

As a result, a lighthouse was built on Enragee Point in 1937, and the light at the southwest end was reduced to a lantern hoisted on a 6-metre pole with a small building at the base. Peter Cormier was the keeper at the south-west light from about 1920, and when the new lighthouse was built, he got transferred to that lightstation as its first keeper.

The station consisted of a combined lighthouse and dwelling, 12 metres high from the base of the dwelling to

This dwelling of the Enragee Point light-station is now gone, but the equipment building is still beside the lighthouse, so the site has the appearance of a lightstation.

the top of the red iron lantern. There was also a barn, a boathouse, and a fog-gun house. The fog signal was an acety-lene gun fired once every minute.

The lighthouse was destroyed by fire on October 19, 1956, and immediately a new octagonal reinforced-concrete tower was built—the existing light tower. Because of the importance of this coastal light, in 1967 it was desig-nated a three-man station and two new dwellings had to be built. In December, the light was changed from kerosene to electricity, and a 400-watt mercury-vapour lamp was installed. A 250-mil-limetre emergency lantern was also installed, and the following year the station got a new electronic foghorn.

Caveau Point Range

Then, just five years after being designated a three-person station, it was reduced to two-person. The keeper's bungalow was declared surplus, sold, and moved off the station in March 1978. Launched on a course towards total automation, it wasn't long before the station was reduced to a one-man station, and in March 1979, the second dwelling and boathouse were declared surplus.

ENRAGEE POINT

ESTABLISHED:	1937
CCG LIGHT #:	867
POSITION:	46° 38' 58.5" N
	61° 01' 37.4" W
	On the northwest point
	of Chéticamp Island
LIGHT:	White flashing,
	F0.3/E3.7/F0.3/E3.7/F0.3
	E15.7
AHW:	22.3 metres
NOM. RANGE:	18 nautical miles
HORN:	B3, S27
DESCRIPTION:	White octagonal
	reinforced-concrete tower
	with sloping sides, 12.7
	metres high with red
	upper portion; nominal
	range of 18 nautical miles.

By 1987, all automatic systems were installed, hooked up, and ready to go. On April 1, 1988, Patsy Lefort and his wife Yvonne packed up all their belongings and left what remained of the station after 42 years of lightkeeping—22 years in Chéticamp Harbour and 20 years on Enragee Point. After they were gone, their dwelling, the old fog-alarm building, and the garage were declared surplus. Everything is gone now but the equipment building, foghorn, and fuel oil tanks.

At the south limit of Chéticamp, turn off the Cabot Trail and cross the causeway to Chéticamp Island, turn right on the dirt road and drive 6 kilometres to the lighthouse.

114 This pair of range lights was originally known as the outer range, situated at the entrance to the harbour about 2 kilometres northeast of the Chéticamp Harbour range. Both towers were originally built in typical wooden pepper-shaker style, each 8.2 metres high base to vane. Constructed by Fulgence Aucoin at a contract price of $447, they were put into operation on October 3, 1897. The first keeper was Germain Chiasson, who earned $120 per year.

This is the rear tower of the range lights at Caveau Point near Chéticamp, Cape Breton Island. The front light is a skeleton mast and white daymark with a red vertical stripe.

In 1950, the characteristic was changed to fixed green, but no further changes were made until 1976, when, for reasons unknown, both towers were changed to skeleton towers. In 1986, because the channel had been changed from the east side to the west side of the harbour entrance, the Chéticamp Harbour range became redundant and was subsequently discontinued. The Caveau Point skeleton towers continued to be used, but in

---

CAVEAU POINT RANGE

ESTABLISHED:	1897
CCG LIGHT #:	862 and 863
POSITION:	————
Front light:	46° 38' 56.8" N,
	61° 00' 03.5" W,
	on extremity of point
Rear light:	223.1 metres from the
	front at 107° 55'
LIGHT:	Fixed yellow
AHW:	Front, 15.5 metres;
	rear, 31.3 metres.
NOM. RANGE:	Unknown
HORN:	None
DESCRIPTION:	Front is a skeleton mast
	with white daymark and
	red vertical stripe, 6.1
	metres high. Rear is white
	wooden pepper-shaker-
	type tower, 8.2 metres
	high, with red vertical
	stripe.

1990, the rear tower was once again listed as a white square wooden structure with a red vertical stripe, 8.2 metres high.

Located right beside the Cabot Trail about 2 kilometres north of the village of Chéticamp. Please respect private property.

St. Paul Island
Northeast
and Southwest

115 Even though the two light-stations on St. Paul Island are 5 kilometres apart, they operate as part of an integrated system and will be described here as one establishment.

St. Paul Island lies in the Cabot Strait, 24.5 kilometres off Cape North at the northern extremity of Cape Breton Island, and 77 kilometres across the strait to Cape Ray, Newfoundland. The maximum length of St. Paul Island is 5.2 kilometres and the width varies between 400 metres and 1.77 kilometres. There are two prominent coves opposite each other at the southern part of the island—Trinity Cove on the west side and Atlantic Cove on the east side. There are also two tiny lakes on the island, and at 147 metres, Mount Groggan, or Coggin Mountain as it is known locally, is the highest peak, and separates the two coves. The northeast light is built on a smaller island about 215 metres in diameter, which is separated from the main island by a 16-metre-wide channel called "the Tittle."

Known as "the Graveyard of the Gulf" in the years before lifesaving stations and lighthouses were established, these treacherous shores where sheer rocky cliffs prevail have brought unknown numbers of vessels to their doom. Those who did make it to shore perished for want of shelter and sustenance. In the wintertime, settlers along the shores of Aspy Bay often watched helplessly as fires burned on the island, lit by shipwrecked survivors, praying for rescuers who would never come—who couldn't come. In the springtime, when the ice had gone, men would go to the island and bury the dead. Two of the earliest recorded wrecks, and most costly in terms of lost lives, were the *Royal Sovereign* and *Viceroy of India*. Both were troop ships during the War of 1812. The *Royal Sovereign* was heading back to England in 1815 with hundreds of returning soldiers when the

ship struck St. Paul Island. Of the 811 men, women, and children on board, only 12 survived.

There had been talk of building a lighthouse on St. Paul Island since about 1817, but it wasn't until after the wreck of the *Jessie* on January 1, 1825, that something was done. The horrific struggle for survival was documented in a diary kept by the owner of the ship, Donald MacKay, who was on board when the ship wrecked. In his diary, he described the hopelessness and despair of survivors desperately trying to get help by lighting huge bonfires. Some lived for almost 11 weeks before dying of exposure and starvation.

In 1831, on the recommendation of the Lighthouse Committee, a lighthouse was built at the south point near where the *Jessie* had wrecked six years

earlier, and in 1832, the New Brunswick government established a lifesaving station at Trinity Cove. In the same year, the government of Nova Scotia also established a lifesaving station on the opposite shore in Atlantic Cove. Neither crew was aware of the presence of the other.

Seven years later, in 1839, the British built another lighthouse at the northeast end of the island. Both lighthouses were large octagonal wooden structures, 12 metres high, and painted white. The south lightstation had a dwelling house for the lightkeeper nearby, and at the north light, the dwelling was connected to the lighthouse tower by a covered passageway.

The first keeper at the northeast light was Donald Moon. He and his family moved to this isolated rock station

The operational part of the northeast St. Paul Island lightstation is shown here. There are also two dwellings and a boathouse not shown. Strangely, there has been no boat on this station for many years.

ST. PAUL ISLAND - NORTHEAST	
ESTABLISHED:	1839
CCG LIGHT #:	1476
POSITION:	47° 13' 35" N
	60° 08' 26" W
	On a rock on the north
	point of the island
LIGHT:	White flashing, F0.3/E9.7
AHW:	38.4 metres
NOM. RANGE:	18 nautical miles
HORN:	None
DESCRIPTION:	White octagonal concrete
	tower, 14 metres high

in 1839. Eight years later, in February, he discovered that his assistant and another hired hand had gone after a seal on the drift ice and were in danger of not being able to get back to the island. He launched a boat with the aid of a female servant, to go to the aid of the two men, and none of the four were ever seen or heard of again. His wife was left alone with a baby; she was discovered several days later, in a state bordering on insanity and great destitution. The commissioner of lighthouses acknowledged that Donald Moon had been a useful and valuable servant.

The first keeper of the southwest light was John Campbell, who continued as keeper, then superintendent for 21 years. His son, Norman Campbell, and then his grandson, followed as keeper. The Campbell family gave a total of 72 years continuous service at the lighthouse.

In 1857, records show that both lightkeepers, Norman Campbell at the south light and Dougald McKay at the north light, were paid £90 salary per year plus another £15 for fuel. Superintendent Samuel C. Campbell, who had overall responsibility for the two lighthouses and a "humane establishment" at Atlantic Cove, received £100 per year plus £15 fuel money and the annual wages for three boatmen of £30 each.

It is interesting to note the supplies that were held at the humane establishment: 6 barrels of pork, 9 barrels of beef, 13 barrels of bread, 9 barrels of flour, 3 barrels of meal, 477 litres of molasses, 62 kilograms of sugar, 2 chests of tea, 12 pairs of blankets, 24 pairs of trousers, 24 pairs of drawers, 48 pairs of socks, 24 pairs of shoes, 24 shirts, 24 coats, and 24 caps. These items were kept in store under charge of the superintendent and issued only to destitute shipwrecked persons cast on the island. Wrecks continued to occur with great frequency, but many of the sailors were saved by the men on the island and the supplies were used up many times over.

With the building of roads interconnecting one end of the island with the

ST. PAUL ISLAND - SOUTHWEST

ESTABLISHED:	1831
CCG LIGHT #:	1477
POSITION:	47° 11' 02" N
	60° 09' 44" W
	On south point
LIGHT:	White flashing,
	once every 4 seconds
AHW:	45.7 metres
NOM. RANGE:	7 nautical miles
HORN:	None
DESCRIPTION:	White circular fibreglass
	tower, 6.1 metres high,
	with red upper portion

other, and the ever-increasing number of people required to operate the light-stations and humane establishment, the population reached about 50 people and a lobster factory was even built on the island. By 1895, a school had been established, and a minister from Sydney began paying visits to conduct services. In 1905, a post office was opened which could claim to be Canada's most unusual mail route. In an article in *In Touch*, Carl Munden wrote, "In order to send the mails to Bay St. Lawrence, a mainland community some 16 kilometres away, the dispatch was picked up by the North

This 8.38-metre iron tower served as the St. Paul Island southwest lighthouse from 1916 until 1988. It is now located, complete with its fourth-order, three-panel Fresnel lens, at the Canadian Coast Guard base in Dartmouth, Nova Scotia.

Sydney/Port Aux Basques ferry, sent all the way to Newfoundland and back as the ferry stopped at St. Paul Island only on the eastern run. At North Sydney it was loaded on a train, taken off at Iona, by mail boat to Baddeck, by stage from Baddeck to Ingonish and finally by courier to Bay St. Lawrence. A distance of approximately 400 kilometres for a location 16 kilometres away."

In 1913, a suspension bridge was built across the Tittle to connect the main island with the small north island. This was certainly a blessing for the families on the north island, who could now have visitors and visit other parts of the main island without being at the mercy of the weather and sea-state, which more often than not would greatly discourage crossing the Tittle in a small boat in either direction. Unfortunately, the bridge didn't last very long, and in its place, a steel cable was suspended across the water carrying a box-like car into which a person could sit and pull themselves across the channel. Later, a breeches-buoy served the same purpose, but, sadly, on December 20, 1955, George Gatza, keeper of the southwest light, went to visit the keeper at the northeast light, and as he hauled himself across the Tittle, the cable broke and he dropped into the water and drowned. That was the end of the connection between the two islands.

In 1916, the southwest light burned down and a new tower was constructed. This was a round cast-iron tower, 8.38 metres high, with a reinforced-concrete gallery. A wire cable was put through the side of the tower and through a ring-bolt to suspend a lead

On leaving St. Paul Island, I got to fly over the southwest station. The tiny fibreglass tower hardly seems sufficient for such an important light. The dwelling has been derelict since June 1964.

weight, which slowly descended 29 metres down the side of the cliff, turning the clockwork mechanism that rotated the lens to give four flashes every 12 seconds. A polygonal lantern housed a fourth-order Fresnel lens, which projected the light 18 nautical miles across the ocean. There was also a six-room dwelling, an oil store, and storage shed on site.

This tower was replaced in June 1964 by the existing 6.1-metre-high round fibreglass tower, which is white with a red band at the top. It has a solar-powered 12-volt system for which no light-keeper is required. The round iron tower was dismantled and moved to the Coast Guard base in Dartmouth, where it is displayed, complete with the three-panel Fresnel lens.

The biggest change at the northeast station occurred in 1961/62. The lighthouse was replaced with the existing octagonal reinforced-concrete tower and a 91-centimetre rotating airport beacon that provides the flashing white light. The tower was completely white until 1966, when the lantern was finally painted red, as it should be. Also built at that time were two new dwellings, an oil store, and a boathouse. The first-order dioptric lens was removed from the old lantern before the tower and old dwelling were demolished, and the site was cleared. It was now a three-family station. In 1967, a new fog-alarm building was built, as was as a 122-metre-long trolley track

and walkway from the lighthouse to the slipway, complete with trolley and a haul-up winch.

In 1973, the airport beacon was replaced with a PRB 46 Pharos rotating beacon. Many bits and pieces of equipment, diesel engines, and generators were changed or altered from here on, all with the intent of eventually automating the station. As inconceivable as it may seem that such an important station should ever be unmanned, the process began on February 8, 1972, when the station was semi-automated and reduced to a two-family operation. The surplus dwelling was subsequently torn down. In June 1977, it became a four-man rotational station with two teams of two men each rotating 28 days on and 28 days off. The foghorn was permanently discontinued on November 1, 1987, and in 1991, the station was de-staffed.

The waters around St. Paul are no less treacherous now than they were 200 years ago, but with modern methods of navigating, such as the global positioning system and other such electronic marvels, we can only hope that mariners will be able to steer clear of danger. But one has to wonder: if a vessel does wreck on this island, if there aren't any people to come to the crew's aid or to find help for them, how many will survive?

116 In 1873, Money Point was selected as the site for a coast light. Construction began two years later. The light was ready in time for the opening of navigation in the spring of 1876. The combined dwelling/lighthouse was built by Jacob Bowser for $3,970. The dwelling was a square wooden one-storey bungalow with a square wooden tower projecting through the roof, and painted entirely white. The building was 10.36 metres high from the base to the top of the lantern, and the light shone from 22.55 metres above high water. A white 12-sided iron lantern topped the tower. The revolving light apparatus was turned by weights, making a complete revolution every 90 seconds. With three of the six lamps fitted with red chimneys, the character was alternating red and white flashes. Taking into account the addition of the lantern and light mechanism, and a small oil stores building, the cost of the station was $6,569.06.

The first keeper of this important lighthouse was John McKinnon, who started on April 9, 1875, at $400 per year.

Standing at the foot of a 475-metre mountain with deep water off the headland, the lighthouse was exposed to frequent violent storms. And even though the station is on the mainland, it was isolated, with nothing but a cart track for more than 9 kilometres from the nearest small settlement, which made it difficult to get supplies. The side of the mountain is very steep, with a 35- to 40-degree grade for most of its elevation. Climbing from the station to the top of the mountain is difficult with nothing to carry, but for a man with a load on his back, it is torturous. The station had a boat from the beginning, but the landing was strewn with large rocks and it was a rare day when the boat could be safely launched, thus it was not a dependable way of getting in and out of Money Point. With ice and snow in the winter months, the station was totally cut off.

In 1906, construction began on a fog-alarm building, but work went agonizingly slow because of the difficult location, and it wasn't finished until a year

later. Because the fog-alarm equipment required an engineer, a home was needed for him to live in, and because the lighthouse itself (which was part of the lightkeeper's dwelling), was in the process of being replaced, it was also necessary to provide a new dwelling for the lightkeeper. The most economical

The current lighthouse on Money Point at Cape North with a 25.4-millimetre rotating airport beacon fitted in the lantern.

means of satisfying this requirement was to build a double dwelling, which cost $2,321, bringing the total expenditure for the fiscal year ending March 31, 1908, to $6,248.57.

In 1907, the old iron lighthouse tower at Cape Race, Newfoundland, was being taken down from where it had stood for 51 years. After reports that over two thousand people had lost their lives in 94 shipwrecks off Cape Race in the 40 years between 1864 and 1904, it was determined that a larger light was needed for this major landfall. The iron lighthouse from Cape Race was destined to have another life at Cape North. It was constructed of 32 iron plates, each weighing 680 kilograms, which had been cast in England in 1855. Eight hundred bolts were

removed and the tower was taken down, section by section, and shipped to Cape North, where it was reassembled and lit again in 1911. That tower was 10.06 metres high from the base to gallery deck, 4.27 metres in diameter. The top of the tower was fitted with a lantern 7 metres high and 3.04 metres in diameter, containing a four-panel third-order Fresnel lens, which was rotated by a weight-driven clockwork mechanism that had to be wound every three hours. The illuminating apparatus was a 55-millimetre kerosene oil-vapour burner.

Construction of a new one-and-a-half-storey bungalow was completed by the fall of 1956, followed by major repairs to the old dwelling, lighthouse tower, and fog-alarm building. The lightstation once again became a two-man operation. In August 1961, diesel generator sets were installed, but it was discovered that they could generate only enough power to supply the two dwellings. The lighthouse had to remain lit by the 55-millimetre oil-vapour burner.

A second assistant lightkeeper was hired in July 1960. He boarded with the head keeper but plans were made to build another dwelling, which was completed in September 1962. At the same time, the tower was painted. For some time, there had been complaints that the solid red colour of the tower blended in too much with the mountain background, and from the sea, could not be readily distinguished. So the colour was changed to a red and white checkerboard design, which positively identifies the tower as the Cape North light to this day.

By the time the tower was 106 years old, it was beginning to show serious signs of deterioration and was leaking badly between the lantern and tower. In 1965, the electrical system was upgraded by installing two larger diesel

---

CAPE NORTH

ESTABLISHED:	1876
CCG LIGHT #:	854
POSITION:	47° 01' 44.2" N
	60° 23' 31.4" W
	On Money Point,
	about 1.6 kilometres
	south-southeast
	of Cape North
LIGHT:	Flashing white,
	once every 5 seconds
AHW:	31.8 metres
NOM. RANGE:	15 nautical miles
HORN:	B6, S54
DESCRIPTION:	Square wooden tower,
	14.32 metres high base to
	vane, with sloping sides
	connected to an
	equipment room. Painted
	white with three broad
	red horizontal bands on
	three sides. The land side
	is all white.

generators, and by March 1966, the entire station was on its own electrical power, including the main light, which was changed from oil vapour to a 400-watt mercury-vapour lamp, and the lens, which was turned by a small quarter-horsepower electric motor. The fog alarm was still operating on its own diesel engines and compressors. A jeep had since been provided for the station, making life much easier, and knowing that a sick or injured person could be taken for treatment provided some peace of mind. Nothing less than a jeep could manage the steep and rock-strewn twists and turns between the foot of the mountain and its summit. A recurring problem developed with the front engine bearings of the jeep, however, and after several incidents, an investigation turned up an interesting explanation for it. Because of the extremely steep grade of the road up the side of the mountain, and the long length of time it took to negotiate the climb, the oil would drain to the back of the engine, leaving the front bearings without sufficient lubrication, causing them to burn out.

In November 1971, a new electronic foghorn was installed, making the diesel engines and compressors unnecessary, and thereby eliminating the need of one lightkeeper. The station was made semi-automatic and reduced to a two-man operation. In 1973, the station was connected to commercial power and $11,500 was spent rebuilding the access road. Another $400 had to be spent to install a chain barrier at the top of the mountain to prevent the public from making the mistake of descending the roadway, unaware of the extreme hazard, not to mention the possibility of not being able to get back out without assistance.

In 1975, Dr. David Baird, director of the museum of science and technology in Ottawa, came looking for a light-

A modern-day, 25.4-millimetre double-ended rotating airport beacon used in many of our lighthouses today—this one is from the Cape North coast light on Money Point in Cape Breton.

house for the museum. It had to be available, it had to be old, and it had to one that could be taken apart and put back together again. It also had to be in good enough condition to withstand the move. Cape North lighthouse fit the bill, and as it was slated for demolition in 1978, the ball started rolling.

In the meantime, the vacant dwelling was declared surplus, sold, and removed from the site in October 1977. Arrangements were made for the construction of a new lighthouse with an equipment building attached. Building began in the fall of 1980, at the same time that the old tower was

being dismantled for its move to Ottawa. After 51 years on Cape Race and 70 years on Cape North, the lighthouse is now at the Science and Technology Museum of Canada where it is beautifully presented on the front lawn atop a reinforced-concrete base, surrounded by huge chunks of limestone to suggest a typical heap of granite boulders on our Atlantic coast. This historic landmark is seen annually in passing by nearly a million people, and museum guides take visitors to the top of the tower to see the beautiful third-order Fresnel lens.

The new lighthouse and attached equipment room which still stands today, were completed on Money Point in January 1981 by Lingan Construction. The lighthouse has a red octagonal fibreglass lantern with a Crouse Hinds 25.4-centimetre rotating airport beacon with a 250-watt metal halide lamp flashing white every five seconds from 31.8 metres above high water. Inside on the main floor there is a workshop and a generator room with two generators, and on the second floor, there's a Sperry videograph fog detector and related equipment. The walls on both floors are panelled. The third floor shows the bare framework with the base of the foghorn protruding through the side to seaward. There is a small bathroom with a chemical toilet. This room was supposed to be used as an emergency shelter. The fourth floor is bare to the outside siding and contains no equipment—above this is the lantern.

Neil's Harbour is situated at the northeast corner of the Cabot Trail at the entrance to a small bay extending inland about 900 metres. It is sheltered from the northeast by Neil Head, a rocky promontory 3 to 6 metres high. An extensive breakwater was constructed off the south

NEIL'S HARBOUR	
ESTABLISHED:	1899
CCG LIGHT #:	851
POSITION:	46° 48' 24" N
	60° 19' 14" W
	On the headland,
	east side of the
	harbour entrance
LIGHT:	White fixed
AHW:	22.3 metres
NOM. RANGE:	10 nautical miles
HORN:	None
DESCRIPTION:	White wooden
	pepper-shaker-type tower,
	10.4 metres high,
	with a red octagonal
	lantern and red tower
	above the gallery deck

The Cape North lighthouse as it appears on the front lawn of the Science and Technology Museum of Canada in Ottawa. Note the third-order Fresnel lens in the lantern.

On September 30, 1987, this station was declared automated and de-staffed, despite a 14-page petition against automation. The houses were quickly boarded up and by 2:30 P.M. that day everyone was gone, including John E. Gwynn, the last keeper of this light. It was a sad day, bringing an end to 111 years of manned lighthouse service. In November 1987, the remaining two dwellings were declared surplus and offered for sale. No interest was shown, so they were burned to the ground by Coast Guard forces in February 1989, clearing Money Point of all structures but the combined lighthouse/equipment building.

Leaving the Cabot Trail at the village of Cape North, drive about 12 kilometres toward Bay St. Lawrence. Watch for a turn off to the right at the hamlet of Bay Road Valley, travel another 9 kilometres to the end of the road near a radio tower. Park here and walk down to the base of the 457-metre mountain and another kilometre along the shore to the lighthouse. That is the easy part. Unless you are fit and in good health, you should not make this hike because coming back up the mountain is a gruelling trek over rough gravel and stones on a very steep incline.

part of Neil Head to protect the fishing fleet from southeast gales. A lighthouse was needed on the outer edge of the head to guide vessels into safe haven.

The lighthouse was built in 1899 under contract by P. McFarlane of Baddeck for $725, and put into operation on September 1 of that year. This is the existing lighthouse, but it showed a fixed red light when it was first lit. The first keeper was Angus A. Buchanan, who was appointed on August 14, 1899, at $150 per year.

In 1934, the characteristic was changed to a fixed white light, increasing the range from 8 to 14 nautical miles. A hand-operated horn had been provided, and the station was now only maintained from April to approximately January 1.

Under the last keeper, Walter Bragg,

Ciboux
Island

the oil lamp was replaced by a 200-watt electric light bulb on November 2, 1956, and six days later, the station was declared automated and de-staffed. In 1964, the light was controlled by a time clock, and in the event of a power failure, it switched to a standby 12-volt battery-operated light. Like at other

Neil's Harbour, with its lighthouse, is a picturesque and much-photographed stopping place on the Cabot Trail.

lighthouses, different lighting systems were used as technology advanced, but not much else changed on the tower since it was built.

This somewhat remote but picturesque Cape Breton community is just at the edge of Cape Breton Highlands National Park, one of the most scenic sections of the Cabot Trail. Take the road off the Cabot Trail into Neil's Harbour, then proceed about 300 metres on Lighthouse Road to the lighthouse.

118 Ciboux Island and Hertford Island together are called the Bird Islands, but locally Ciboux Island is also known as Bird Island, and few people actually know it by its proper name. The two islands are long and narrow and lie end to end. Hertford Island is 1,300 metres long and Ciboux Island is 1,700 metres long, with 900 metres of shoal water separating them. Their maximum width is no more than 100 metres. This is an extremely dangerous place to navigate, as a reef and shoal extends 2,200 metres beyond the outer point of Ciboux Island. The lighthouse is located at the outer end of the islands and serves as a coastal light, which guides traffic into St. Ann's Harbour and the Great Bras d'Or Channel into the lake.

CIBOUX ISLAND	
ESTABLISHED:	1863
CCG LIGHT #:	844
POSITION:	46° 23' 06.2" N
	60° 22' 28.2" W
	North end of the island
LIGHT:	Flashing red, F2/E10
AHW:	27.2 metres
NOM. RANGE:	5 nautical miles
HORN:	None
DESCRIPTION:	White circular fibreglass tower, 9.1 metres high, with two red horizontal bands, one two- thirds of the way up the tower and the other at the top

First lit on November 26, 1863, the octagonal iron lantern showed alternate red and white flashes once every minute from 23.47 metres above high water. The tower was 10.05 metres high base to vane, and the dwelling was a separate building. Malcolm Morrison was placed in charge as keeper and paid $400 annually. When the coast was completely blocked with ice, he was instructed to discontinue the light

until an opening appeared in the ice or he saw a vessel. A safe landing from which to haul up the boat was absolutely essential, yet it took until 1869 to get a strong sloping pier. A couple of years later, a crane was erected on the cliffs for the purpose of landing

The Ciboux Island light looks very similar to that on Gregory Island, but a trained eye will detect differences other than the fact that this tower is at the 18-metre summit of a much larger island. Access is limited because the island is a bird sanctuary.

stores. Sadly, in October 1870, Morrison was killed when his gun burst. His widow continued to keep the light until the following June 30, when Angus Ross was appointed as keeper.

In 1939, a new combined lighthouse/dwelling was built. The square

Carey Point Range

two-storey dwelling had a red octagonal iron lantern mounted on the roof, which was visible from all points of approach. In 1952, the oil-burner light was changed to a 12-volt electric lamp supplied by two banks of 10 large single-cell batteries in parallel with a lamp changer and flasher. The batteries would last six to eight months before they had to be changed. The station was de-staffed at this time. Unfortunately, vandalism became a serious problem and the building was slowly being destroyed. In 1971, it was declared surplus and a skeleton tower was erected for the light. The old lighthouse/dwelling was bought by private interests, stripped of anything salvageable, and left to rot for several years before it was finally demolished. The 1971 Millard skeleton tower was 9.75 metres high with a watertight marine lantern on top. The tower supported a daymark of red and white horizontal slats; the bottom was enclosed and painted red.

Not considered substantial enough for such an important light, in 1980, the tower was replaced with the existing fibreglass tower, bolted to a concrete pad that was poured over the cistern part of the old dwelling foundation. It was still a 12-volt system, but instead of 20 large single-cell batteries, the light was now provided by two ordinary 12-volt car batteries kept charged by a small 20-watt solar panel.

Ciboux and Hertford islands are now a wildlife management area. Between April 1 and August 15 landing is forbidden without the permission of the Canadian Wildlife Service. Tour boats operate from Big Bras d'Or in the summer, but do not land on the islands.

119 The narrowest part of the channel into Great Bras d'Or occurs at Carey Point. At most it's only 300 metres wide between Carey Point and Noir Point, and there's a tidal current of 2 to 2.5 knots. Carey Point is a shingle beach with a shoal extending out 1,550 metres along the west side of the channel. On many parts of the shoal, there is only a metre of water at low tide and thus is very dangerous. It was for this reason that a pole light was erected here and put into operation on September 20, 1886. The small lantern was hoisted on a mast 7.62 metres high, with a white shed at its base. James Carey was appointed keeper on August 18, 1886, at $46.66 per season, or $60 per year.

CAREY POINT RANGE	
ESTABLISHED:	1886
CCG LIGHT #:	802.5
POSITION:	46° 17' 35.2" N
	60° 25' 07.8" W
	On the west side of the
	north entrance to Great
	Bras d'Or
LIGHT:	White, red, and green
	sector
AHW:	8.7 metres
NOM. RANGE:	Unknown
HORN:	None
DESCRIPTION:	White circular fibreglass
	tower, 6.3 metres high,
	with a red vertical stripe

When the Great Bras d'Or range lights were established directly across from Carey Point in 1903, the Carey Point light was no longer necessary and was discontinued at the opening of navigation that year.

In 1972, range lights were established on Carey Point, at almost the exact same place as the previous light. Both towers are circular and made of fibreglass. The front one is 3.8 metres high, and the rear is 6.3 metres high and 165

This is the rear tower of the Carey Point range. Note the sector light mounted on top.

metres from the front tower. Each has a vertical fluorescent red stripe as a daymark and shows a fixed yellow light at night.

In 1988, the range lights were discontinued and the rear tower was fitted with a sector light. The top part of the front tower is boxed in and painted red; otherwise, both towers remain unchanged and still serve as excellent daymarks and daytime range markers.

View the towers across the channel from the Great Bras d'Or range lights. Otherwise, at the west end of the Seal Island Bridge, which is at the bottom of Kelly's Mountain, turn off Route 105 at the hairpin turn and drive about six kilometres to New Campbellton, where you can park and hike about 600 metres to the towers.

Great Bras d'Or Range

120 The channel into Great Bras d'Or, used extensively by large gypsum ships, is extremely narrow at this point, with a severe tidal current of 2 to 2.5 knots. Two aligned lights lead vessels clear of Middle Shoal and Carey Point Bar on the west side, and Black Rock Shoal on the east. The towers were erected under contract by P. L. McFarlane of Baddeck at a cost of $1,500. Malcolm McLean was appointed the first keeper of the front light, and Alexander Fraser was made keeper of the rear light, both on January 13, 1903.

Over 62 of Nova Scotia's lighthouses are square wooden structures with sloping sides, affectionately referred to as "pepper-shaker" lights. Although the front tower of this range can be described that way, the rear tower, though similar, is such an imposing size that it can hardly be classified as a pepper-shaker-type lighthouse. At 16.8 metres base to vane, it is the tallest square wooden tower in Nova Scotia, and actually taller than some of the octagonal reinforced-concrete towers. It is four storeys high, with a 2.9-metre-high square wooden lantern on top. The lights used duplex oil-lamps until November 7, 1956, when they were

This is the front tower of the Great Bras d'Or range, across from Carey Point. The rear tower can just be made out in the distance.

GREAT BRAS D'OR RANGE	
ESTABLISHED:	1903
CCG LIGHT #:	803 and 804
POSITION:	46° 17' 25.4" N
	60° 24' 50.8" W
	Front tower is on Noir
	Point; rear is 514 metres
	from the front
LIGHT:	Fixed green
AHW:	Front, 12.5 metres;
	rear, 20.1 metres.
NOM. RANGE:	8 nautical miles
HORN:	None
DESCRIPTION:	Front is a white wooden
	pepper-shaker-type tower,
	8.8 metres high.
	Rear is a square white
	wooden tower with
	sloping sides, 16.8 metres
	high. Both towers have a
	red vertical stripe on the
	seaward side.

This is the rear tower of the Great Bras d'Or range. This pepper-box tower is different from others of its type because of its great size.

made electric, increasing the intensity of the light. But at the request of pilots, the colour was changed from fixed white to fixed green to avoid confusion with other lights in the area. In December 1957, the incumbent keeper of the rear light, John R. Squires, was offered the job of caretaker for both lights at $150 per year, in preparation for total automation. Three months later, both lights were fitted with sun switches, battery-operated lights were installed in case of a power failure, and they were officially made unwatched. The previous front lightkeeper, O. S. Douglas, took over the caretaker job from Squires on June 17, 1959, until caretaker services were terminated in November 1969. The vertical red stripes were added to both towers in 1984.

At the northeast end of the village of Big Bras d'Or, watch for Ferry Road. Travel 300 metres to the end, from which you will see the rear tower; 515 metres up the shore is the front tower. Notice the Carey Point towers across the channel.

Black Rock
Point

121 Black Rock Point, in line with Table Head, leads in the fairway between shoal water at the entrance to the Great Bras d'Or. A light on the point was recommended by the Committee on Navigation Securities in May 1866, as a great benefit to vessels trading to the Great Bras d'Or.

The lighthouse, completed in July 1868, was a one-storey building, 7 metres high, with a hip roof. The light shone from a three-sided window that projected from the seaward side of the roof. The fixed white light had four lamps and reflectors, two facing seaward, one across the channel, and one toward the harbour. There was also a storehouse with a shed on one side for a stable, and a 4-metre station boat.

BLACK ROCK POINT	
ESTABLISHED:	1868
CCG LIGHT #:	799
POSITION:	46° 18′ 18.6″ N
	60° 23′ 32.3″ W
	South side of entrance to Great Bras d'Or
LIGHT:	White flashing, F0.5/E4.5
AHW:	22.8 metres
NOM. RANGE:	17 nautical miles
HORN:	B3, S27
DESCRIPTION:	White square tower attached to a white rectangular building, 10.8 metres high

Access to the station was by water, and from the landing to the lighthouse, there was a road about 150 metres long up a sloping bank.

Donald Morrison became the first keeper in 1868, and earned $359.60 a year. As often was the case, the living conditions were cramped, and the occupants were supplied with only the bare necessities—even a separate kitchen was not considered essential. It took eight years before an addition to the lighthouse for a kitchen was autho-

The replacement lighthouse at Black Rock Point was built in 1977. The square building on the right has a sector light mounted on the roof.

rized. Oil and larger stores were kept in the barn, which contained straw on the upper floor and was half-full of hay on the lower floor where the cattle were kept.

In 1878, because of its location, shape, and colour, the lighthouse was not easily distinguishable as a daymark, so it was painted red with a white cross.

In 1937, a new two-storey lighthouse was built. Commodious in comparison to the old, it was 7.62 metres square, surmounted by a 1.6-metre square wooden lantern strengthened by four iron corner posts. It was 10.35 metres high, base to vane. A hand-operated horn was supplied to answer vessels' signals. In 1961, it was reported that each year there were more than 100 large ships and numerous small craft entering the Great Bras d'Or, so the hand-operated horn was replaced by a 2-mile electric horn. An assistant keeper had been employed at this station since 1963, but it wasn't until 1968 that he finally got a three-bedroom wood-frame bungalow in which to live.

The process of automation began in

1972, when the station became semi-automated and reverted to one light-keeper. In 1977, a new rectangular equipment building was built 38 metres east of the old lighthouse. A white, 2.9-metre-square, 10.8-metre-high tower was built on the corner of the building, and a 25-centimetre rotating airport beacon was positioned on the open gallery deck. An octagonal lantern was installed in the spring of 1987, completing the lighthouse that exists today. The Stone Chance electronic horn was changed to a Swedish

This is the 1937 lighthouse from Black Rock Point, now privately owned and sitting just a few hundred metres along the shore to where it was moved by the owner.

Point Aconi

AGA electronic horn, so much more powerful, and with such increased effectiveness, that a resident 1.6 kilometres away across the water complained about the loud sound, whereas before he never heard a horn at all.

In 1979, the old two-storey lighthouse was sold and moved from the site. It is now located just a few hundred metres down the shore, restored and maintained in excellent condition. It can be viewed from the road, but the privacy of the owner must be respected. In 1980, the horn was made seasonal, and since 1985, the station has been maintained only from May to January. When de-staffing became imminent, Frank Kozera, the last keeper at this station, asked the government to allow him to remain living in the dwelling under a lease agreement, but he was refused. So on July 16, 1990, Frank Kozera locked up the premises and walked away from the station he had kept for 13 years, ending 34 years as a lightkeeper. In October 1991, the dwelling was bought and removed from the site. All that remains at the station is the lighthouse/equipment room and foghorn. Down by the bank, however, are a sector light, established in 1964, and its equipment room.

From the Big Bras d'Or, drive 2.2 kilometres out the Black Point Road, turn left onto a narrow dirt road, and continue about 600 metres until you come to a gate. Park here and walk a short distance to the lighthouse, where there's a beautiful view across the water to the 1,000-metre-high hills of Cape Dauphin.

122 The first structure to be called the Point Aconi lighthouse was actually built about 1.6 kilometres south of the point, on High Cape. Its purpose was to mark the entrance to Little Bras d'Or, about 900 metres south of the lighthouse, and was actually referred to by the Nova Scotia Pilot as the High Cape lighthouse. Built by John A. Moore for a contract price of $500, the square wooden building was 6.1 metres high with a small dwelling attached. The first lightkeeper was George Bonner, appointed at $150 per year. It showed a fixed red light from an octagonal lantern 28 metres above high water. In 1893, a small room, 3 metres by 4.27

extends some 1,400 metres from the point, and to mark the east point of the entrance to the passage into the Great Bras d'Or. The structure was a fluorescent-orange skeleton tower, 10.4 metres high, with two white slatwork daymarks that had a fluorescent orange vertical stripe. It had been a three-man station, but at some point reverted to a

Erosion is occurring at such a rapid rate at Point Aconi that it will no doubt be necessary to move this lighthouse in just a few years. It is quite easy to do, however, as the tower is simply bolted through a flange at the base to a concrete pad. The cliff face is black from the coal seam that runs parallel to the surface the full length of the point.

metres, was built on the north side of the tower, improving living conditions considerably. The whole building was then re-shingled and painted. In 1897, the oil-store building had to be moved back from the eroding bank. Other than these details, very little was recorded regarding the operation of this station. In about 1946, the light-station was discontinued in favour of a gas-lighted whistle buoy off the point.

A lightstation was eventually established on Point Aconi itself, for the main purpose of warning vessels clear of a treacherous rocky shoal that

POINT ACONI	
ESTABLISHED:	1874
CCG LIGHT #:	796
POSITION:	46° 20' 09.5" N
	60° 17' 35.1" W
	On the point
LIGHT:	Fixed white
AHW:	25.6 metres
NOM. RANGE:	12 nautical miles
HORN:	B6, S54
DESCRIPTION:	White circular fibreglass tower with red octagonal lantern, 11.5 metres high

Sydney Range

one-person station with the skeleton tower, fog-alarm building, and one dwelling. The other two dwellings had been sold to private interests and moved down the road away from the station. The last keeper was Carl D. Goyetche, a lightkeeper since 1956 who served on this station with his family from 1979 until it was de-staffed in 1990. In 1989, the existing fibreglass tower replaced the skeleton tower, and soon after, Goyetche left, and the last dwelling was moved off the station, leaving only the foghorn and fog-alarm building with the lighthouse. The fog-alarm equipment and emergency diesel generator are automatic.

Point Aconi consists of coal-bearing strata, evident by a very visible coal seam the full length of the point about half way down the face of the cliff. The Prince Colliery is nearby. The point is quickly yielding to the sea through erosion, and as the shale and sandstone breaks and falls to the base of the cliff, fossilized plants are easy to find, lying exposed for the first time in 300 million years.

Take Exit 17 off Route 105 onto Route 162, drive to the end, turn right, then proceed to the stop sign, and turn left to the lighthouse.

123 Sydney Range, particulartly the front tower, is among the most distinctive lights in Nova Scotia. The front tower is a large octagonal tower most often seen as a coastal lighthouse. The rear tower, with the gallery deck only on the front side, also makes it distinctive. The reason for the configuration of these two towers is not recorded.

In the early part of the twentieth century, steamship lines ran between Sydney and the St. Lawrence River ports of Quebec City and Montreal, to Halifax, St. John's, Newfoundland, and Boston. There was also steamship service three times a week between North Sydney and Port-aux-Basques, Newfoundland, not to mention the vessels that serviced the ports of the Bras d'Or Lakes and those that served the coal industry and steel company. In

SYDNEY RANGE	
ESTABLISHED:	1905
CCG LIGHT #:	782 and 783
POSITION:	46° 10' 48.6" N
	60° 15' 00.7" W
	Front tower is on the
	south side of the west arm
	of Sydney Harbour;
	rear tower is 766 metres,
	213° 34' from the front
	one
LIGHT:	Fixed yellow
AHW:	Front, 18.3 metres;
	rear, 37.1 metres.
NOM. RANGE:	Unknown
HORN:	None
DESCRIPTION:	Front : Wooden octagonal
	tower with sloping sides,
	17.7 metres high.
	Rear: Square wooden
	tower with sloping sides,
	12.2 metres high. Both
	towers are painted white
	with a vertical fluorescent
	orange stripe for a
	daymark.

A six-place lamp changer, similar to the one that was in the front tower of the Sydney Range light. When the operating lamp fails, another one is rotated into position. There are several different styles of this apparatus, depending on the size of the lamp bulbs. Four-place changers using lamps this size are the most common.

the 1960s, the Sydney Steel Corporation was considered the largest self-contained steel plant in North America, producing more than one million tons of steel ingots annually.

Both towers were built in 1905 by P. L. McFarlane of Baddeck for $2,124. The front tower, 1.6 kilometres west of Edward Point and 0.8 kilometres east of Dixon Point, is 50 metres from the water's edge inside the sandbar. Note that the sandbar has now joined the mainland, creating MacInnis Pond between the light and the North West Arm. The rear tower is 766 metres from the front, and both of these towers still exist.

Strangely, there was a lightkeeper for each tower. The first keeper of the front tower was S. Rudderham, who earned $250 per year, and the first keeper of the rear tower was A. J. Lewis, who got $150 per year.

In December 1947, after 42 years in operation, the superintendent of pilots requested that the colour of the towers be changed to international orange because it was difficult to see them in the daytime. It must have been an exceptionally snowy winter that year because a notice to mariners dated August 30, 1948, states that the colour had been changed—not to international orange, but to yellow! No other lighthouse in Nova Scotia is known to have ever been painted yellow. The choice was not very well received, because after two years, the towers were painted white again, only this time with two red horizontal bands, which since 1908, was the most accepted means of providing an effective daymark.

In 1956, extensive repairs were undertaken, including new concrete foundations, floor joists, shingling, eve troughs, canvas, flashings, and painting. Automatic standby lights were also installed.

In 1965, Roy Lewis, who had been keeping both lights at the time, was let go as keeper and appointed caretaker,

There is no more handsome a range light tower anywhere in Atlantic Canada than this front tower of the Sydney range.

as the lights were now fully automated. The physical appearance remained much the same until 1972, when the horizontal red stripes were changed to a single red vertical stripe only, 2.4 metres long. It was doubled in length to 4.8 metres in July 1977, and still red. But, eventually, it settled at the current colour scheme of a fluorescent orange stripe running the full height of the towers on the seaward side. It's amazing that the stripes weren't always full length and vertical, considering that in daylight, lining up the towers was so important for safe passage.

About 3 kilometres past the Coast Guard College on Route 239, just as you near the North West Arm, the front tower should come into view on the right, less than 100 metres from the road. A further 500 metres and the rear tower is visible on the left, slightly more than 300 metres from the road.

The rear tower of the Sydney range is quite different from the front one, as there is only a gallery deck on the front side of the tower. But with no windows to clean on the other three sides, there really was no need for a gallery deck all the way round. No other lighthouse in Nova Scotia is built to these specifications.

124 In 1872, a lighthouse was built on the west end of South Bar, on the west side of Sydney Harbour. It was a square wooden tower with a dwelling attached. The tower was 6 metres square, painted white, and surmounted by an octagonal wooden lantern. It was constructed by T. M. Leslie for $482 plus another $166.18 for

SYDNEY BAR	
ESTABLISHED:	1872
CCG LIGHT #:	778
POSITION:	46° 12' 20.7" N
	60° 13' 07.1" W
	On the pier at the west
	extremity of
	Southeast Bar
LIGHT:	Fixed green
AHW:	8.9 metres
NOM. RANGE:	10 nautical miles
HORN:	B2, S18
DESCRIPTION:	Triangular skeleton mast
	on the northeast corner of
	a square white cement-
	block building, 9 metres
	high from high water to
	the top of lantern.

the illuminating apparatus. The first keeper was George Nunn, who earned an annual salary of $200. In 1873, a small ballasted cribwork was built to protect the lighthouse, an oil store was constructed on a good stone foundation, and a 4.57-metre station boat was supplied. However, it became a continual battle to maintain the cribwork against the elements.

In 1878, an oil burner that was added to improve the light caught on fire, destroying the lantern. The tower survived, but the repaired lantern and roof leaked so badly that in 1888 a new tower had to be built. The upper half of the old tower was attached to the new tower to provide the keeper with a living room.

By 1912, the station required another new lighthouse—this one was a square hip-roof dwelling surmounted by an octagonal lantern, built on a 4.57-metre cribwork pier with a concrete exterior, in the water off the end of the bar. Chappell Brothers Ltd. of Sydney did the job for $7,350 plus another $1,000 to build protection for the pier. After much repairing of the cribwork, in 1925 it was decided that a

Sydney Bar light, with North Sydney and the Newfoundland ferry terminal across the harbour. The helicopter landing pad built on top of the light building makes a great roosting place for gulls and cormorants. It is difficult to make out the green light at the right corner of the landing pad.

new concrete pier needed to be built and that it would be located some 6 metres inshore from the old one. It was built by A. E. Cunningham, and the lighthouse was moved onto it in 1926.

By 1951, the lightkeeper was living in his own home about 1.6 kilometres down the road. In November 1952, a raging, howling northeast storm took the station dory as well as two sheds. About 60 metres of the bar washed away, so it was no longer possible to get to the lighthouse on foot.

In 1963, another new lighthouse was required. This was a square wooden tower 11 metres high, 3.96 metres square from top to bottom, topped by an octagonal iron lantern.

Another storm in January 1965 washed out over 180 metres of the outer bar, toppling five power poles, and prompting the government to install an emergency diesel generator set.

Finally, in 1973, with the goal of automating the light, the existing pier was encircled with sheet-steel pilings to a diameter of 12.2 metres, filled with concrete, and the existing lighthouse was built—a concrete building that measures 6.09 metres square, 5 metres high with a skeleton mast on the northeast corner of the deck.

About 4 kilometres north from the outskirts of the community of Whitney Pier, watch carefully for a narrow dirt road to the left, which will take you about 300 metres to the base of the bar on Daly Point. Park your car and walk to the end of the bar, about 1,400 metres. Unless you are extremely lucky with the condition of the sea and the tide, you still won't be able to get within 350 metres of the light.

125 The point of land where the Low Point lighthouse is located is both low lying and flat. Consequently, the lighthouse has been called both Low Point and Flat Point in official lists of lights, and is still known by either name among the local residents. Located near New Victoria, on the east side of the 6-kilometre-wide entrance to Sydney Harbour, the point is about 1 kilometre wide at its base, and extends 600 metres to the lighthouse.

The original lighthouse was built at a cost of £770. The tower was wooden, and 15.54 metres high, base to vane. During its first winter the lead roof was blown off in a heavy gale and the light was out until the lantern could be

Low Point	
Established:	1832
CCG Light #:	775
Position:	46° 16' 01.4" N
	60° 07' 33" W
	East side of the entrance
	to Sydney Harbour
Light:	White flashing, F0.5/E4.5
AHW:	23.8 metres
Nom. range:	26 nautical miles
Horn:	B3, S3, B3, S51
Description:	Octagonal white
	reinforced-concrete tower,
	21.9 metres high

replaced with a new iron lantern. It was so excessively cold that the lightkeeper, Robert McNab, put pans of hot coals around the inside of the lantern to keep his light going, but it was nearly impossible to keep up a flame from poor-grade oil when the temperature was minus 25 to 30 degrees Celsius. In 1856, McNab complained that there had been no repairs or improvements of any consequence in the 19 years of the light's operation. In particular, the tiny dwelling required considerable repair, and the light leading into the increasingly busy Sydney Harbour was considered to be inadequate. The tower did, however, provide an excellent daymark with its eight sides painted alternately red and white. New lamps were supplied immediately, which did improve the light, but it was another seven years before a new octagonal iron lantern was installed, providing the room necessary for larger oil burners and reflectors.

In 1878, it was once again necessary to increase the size of the lantern; to accommodate it, the tower had to be strengthened structurally. A temporary light was fitted 4.87 metres below the lantern deck while new frames and knees were fitted under the gallery deck. The new iron lantern was 12-sided, 2.95 metres in diameter, and able to hold the new lighting apparatus of 13 burners, each with its own 40.6-centimetre reflector. A light was first shown from the new lantern on July 13, 1878, and with all the buildings repaired and painted, the station was

A close-up of the classic round iron lantern atop the Low Point lighthouse. It is the only one like it left in Nova Scotia.

This is the Low Point lighthouse and fog alarm—also known as Flat Point, for obvious reasons.

in first-rate order.

A steam fog-horn was established at this station in 1903, followed by many alterations and additions over the years to the horn and lighting mechanisms as technology advanced. One of the more serious problems that plagued this station, as it did many others, was erosion. Through the years, upwards of half a million dollars was spent on building and maintaining the breastworks and cribbing.

In 1938, the wooden tower came to the end of its days and the existing reinforced-concrete tower was built in its place with the lens and lighting apparatus from the old tower. In 1953, a new dwelling was built for an assistant keeper and electric power was brought to the station. By 1954, the station consisted of the lighthouse tower, fog-alarm building, stores building, oil stores, head keeper's dwelling, and the assistant keeper's dwelling. The old house was torn down, the materials used for general improvements around the station. In 1962, with the addition of a diaphone horn and associated machinery, a third lightkeeper

was taken on and a third dwelling built to accommodate him and his family.

In 1970, with automation the objective, an electronic horn was installed, eliminating the need for engines and compressors used with the diaphone horn—and the third keeper. His dwelling, now surplus, was sold and removed from the station in August 1977. Further downgraded to a one-person station in January 1979, the older two-storey dwelling was first converted to a survival station, then sold and removed in 1987. In the meantime, the third-order Fresnel lens was replaced in October 1984 by a 91.44-centimetre rotating airport beacon. The lens, considered a relic of the past, was moved to the Coast Guard base in Dartmouth, where it sits, largely unnoticed in a dimly lit corner of the building entrance. The round, iron, first-order lantern remains atop the lighthouse tower, the last classic lantern of this type still in use on an operational lighthouse in Nova Scotia.

James H. Jobe, a lightkeeper since 1959, worked all but three years at Low Point until October 1988, when the station was officially de-staffed. Jobe and his wife, Jean, leased the last remaining dwelling, where they stayed on as unofficial, unpaid lightkeepers, you might say.

From Route 28 in New Victoria, proceed on Browns Road for about 660 metres, then turn right. At about 650 metres, take a left turn and drive about another 500 metres further to the lighthouse.

Glace Bay
North Breakwater

126 Glace Bay is an important year-round fishing port with 25 fishing boats in the harbour. Most of them are Cape Island style boats, 10 to 12 metres in size. Many of the men fish for lobster from a small open boat during the season, then as a captain or crew on larger vessels the rest of the year. Boats enter the harbour through a narrow channel between two breakwaters, which continues to be very narrow for its full length, with most of the wharves occupying the 400-metre length of the inside face of the north wall. The dredged channel is about 30 metres wide with a depth of about 4 metres.

GLACE BAY NORTH BREAK WATER	
ESTABLISHED:	1956
CCG LIGHT #:	774
POSITION:	46° 11′ 56.5″ N
	59° 56′ 54.2″ W
	On the outer end of the
	north breakwater
LIGHT:	Fixed green
AHW:	9 metres
NOM. RANGE:	Unknown
HORN:	B2, S18
DESCRIPTION:	White circular fibreglass
	tower with red upper
	portion, 5.3 metres high

A lighthouse and fog-alarm building were built on the north breakwater and put into operation on February 29, 1956. It cost $2,015 plus another $1,776 to supply power from town to the fog-alarm building. The lighthouse was a square concrete tower mounted on a square concrete building on the end of the government wharf. It was 3.35 metres square and 5.48 metres high with a small 1.22-metre-square tower from which shone a fixed green light supplied by commercial power. There was also a small battery-powered emergency light. Lipkus Fisheries requested the loan of a hand-operated foghorn from W. J. Manning, chief of

aids at the time, so when the lighthouse was established, it would have a horn too.

In August 1969, this light was fitted with automatic lamp changers and left on continuously. But with no one to man the horn, the decision was made

The little square building and light is gone from the wharf in Glace Bay Harbour, replaced by this light on the end of a new breakwater at the harbour entrance.

to retain head keeper Michael McGillivary and hire a casual keeper for 12-hour shifts.

The harbour was greatly improved by the construction of a new stone breakwater, and a new light tower and horn were built on the end of it in June 1990. The 300-millimetre lantern on top of the tower has a four-place light changer that is supplied by commercial power. A diesel generator in an equipment house on shore automatically

supplies emergency power if the commercial power fails. Local mariners appreciate the 1,000-watt horn and claim that the little light is the best of its kind on the coast.

This pretty little harbour is a busy and exciting place to visit during the opening days of lobster season in mid-May. Boats loaded high above the gunnels with lobster traps exit the harbour, running at full throttle to get the traps set before hurrying back into harbour for another load.

The lighthouse is easily found on the waterfront in the centre of town, and quite picturesque despite being just a small fibreglass tower.

Flint Island

127 Over time, erosion has separated Flint Island into two halves, between which there is about 150 metres of turbulent water strewn with treacherous rocks. It's a very dangerous place, as even in fine weather the ocean swells break on all sides of the island, especially on the western end, where an uneven bottom together with irregular tidal currents running at about two knots produces a strong rippling effect and breaking seas. The main part of this sandstone island, where the lightstation is located, is about 250 metres in length with an average width of about 45 metres, narrowing at one point to 15 metres and coming to a sharp point at each end, like the prow of a mighty ship. There is nothing irregular about the top of the island, which is perfectly flat and about seven metres above high water, with not a tree or shrub of any kind. From certain seaward vantage points, the main part of the island looks like a giant aircraft carrier with the lighthouse forming what looks like the superstructure. The nearest mainland is Northern Head on uninhabited Cape Perce, 3.3 kilometres to the west. Perce is pronounced Percy and is so spelled by the locals. Port Morien lies about nine kilometres to the southwest.

At the time it was established, the lighthouse was of great importance to vessels trading to the coal ports between Cow Bay and Bridgeport. Of the several lighthouses that were recommended in 1856, it was the only one built in Nova Scotia that year. The first lightkeeper was George Cann, who was given an annual salary of £60 and an additional £20 for fuel. The first winter was terrible because the dwelling house had not been properly finished. Although they had ample room, the keeper and his family suffered a great deal from the cold and, in fact, burnt out the new cooking stove

from trying to keep warm. Cann also wanted a higher wage, as he had to pay a hired man out of his own small salary to help haul the boat up the cliff where it would be safe. The lighthouse was a wooden octagonal tower separate from the dwelling, which was a good thing because on the night of August 31, 1864, the lighthouse was destroyed by fire. The keeper reported that he was unable to state the cause of the accident. A new lighthouse had to be built as soon as possible.

The second lighthouse was much the same as the first, a white wooden octagonal tower 13.1 metres high base to vane, situated 45.7 metres from the dwelling. The new station also required

FLINT ISLAND	
ESTABLISHED:	1856
CCG LIGHT #:	770
POSITION:	46° 10' 49" N
	59° 46' 16" W
	Off Cape Perce
LIGHT:	White flashing, F0.5/E4/F0.5/E20
AHW:	21.3 metres
NOM. RANGE:	16 nautical miles
HORN:	B3, S27
DESCRIPTION:	White octagonal reinforced-concrete tower with sloping sides, 18 metres high

a store house and a tank in the cellar for water, which was sometimes brought in from the mainland.

There was always some risk in taking supplies to Flint Island, as demonstrated in December 1869 when some men were carried out to sea and for nine days suffered from exposure, leaving them severely frost-bitten and crippled for life. In 1873, owing to the isolation and difficult character of the station, lightkeeper Benjamin Heney had his salary increased, by order in council, from $400 to $500 per year.

All is tranquil at the lighthouse on Flint Island, belying the dangers all around this island for the lightkeepers and their families. Now that the dwellings are gone and the landing has washed away, it is highly unlikely that anyone will ever live on this island again.

The boat slip was continually being damaged beyond safe use and extensive repairs were ongoing. It was also mentioned in the records that purchase blocks and hauling gear were needed. The slipway was long and steep and one wonders how the boat was ever hauled up without such gear.

By 1909, so much was lacking and so many repairs were required at the station that it was completely rebuilt, starting with a 7.62-centimetre duplicate diaphone plant, operated by two 12-horsepower oil engines installed in a wooden fog-alarm building, together costing over $11,000. In 1910, the third lighthouse was built on Flint Island—a hexagonal reinforced-concrete tower with six flying buttresses and surmounted by a round iron lantern, overall 18.9 metres high. A wooden boathouse, an oil store, and outbuildings were built by contractor F. Silver. Then in 1912, a new double dwelling was built under contract to A. McAskill of Glace Bay at a cost of $4,300. The lightkeeper himself built two new slipways in 1916.

Of all the tragedies to befall any Nova Scotia lighthouse-keeping family, the

Martell family suffered the most. They moved to Flint Island on September 22, 1927, when John J. Martell was appointed head keeper. They were a family of ten: John and his wife, Amy, and eight children. Four more children were born on the island and three died there. Fifteen-year-old Raymond drowned on March 23, 1933, and 13-year-old Ethel was drowned on October 15, 1935. Harold, one of the younger children born on the island, had a ruptured appendix in January, year unknown, and despite his father's valiant effort to get him ashore across the ice, it was too late and the little fellow died of peritonitis. The only way to communicate with the shore was for the lightkeeper to stop the light rotating and show a fixed light as a signal that there was trouble. But what could they do on the mainland when the way to the island was blocked by ice? This family suffered several other near-fatal incidents in their 18 years on that sta-

tion. It was always an anxious time when someone left the island until they were safely back on it.

In August 1950, Frank Langille was hired as head keeper, and his assistant was George Campbell. They were both drowned on November 13, 1950; neither body was ever found.

In building the third lighthouse, it is

Like an aircraft carrier at sea, Flint Island actually looks like it is moving through the water at a great speed as shoal water breaks all around.

likely that ocean water was used to mix the cement because in 1954 it was noted that the building was in poor condition and should be replaced. Furthermore, a 1961 status report stated the condition of both the double dwelling and lighthouse tower as poor and and that they needed to be replaced as soon as possible.

On August 29, 1961, a temporary acrylic lantern was installed on the roof of the dwelling while construction began on a new lighthouse. On July 13, 1962, the light was lit from the fourth new Flint Island lighthouse, 15 metres south of the old tower, which was then demolished. This new, octagonal tower is still standing today. Made of reinforced concrete, it has sloping sides and an octagonal red aluminum

lantern; it measures 18 metres high, base to vane. Three new dwellings for the head keeper and his two assistants were built at the same time—two one-storey bungalows and a one-and-a-half-storey bungalow—creating a first-class station. The fog-alarm building, oil store, and boathouse were still in good condition, so all that was required were repairs to the skidway and a more suitable station boat.

In 1963, two diesel engines and compressors were installed for the new fog alarm equipment, and two diesel generator sets provided the station with electric power. A 1,000-watt bulb replaced the 55-millimetre oil-vapour lamp, which was then fitted as an emergency standby, and the reflectors could be turned by a small electric motor, eliminating the need to wind the weights that drove the clockwork turning mechanism to the top of the tower every four hours.

Robert and Gerry Spears, and their two small children moved to Flint Island in 1960 when Robert was appointed assistant keeper. He was promoted to head keeper in June 1968. Big changes were in the offing starting in November 1971, when a new electronic foghorn was installed replacing the type F diaphone, much to the dissatisfaction of mariners. This was progress though, and with the engines and compressors associated with the diaphone no longer required, the station was reduced to a two-person operation. In 1977, the 15-year-old spare dwelling was declared surplus. Understandably, there were no offers to purchase, so the building was sold to Spears for salvage. In late 1980, consideration was given to making the station rotational, meaning that the families would be moved off and two pairs of two keepers would alternately man the station—28 days on and 28 days off. One house could be modified to accommo-

Scatarie

date both keepers and the other could be disposed of. But after another five years of agonizing over the operation of the station, Flint Island was fully automated and de-staffed in April 1985. The following month, the remaining two dwellings and boathouse were declared surplus.

In March 1982, after 22 years on Flint Island, Robert and Gerry Spears were transferred to Scatarie Island lightstation. The Spearses now have a home in Port Morien, where they can see Flint Island from their window. At least ten times a day, Gerry looks out at the island and recalls happy times, such as the day the family got to move into their new dwelling, which had beautiful hardwood floors that they never walked on with shoes. Some time in May 1986, Gerry walked to the window, as she was in the habit of doing, and was horrified to see a fire raging on Flint Island. She thought of all the years of loving care they had put into that station, and of her beautiful hardwood floors burning up.

The island can be seen from nine kilometres away at Port Morien. A determined person who likes hiking could get to within about 3.5 kilometres of Flint Island by walking a trail from Schooner Pond on Cape Perce out to Wreck Point, or by boat, but landing is definitely not recommended—this comes from personal experience.

128 Located at the eastern tip of Scatarie Island, this is the most eastern lighthouse in Nova Scotia. The island itself is separated from Cape Breton by the 1.93-kilometre-wide Main-à-Dieu Passage. It is triangular in shape: the north shore is the longest at 9.8 kilometres, the south shore is 7.7 kilometres long, and the east shore is 5.1 kilometres long.

By about 1910, there were 16 or 17 families with homes established on Scatarie Island. There was a school and a church, and mail service was established in 1884, and eventually even a little store opened up by the wharf. Everyone had a couple of cows, a few sheep, and chickens. They raised their own potatoes, turnips, cabbage, and hay for the cattle. The teacher was paid $200 for the year from which $10 a month was paid for room and board. The lightkeeper was paid $385 per year. In the summertime, many others would come to the island to fish. They would split, salt, and dry the fish for which there was a good market. Gradually, however, fresh fish came into favour and the population of the island began to decline from about 40 homes to just a few families that would winter over. The post office closed in 1957, and the fate of the remaining population was pretty much decided. The last to leave, of course, were the lighthouse keepers. The lightstation was de-staffed and automated on October 9, 1987.

The first lighthouse on the east end of Scatarie Island was built in 1839. The wooden octagonal tower, painted white and topped by a red circular iron lantern, measured 22.25 metres, base to vane. In an 1857 report, the station was described as also being a "humane establishment" with a comfortable dwelling for the keeper, a stores building, a house of refuge, two barns, and a boathouse. Lightkeeper Edmund S.

Dodd was referred to as the superintendent of the island because not only was he responsible for the station, he was also in charge of three boatmen to whom he paid yearly wages of £30 each. His own annual salary was £100 plus a £15 fuel allowance. Provisions consisted of 1 barrel of pork, 1 barrel of beef, and 8 barrels of bread. For clothing, there were 18 common blankets, 18 pairs of coarse trousers, 2 monkey jackets, 7 pea coats, 5 blue Guernsey frocks, 12 blue flannel shirts, 12 pairs of stockings, 15 pairs of mittens, 9 comforters, 6 white Guernsey frocks, 20 pairs of soldier's trousers (meaning old), and 12 pairs of small shoes.

Between 1865 and 1870, there were 12 wrecks on Scatarie Island, pointing

SCATARIE	
ESTABLISHED:	1839
CCG LIGHT #:	767
POSITION:	46° 02′ 05″ N
	59° 40′ 36″ W
	Northeast point of
	Scatarie Island
LIGHT:	Flashing white, Fl/E29
AHW:	19.5 metres
NOM. RANGE:	23 nautical miles
HORN:	B2, S3, B2, S3, B2, S48
DESCRIPTION:	White square wooden
	tower with sloping sides,
	16.05 metres high

out the need for a humane establishment. Three boats were kept at the station: a 5.48-metre life boat, a 5.18-metre whale boat, and a small 4.57-metre flat boat. One year, the barque *Star of the West* was wrecked here in thick fog, and the brig *Una* was wrecked on the south side shortly after. Both crews got ashore in their boats and were taken care of at the lighthouse. Only the captain of *Star of the West* was lost—drowned when he apparently fell out of the boat while coming ashore. In 1874, the superin-

The square tower with sloping sides at the eastern tip of Scatarie Island is a very important light and the largest of this style ever built in Nova Scotia, see how it dwarfs the one-and-a-half-storey bungalow.

tendent recommended that a fog whistle be considered for the station. Three years later and still no fog alarm, the Norwegian barque *Zaurak* hit the rocks at the east side of the island during a thick fog. The captain and 12 crew were on the island for five days.

The first reference made in the records to any kind of fog signal was in 1879—a gun was described as so honeycombed as to be unfit for use, and the wooden carriage was altogether rotten. Finally, in 1881, a steam fog-whistle was put into operation and Malcolm Ferguson was appointed fog-alarm engineer from September 16, 1881 until 1886, when it became the responsibility of the lightkeeper. He was also responsible for a Dobbins pattern, self-righting lifeboat, but in the case of an emergency, with no organized crew, he had to use anyone he could find to help out.

In 1916, the old steam plant for the horn was replaced by an oil engine for a diaphone horn. It seems incredible that only now the station got an assistant keeper. In 1924, a new double dwelling was built to accommodate the lightkeeper and his assistant.

In 1953, a new lighthouse tower was constructed—a huge skeleton tower with enclosed stairway in the centre, rising 14.63 metres from the ground to the gallery deck and with a 3.75-metre-high circular iron lantern, making the tower an overall height of 18.39 metres. A 55-millimetre oil vapour burner provided the light that was projected through three reflectors turned by a weight-driven clockwork mechanism.

On September 28, 1957, fire totally destroyed the double dwelling in which two persons were burned, one critically, and almost claimed the lives of six children ranging in age from 4 to 16 years. While head keeper Raymond Ringer was on vacation, a 16-year-old, who had been hired as an assistant, attempted to start the kitchen range, unaware that the coals in the stove were live. He doused them with kerosene, resulting in a terrific blast that showered the place with flames and rendered him a living torch. Acting head keeper Ronald MacIsaac was a hero that day, badly burned about the hands and arms as he beat out the flames that enveloped the young assistant. Managing to grab a blanket off a nearby bed, he finally extinguished the flames that engulfed the young man. After moving him to a safe place, MacIsaac went to assist his wife and several children to safety,

then rushed to the side of the house, placed a ladder under an upstairs window, and helped the remaining children to the ground below. Shortly after the last child was out of the house, the entire roof fell in. Despite the neighbours' efforts, nothing was saved and the dwelling burned to the ground. The young assistant died two days later; Ronald MacIsaac completely recovered. Two other men played a heroic part in the disaster. Jim Trim and Charles Wadden set off in a 7.62-metre open boat in heavy seas and 40-knot gale-force winds to transport the two badly burned men to Main-à-Dieu, some 14 kilometres away, from where they were quickly transported to a hospital in Sydney.

Jim Trim volunteered to keep the light lit until arrangements could be made for a more permanent solution. The Coast Guard ship *Lady Laurier* was scheduled to proceed to Scatarie Island with supplies to make temporary accommodations for the keeper and his assistant in the fog-alarm building. In May 1958, tenders were called to build two new dwellings. These two one-and-a-half-storey dwellings were ready for occupancy in March 1959. A third dwelling of the same design was contracted, cancelled, and contracted again, and finally ready in September 1964. The year before, two diesel generators were installed and the station had electricity. A 91.44-centimetre airport beacon with a 1,000-watt bulb was installed as the main light and a 12-volt emergency light was established on a 3-metre Millard skeleton mast atop the main tower. On July 12, 1971, an electronic foghorn was installed in preparation for semi-automatic operation. Despite many complaints about the feeble sounding horn, the Coast Guard went ahead with removing the diesel engines and compressors for the old foghorn and the station was offi-

Louisbourg

cially classified semi-automated. On February 8, 1972, it was downgraded to a two-man station. They did extensive audio range tests with the horn and as a compromise, added four emitters to the other four, set at a different angle but blown in unison. Later, a more powerful electronic horn was installed, a 2-kilowatt Swedish AGA horn.

On March 25, 1977, the spare dwelling was declared surplus, sold, and removed from the site in accordance with the sales agreement. Another big change came on November 30, 1981, when a new combined lighthouse tower/equipment building was accepted from the builder. This is the existing lighthouse, which has a large 3.85-metre-high red octagonal lantern and 91.44-centimetre rotating airport beacon. The main floor contains three diesel generators and a workshop; the panelled room on the second floor is tiled and contains the fog-alarm equipment. The second floor was a survival room with food and essential clothing for department personnel who got stranded. The third floor is also panelled with plain plywood—a very neat, clean, and spacious room with just a couple of switch boxes and the monitor for the main light. The fourth floor is empty except for a steep ladder leading up into the lantern.

Robert and Gerry Spears were the last lightkeeping family on this station when it was officially de-staffed in 1987, leaving the island totally uninhabited for the first time in 148 years.

Not visible from the mainland.

129 Lighthouse Point is within the bounds of the Fortress of Louisbourg National Historic Park at the southeast point of a headland on the east side of the harbour. Four kilometres long and 1,500 metres at its widest point between Battery Point and Battery Island, this extensive harbour is ice-free, well-protected, deep, and close to the fishing banks. That's what attracted the French to settle here in the 1700s. They built the very first lighthouse in Canada in 1734, the second in all North America. The first was the Boston Harbour light on Little Brewster Island, built in 1716.

The French lighthouse at Louisbourg was a round stone tower 16.46 metres high. It had a 4.87-metre-high lantern

LOUISBOURG	
ESTABLISHED:	1734
CCG LIGHT #:	756
POSITION:	45° 54′ 24.4″ N
	59° 57′ 32.7″ W
	On Lighthouse Point,
	north side of the entrance
	to the harbour
LIGHT:	Flashing white,
	once every 9 seconds
AHW:	32 metres
NOM. RANGE:	17 nautical miles
HORN:	B2, S18
DESCRIPTION:	White octagonal
	reinforced-concrete tower,
	16.8 metres high

and a 3-metre-high ventilator and vane, for an overall height of 24.33 metres. It was 7.31 metres in diameter at the base, and consisted of four tiers, each about 30 centimetres less in diameter, tapering to 6.4 metres at the top. Within the lantern, a circle of wicks was set in a copper ring mounted on cork floats in sperm oil, which provided a light that could be seen a distance of 6 leagues (about 29 kilometres) in clear weather. Unfortunately, the lantern's wooden

construction and its relatively small size for so many flames was its undoing. On September 12, 1736, it caught fire and the entire structure was gutted.

So important was this lighthouse that work was begun immediately to replace it. The tower remained virtually the same, but with a much larger lantern, 7 metres high by 5 metres in diameter. Built entirely of non-combustible materials, it was designed with 6 stone pillars topped by a vaulted brick roof covered with lead. When it was completed in July 1738, the tower was 26.82 metres high, base to vane. It survived the first British siege of Louisbourg in 1745, but was so badly damaged by the second siege in 1758 that it was never repaired and subsequently fell in ruins.

By the time another lighthouse was built on this site 84 years later in 1842, there were already 15 other lighthouses strategically placed around Nova Scotia's coast, including the one on Sambro Island at the entrance to Halifax Harbour, which was being built in 1758 as Louisbourg was being destroyed. The Louisbourg lighthouse was quite different from the others being built at about the same time. A huge square building with a foundation built on bedrock, it had only a partial basement, though it was otherwise commodious with two full floors and a half floor. The building was painted white with a black vertical stripe on the east, south, and west sides for a daymark and had a lantern on top. The first keeper was Lawrence Kavanagh, hired at a yearly salary of £100 plus a fuel allowance of £15. It was considered both an important harbour light and coast light, as it marked the only safe harbour between Scattarie and Arichat.

In February 1902, a small white house was built on a knoll at the edge of a cliff 122 metres south of the lighthouse, in which there was a compressed air siren. The engines were contained in a red brick building 10.66 metres north of the siren house. The siren gave a double blast every two minutes, consisting of a low note followed by a high pitched note. This was replaced in 1908 by a diaphone that gave two 3-second blasts every 75 seconds. Then in 1922, fire struck once

Two lighthouse foundations have been stabilized at Louisbourg, and plaques have been mounted to identify them. The foundation at the base of the lighthouse is from the first lighthouse in Canada, the second in all North America, which first showed a light in 1734. The other, to the left of the picture, was the 1842 lighthouse.

again and the lighthouse building was destroyed.

In 1923, the new station—the existing reinforced-concrete tower and a wooden dwelling—was ready. The dwelling, a two-storey duplex, just 38 metres south of the lighthouse, was accommodation for the lightkeeper and the engineer who ran the fog-alarm system.

Many changes occurred over the following 34 years. The fog alarm and light systems were continuously

improving, but the biggest advance came when commercial electric power was connected on November 22, 1957. In 1960, two assistants were hired. Nine years later, three new dwellings replaced the duplex dwelling, and the old dwelling, an oil shed and garage, all built in 1924, were declared surplus and removed from the station. In 1961, a new fog-alarm building replaced the one built in 1902. Strangely, no sooner had the station been brought up to date when serious consideration was being given to automating it. With the installation of an electronic foghorn, there was no need for someone to run the engines and compressors, so in 1971, the second assistant lightkeeper was let go. With further upgrading of the lighting apparatus and fog-alarm equipment, the station reverted to a one-person station in 1978. One surplus bungalow was sold and removed from the station, and a second was transferred to Parks Canada. In 1988, the lighthouse tower was altered to accommodate all the station equipment and the fog-alarm building was demolished. The demolition of all other surplus structures was carried out in January 1989, and on September 28,

1990, the station was de-staffed. The third bungalow was sold to private concerns and moved off the station.

The last keeper, Roy Forgeron, a lightkeeper since 1962, moved to this station with his wife and family of six children in October 1966, and served there until it was de-staffed in 1990. He said, "It was a good life, but the last 12 years were hard, with being the lone keeper I was tied down seven days a week. The work was not too demanding, but you always had to be here. There were always lots of visitors, as Parks Canada people would send them over here from the fortress. Sometimes I would climb the tower with visitors 30 or 40 times a day." In 1965, over 17,000 people visited the lightstation, and in 1969, it was claimed that upward of 30,000 tourists visited the site.

Since that time, the foundations of the previous lighthouses have been stabilized and preserved. There are plaques placed around the site that provide good information about the lighthouses as well as the history of the area. Since it is part of the overall Fortress of Louisbourg National Historic Park, it is well worth taking the time to visit. The fortress, renowned as the largest historical reconstruction in all North America, takes you back in time to 1744.

Drive through the town of Louisbourg and turn at the Visitor Information Centre towards lighthouse point. A winding road takes you about 3.5 kilometres to the lighthouse parking lot.

Main-à-Dieu

130 Main-à-Dieu Passage is about 1.6 kilometres wide between Moque Head and West Point, Scatarie Island. It contains several shoals and rocks, and the channel is no more than 640 metres wide at its narrowest point. It saves no time or distance for vessels travelling to and from the southwest and Mira Bay. Today, mostly local fishermen use the passage, but back in 1869, it was apparently considered important enough for the superintendent of lighthouses himself to recommend that a light be erected there.

Construction of the lighthouse was completed in 1870 at a cost of $2,312.39. But because there was a problem landing the lamps, which came from Montreal, on the west end of Scatarie Island, lighting was delayed until August 1, 1871. James Burke was placed in temporary charge of the light, but was soon appointed as its permanent keeper at $300 per year.

The lighthouse was a white square wooden tower 12.2 metres high with a dwelling attached. It had a very small octagonal iron lantern, 1.37 metres in diameter, with oil lamps showing a red light to seaward and a white light to the north. An oil store building was also part of the station. The keeper must have experienced some very rough weather in the first three years because a report from December 19, 1874, indicates that the tower had to be strengthened with four wire stays, the roof of the lighthouse and the lantern base had to be re-shingled, and a retaining wall of rough stone had to be constructed around three sides of the building. It was also noted that a storehouse was needed at the landing to receive supplies. As the landing was some distance from the lighthouse, a road was also required.

In 1935, a new lighthouse was built at the station. It was standard for the

Main-à-Dieu light is just one of 14 standard 9.1-metre fibreglass towers in Nova Scotia.

MAIN-à-DIEU	
ESTABLISHED:	1871
CCG LIGHT #:	766
POSITION:	46° 00′ 13″ N
	59° 47′ 42″ W
	On west point of
	Scatarie Island
LIGHT:	Flashing white, F0.5/E3.5
AHW:	24.7 metres
NOM. RANGE:	7 nautical miles
HORN:	None
DESCRIPTION:	White round fibreglass
	tower with two horizontal
	red bands, one at the top,
	the other about mid-
	point, 9.6 metres high

time, a square two-storey dwelling surmounted by an octagonal iron lantern, 10.52 metres high base to vane. Eliza J. Campbell was appointed to watch the light when her husband Ben died in 1945. She was the last lightkeeper at this station, having lived there all alone for 20 years, until it was rigged for automatic operation in 1965. There is no record of her having any difficulty managing the job, but it must have

been worrisome. Even though there were lightkeepers at the other end of the island and there was a telephone connecting them, they were still 10 kilometres apart.

The automated light was operated by two parallel banks of 10 large single-cell batteries, with a sun switch to turn the light on and off. The building was boarded up and secured with a strong padlock, but this didn't stop vandals from wilful destruction. On November 27, the lighthouse was found with the padlock and hasp blown off by shotgun blast, the plywood pried off the windows, the glass broken, the tower door broken open, and five of the lantern glasses smashed out. This went on for six years—intermittent periods of vandalism followed by repairs—but by April 1978, the building was beyond repair. It was declared surplus and offered for sale. By May 1979, there were no offers, and permission was given to dispose of it by the most appropriate means.

On October 5, 1979, a new light was established approximately 12 metres from the old one. This is the existing fibreglass tower, which is battery-operated and charged by a solar panel.

The lighthouse can be seen across the passage from the village of Main-à-Dieu.

Gabarus

Rouse Point

131 Gabarus is a small fishing village of about 110 people situated 5 kilometres across the bay from the Fortress of Louisbourg National Historic Park. The harbour lies between Rouse Point and Harbour Point, and is the only secure boat harbour in all of Gabarus Bay. It can be used solely by small craft, however, as there is only 1.5 metres of water in the narrow buoyed channel leading into the harbour. The lighthouse marks the harbour and the good anchorage in Gabarus Cove behind Harbour Point.

The lighthouse is the only wooden hexagonal tower in Nova Scotia and one of only a few remaining original nineteenth-century lighthouses in this province. This lighthouse was built under contract by Neil McNeil and put into operation on November 1, 1890. The contract price was $650, but extras brought the total expenditure to $748.33. The first lightkeeper was John Hardy, appointed on November 22, 1890, at $150 per year. Hardy apparently lived in his own home, as the only other building at the station was an oil store near the lighthouse.

The light was produced by a kerosene-oil duplex burner, which burned about 360 litres of oil annually, until commercial power was brought

to the lighthouse in 1964. Two storm lanterns were installed with a changeover relay to switch to a second light if the first light failed. The light-

There are only two hexagonal lighthouses in Nova Scotia. This, at Gabarus, is one of them.

keeper, Michael B. Morrison, who had been keeper since 1950, was no longer required, but a caretaker was hired to keep an eye on things for $60 per year. On April 12, 1988, the storm lanterns were replaced by a light operated by a sun switch, classifying it as fully automated. Unfortunately, in an attempt to discourage vandals, the floor-level windows were closed in on the side of the tower opposite the door, somewhat altering the aesthetic appeal of a unique tower in such a photogenic site overlooking the harbour and village.

Easily seen from just about anywhere in the village of Gabarus, the lighthouse can be reached by Harbour Point Road and a short walk up the hill.

132 It is amazing that a light was never established on Rouse Point before 1983, because without local knowledge, any vessel approaching at night from the west seeking Gabarus Harbour would have to sail halfway across Gabarus Bay before Harbour Point light would come into clear view. A light on Rouse Point, on the other hand, would make it possible to turn into the harbour soon after passing Cape Gabarus—reducing the trip by several kilometres. Gabarus Harbour is the only secure boat harbour in the 64-square-kilometre expanse of Gabarus Bay.

Another nondescript, functional light, the one at Rouse Point. The fog detector sticking out the front of the building starts the vertical bank of four 100-watt Stonechance emitters blowing. On the roof is a 200-millimetre DLD (Dominion Lighthouse Depot) gas light that has been converted to electricity.

A light on Rouse Point was never considered very important because local fishermen were more concerned about the frequent summer fogs along the Atlantic Coast. In 1978, about 40 fishermen representing 28 boats in the area requested a horn on Rouse Point. In July 1982, after four years of lobbying, a tiny wooden building was constructed on a concrete foundation, and fitted with an electric light in a 200-millimetre gas lantern at the seaward end of the roof. A small electronic horn

GABARUS	
ESTABLISHED:	1890
CCG LIGHT #:	753
POSITION:	45° 50' 37" N
	60° 08' 52" W
	On Harbour Point,
	south side of the bay
LIGHT:	Fixed red
AHW:	16.5 metres
NOM. RANGE:	8 nautical miles
HORN:	None
DESCRIPTION:	White hexagonal wooden
	tower with sloping sides,
	9.7 metres high

Guyon Island

was also mounted on a cement pad beside the building. The Coast Guard maintained this small station, as no lightkeeper was required.

The very next year, a severe storm badly damaged the light, horn, and the building when a substantial portion of the bank was washed away. A notice

ROUSE POINT	
ESTABLISHED:	1983
CCG LIGHT #:	752.6
POSITION:	45° 50′ 35.7″ N
	60° 07′ 59.1″ W
LIGHT:	Fixed yellow
AHW:	9 metres
NOM. RANGE:	8 nautical miles
HORN:	B3, S3, B3, S51
DESCRIPTION:	White rectangular wooden building, 3 metres high

was posted that the station would be permanently discontinued at the end of the season, which was May 1 to December 15. After very strong protests were heard from the fishermen through the president of the Fisherman's Association, the notice of intent to discontinue was cancelled and the horn was back in operation by the beginning of the next fishing season.

Proceed through the small community of Gabarus on Route 327 until you reach the sea wall. From here, proceed on foot along a path for about 400 metres to the light on the point.

133 Approximately 700 metres long by 200 metres wide, Guyon Island, bare of trees, is a very dangerous low-lying island with a shoal that extends about 730 metres eastward. Although only 1.6 kilometres south of Winging Point, the nearest point on the mainland, Guyon Island seems completely isolated. For more than 6 kilometres in either direction, this part of the coast is totally uninhabited, and in the dark of night, not a single light can be seen on shore. Even the flashing white light of Louisbourg lighthouse 18 kilometres to the northeast and the fixed white light of Fourchu Head 11 kilometres south-

GUYON ISLAND	
ESTABLISHED:	1877
CCG LIGHT #:	750
POSITION:	45° 45′ 58″ N
	60° 06′ 48″ W
	210 metres from the west end of the island
LIGHT:	Flashing white, once every 20 seconds
AHW:	16.2 metres
NOM. RANGE:	15 nautical miles
HORN:	B6, S54
DESCRIPTION:	White octagonal reinforced-concrete tower, 12.8 metres high

west, both at the outer limit of their nominal range, can barely be seen on perfectly clear nights.

In 1876, a contract for the construction of a lighthouse on Guyon Island was given to John G. Sinclair for $2,980. The building was a square wooden tower 16.46 metres high with a wooden dwelling attached. The total cost, including a 12-sided iron lantern and the lighting apparatus, was $5,668.60. The station was also provided with an oil store and a 4.26-metre station boat. On April 28, 1877, Robert B. Winton became its first keeper at $400 per year.

In 1923, a white square wooden fog-alarm building was built and a dia-

The lighthouse tower at Guyon Island is well secured against intruders.

phone horn installed together with the necessary oil engines and air compressors. An assistant lightkeeper was also hired at this time, and a bridge was built across the gully to make access to the main part of the island easier. A new combined dwelling/lighthouse was built in 1927—a square two-storey wooden dwelling with two vertical red stripes, surmounted by a lantern.

Another building boom occurred in 1937, when a new oil store, a storage shed, and a boathouse were built. The elements must have been particularly hard on the buildings on Guyon

Island, because the total reconstruction of the station was planned and completed in 1964. The reinforced-concrete tower and two bungalow-style dwellings still remain at the site. In February 1966, the type B diaphone

Guyon Island lightstation's fog-alarm building, equipment building, horn, and huge solar panel, and the lighthouse tower itself. Two dwellings, a boathouse, and another small shed also still existed on this island in 1992.

foghorn was replaced by a larger type F diaphone, together with correspondingly larger diesel engines and compressors to deal with the annual average of 1,844 hours of fog on this shore. Then two months later, in April 1966, two diesel generator sets were installed and the station became electrified using its own generated electricity. A 1000-watt lamp was fitted in the tower in place of the oil vapour lamp, greatly improving the brilliance of the light. In 1969, a new boathouse was built and extensive repairs were made to the fog-alarm building.

It was all downhill from there. When a new electronic foghorn was installed in 1971, it was just four months until the station was classified semi-automatic and reduced to a two-man operation. Following many complaints from local seafarers about the less effective foghorn, the Coast Guard added a second bank of four 100-watt emitters, which were still far from satisfactory. Nothing has ever been able to compare to the diaphone air horns, but they

took engines and compressors, not to mention an additional person to run them. Full automation was on the way. In 1981, a submarine power cable was laid to the island, but in April 1986, the station was changed to solar power to charge the banks of large, single-cell batteries that provided power to the light and horn.

The station was de-staffed, and immediately two dwellings, two storage buildings, and the boathouse were declared surplus—the 1927 dwelling already long gone. The surplus buildings were offered for sale, but given the isolated location, it is not surprising that no interest was shown. In 1997, all the buildings still remained on the island; with the introduction of the alternate use program, perhaps someone will restore them. Considering how difficult it is to access the island, however, it is hard to imagine how these buildings could be put to some useful purpose.

The fact that strange things have been known to happen on Guyon

Island doesn't help matters. Some lightkeepers have apparently heard frightening sounds and have seen ghostly white figures wandering around the station. One lightkeeper even took to firing a shotgun at the figures. At one point, strange happenings and noises were occurring with such frequency that the RCMP was brought to the island to investigate. To this day, no one knows what caused all the fuss, or if they do, they aren't saying. I spent six days and five nights alone on Guyon Island—three nights longer than I wanted to—but I'll never admit to anything strange happening. Who would believe me?

Not visible from any accessible part of the mainland.

Fourchu Head

134 Fourchu Head is rocky with a grassy hummock on the higher ground where it rises to 12.2 metres above high water. Except for some stunted spruce, it is a barren islet connected to the mainland by a 260-metre-long rock seawall that protects the approaches to Fourchu Inlet. The lighthouse marks the south side of the entrance and channel into Fourchu Harbour. Crossing the seawall should not be attempted during stormy weather, as the sea breaks clean

FOURCHU HEAD	
ESTABLISHED:	1907
CCG LIGHT #:	747
POSITION:	45° 43' 03" N
	60° 13' 48" W
	Near the east extremity
	of head
LIGHT:	Fixed white
AHW:	14.6 metres
NOM. RANGE:	11 nautical miles
HORN:	One faces 065° and the
	other faces 170°. They
	sound in unison: B3, S27.
DESCRIPTION:	Round white fibreglass
	tower with two red
	horizontal bands, 9.8
	metres high

across it. Even in fair weather, crossing the top of the seawall can be extremely treacherous; however, in fine weather at low tide, crossing can be easily accomplished by walking alongside the seawall on the lee side.

The lighthouse tower was established near the end of the point, 39.6 metres back from the high-water mark on land that is 6 metres above high water. It was a typical pepper-shaker tower built under contract by Lawrence Mury of Amherst West at a cost of $700. There was also a small, four-room, wooden dwelling and a small storage shed at the station, which was manned by Albert Hooper from April to January for an annual wage of $120.

Nothing much changed until 1956, when the station got a small fog-alarm building and a type B diaphone horn, which gave two two-second blasts every minute. In 1964, a new dwelling was built for the head keeper, and the assistant who was hired because of the extra workload with the horn had his own dwelling. A metal engine room was built for two diesel generator sets that provided electrical power to the island, and the battery-supplied light

Standing out against the fog bank as it rolls in from the sea, the two horns at Fourchu Head light are about to start blowing in unison a three-second blast every half-minute.

was replaced by a much more powerful light.

On February 23, 1967, a 27.43-metre trawler came ashore about 1.6 kilometres west of the station. Sadly, 10 men were lost. The lightkeepers relayed radio-phone messages while search and rescue searched for bodies. Lightstation personnel recovered two bodies themselves.

In 1970, Fourchu Head was connected to commercial power to supply the main light, and a 12-volt battery operated system was installed as a standby

light, thus the station became semi-automated. In October 1974, an electronic foghorn was installed, bringing the station another step closer to full automation. The original lighthouse, which had served a total of 72 years, was replaced in 1979 with the existing circular fibreglass tower. With a remotely monitored automatic diesel generator back-up, automation and de-staffing was imminent. Even so, five more headkeepers served at this station

in its final 10 years, ending with Robert Spears and his wife Gerry, who witnessed the deterioration of the surplus buildings until they were posted off on October 11, 1988. The two dwellings were then declared surplus and advertised for sale, to be removed from the site. Three different individuals expressed interest, but one by one failed to honour the terms of the agreement. As a result, the Coast Guard's real estate division authorized the disposal of the buildings.

To view the light, drive through the village of Fourchu 2 kilometres to the seawall. If the weather and tide are right, and you possess an adventurous spirit, you might cross the seawall for a closer look.

Jerome Point

135 This light was built to lead vessels through numerous rocky shoals scattered about St. Peters Bay as they headed towards St. Peters Canal. The canal cuts through an isthmus about 800 metres wide, which connects Bras d'Or Lake with St. Peters Bay and the Atlantic Ocean. Although the canal was opened in 1869, it wasn't until 1883 that the lighthouse was built. Lawrence J. O'Toole of St. Peter's built the lighthouse under contract for $1,300. It had a square tower 12.2 metres high with an octagonal iron lantern on top. The first man to keep the light was John D. Matheson, for $200 a year. The keeper's dwelling was

JEROME POINT	
ESTABLISHED:	1883
CCG LIGHT #:	734
POSITION:	45° 38' 53" N
	60° 52' 24" W
	Near the head of St. Peter's Bay on the point at the east entrance to the canal
LIGHT:	Fixed red
AHW:	16.5 metres
NOM. RANGE:	8 nautical miles
HORN:	None
DESCRIPTION:	White wooden pepper-shaker-type tower, 10.9 metres high

in May 1960, the light was made unwatched and a caretaker was hired. Two years later, in 1962, the job was entrusted to the lockmaster at the canal. The following year, the keeper's dwelling and property were deeded to the canal authority, and the lighthouse, which is located within the provincial park, officially became unwatched in February 1965.

Once the lighthouse was fitted with a four-bulb automatic changer and a sun switch to turn it on and off between May and November, it could operate for long periods of time with minimum attention.

In the town of St. Peter's, at the east end of the canal bridge, turn into Battery Provincial Park and proceed just a little over one kilometre to a parking area at the lighthouse. Be advised, provincial parks are seasonal.

This is Jerome Point lighthouse in Battery Provincial Park. The town of St. Peters, the canal, the park, and the lighthouse all combine to make a beautiful and interesting place to visit.

attached to the light tower, and he was provided with a hand-operated horn to answer vessels' signals.

Aside from minor repairs and regular maintenance, little has been recorded about this light in its early years. It was then generally known as St. Peter's Bay light, which could

account for some records having gone astray.

Lightkeeper David A. McNeil, who had been appointed on September 13, 1935, witnessed the end of the old lighthouse he had kept for 21 years. However, he got to live in a new dwelling and was keeper of the current lighthouse on Jerome Point for two years, until his retirement on March 31, 1958. Both dwelling and existing lighthouse were built in 1956 and were connected to commercial electrical power.

A temporary keeper was hired; then

Gregory Island

136 Originally known as Freestone Islet, Gregory Island is actually an extension of the northwest end of Doctor Island, with less than 200 metres of very shallow water covering a bar between them. The island is tiny and low lying with a maximum height above high water of no more than 1.8 metres. Triangular in shape, the north side is the longest at about 120 metres. There is a small pond in the middle of the islet, and nearby, there are the foundation ruins where the lightkeeper's dwelling stood from 1913 to 1952. This light is considered key to a series of lights established in the early summer of 1884. Increased traffic since the opening St. Peters Canal, including a number of steamships carrying passengers and mail between Port Mulgrave and Sydney, required the route to be lit at night, and a series of pole lights was ordered to mark the principal turning points. On Freestone Islet (Gregory Island), a small shelter 3.65 metres by 4.87 metres was built for the accommodation of the keeper. The light was a small lantern hoisted on a mast 7.62 metres high, with a white shed at its base.

The first keeper was Lauchlin Morrison, who was paid $135.10 a year. His life could not have been easy in such spartan conditions, but after he died in 1897, a permanent lighthouse was erected and put into operation in October 1898. The new lighthouse was a square wooden tower with a square wooden lantern on top, making it 10 metres high, base to ventilator. It was constructed by Alexander McCuish of St. Peter's, whose contract price was $387. Widow Morrison continued to keep this light after her husband's death, until May 1907. It was not until 1913 that a new dwelling was built by J. L. Campbell of St. Peter's at a cost of $794. In 1910, the name was changed from Freestone Islet to Gregory Island, though the reason is not clear.

In 1951, the oil lamp was changed to a battery-operated light with a four-place lamp changer, a flasher, and a sun switch to turn the light on and off. The last keeper, William Digout, was subsequently informed that he would not be required after May 31 of that year. He was given permission, at a nominal cost, to remove the buildings from Gregory Island to French Cove for his own use, which he accomplished by October 17, 1952.

By the fall of 1970, the southwest corner of the lighthouse had been undermined and it was necessary to construct a rock and mortar foundation across one side of the structure. Further repairs were not considered to be cost-effective, so in 1979 it was decided that the old tower would be demolished and burned on site. The light would have to be temporarily discontinued until a new tower could be constructed. In 1982, for additional support against high winds, the existing fibreglass tower was bolted into place on a concrete pad with eight steel guy-wires from the upper part of the tower to anchors in the ground. A watertight marine lantern is mounted on the open deck at the top of the tower, supplied by two 12-volt batteries that are kept charged by a small solar panel. Equipped with a flasher and a sun switch to turn the light on and off, it is maintained only from May 1 to December 15.

Can be seen from Cape George 3 kilometres away.

It is difficult to imagine that there was ever a dwelling and lighthouse on this tiny low-lying stone and gravel bar called Gregory Island. Note that the tower has to have eight steel-wire guys to secure it against high winds.

GREGORY ISLAND	
ESTABLISHED:	1884
CCG LIGHT #:	841
POSITION:	45° 42' 38.2" N
	60° 48' 03.9" W
	On the west end of islet
LIGHT:	Red flashing, F0.5/E3.5.
AHW:	10.9 metres
NOM. RANGE:	5 nautical miles
HORN:	None
DESCRIPTION:	White circular fibreglass tower with two red horizontal bands, one about two-thirds the height of the tower and the other at the top. The tower is 9.1 metres high.

McNeil Beach

The original light at McNeil Beach was a small lantern hoisted on a pole 7.62 metres high with a small white shed at its base. It showed a fixed red light at 10 metres above high water. The light was intended to guide vessels through a difficult channel only 180 metres wide between the Seal Reefs and Boulardarie Island in the Great Bras d'Or. There is a good depth of water, between 12.8 and 23.8 metres, but the fairway is narrow, and there is a tidal current of 2 to 2.5 knots. Lauchlin McNeil was appointed first

through a ruby chimney at 9.45 metres above high water, and could be seen 8 kilometres away.

In 1961, the 761-metre-long, 37-metre-high Seal Island Bridge was built, and the channel below was marked by lighted buoys, rendering the lighthouse more or less redundant. It was, therefore, discontinued as an aid to navigation and bought by private interests. Although it no longer serves any official purpose, it certainly has become an attraction. Anyone travelling the route across the bridge will

a look-off on Kelly's Mountain. Or you can leave your car at the small parking place at the east end of the bridge and take the path down to the beach and to the lighthouse. It is not a very difficult hike, but you should be reasonably fit and wear appropriate footwear.

McNeil Beach	
Established:	1884
CCG Light #:	Unlisted in current list of lights.
Position:	46° 13' 55" N
	60° 29' 15" W
	On the north side of Boulardarie Island.
Light:	Unlit
AHW:	Unknown
Nom. range:	Unknown
Horn:	None
Description:	White wooden pepper-shaker-type tower, 10 metres high

The McNeil Beach lighthouse, although privately owned and no longer in use, has become such an attraction and so enhances the scenic view from Kelly's Mountain that we can only hope it will be kept in good condition and perhaps an alternate use for it can be found.

keeper of this light on August 1, 1884, at a salary of $150 per year. It was no coincidence that the keeper's name happened to be the same as that of the lighthouse site.

The pole light was replaced in 1909 by the existing pepper-shaker tower, erected under contract by L. Mury of West Arichat at a cost of $780. An oil lamp provided the fixed red light

appreciate the lighthouse and the beauty of the area. Unfortunately, because it is private property, there is no control over its disposition and it has been allowed to deteriorate. A small one-storey addition attached to the side of the tower was in a dilapidated state by 1988—all the glass was broken out of the lantern, there were holes through the gallery deck, and the guard railings were broken or missing. A few years later, the attached building had been removed and there was evidence that repairs had been made to the tower. It would be a pity if it were lost.

There is a beautiful view of Seal Island Bridge and the lighthouse from

Man of War Point

138   Man of War Point lighthouse is located on the beach on the western side of Boularderie Island, some 7 kilometres below the Seal Island Bridge, where the Great Bras d'Or narrows from about 1,800 metres to 725 metres in width.

The 1912 lighthouse was described as a pepper-shaker-type tower, built under contract by P. L. Macfarlane of Baddeck at a cost of $974. The first lightkeeper was Malcolm N. McLeod, appointed on January 5, 1912, at $120 per year.

This lighthouse was destroyed by fire in 1925. A temporary pole light made do while a new lighthouse was being built—the one that still stands today.

MAN OF WAR POINT	
ESTABLISHED:	1912
CCG LIGHT #:	810
POSITION:	46° 11' 14.4" N
	60° 33' 10.1" W
	On the beach
LIGHT:	White flashing, F0.5/E3.5
AHW:	8.2 metres
NOM. RANGE:	7 nautical miles
HORN:	None
DESCRIPTION:	White wooden
	pepper-shaker-type tower,
	7 metres high

In 1965, the light was converted from oil to acetylene gas, and the characteristic changed from fixed to flashing, thus increasing the life of each gas tank by 10 times. By using a sun valve to turn the light on only when it was dark, the life of the gas tank was extended even more. When it was classified as seasonal—operating from April 15 to January 31—a lightkeeper was no longer necessary. Alexander McKenzie, the last keeper at the light, was only part-time anyway, as he didn't live at the light and only went to tend it twice a day, once to light it and once to snuff it. He continued on for three more years as a caretaker, but it was

Another light tower that has recently become privately owned is this one at Man of War Point. Its disposition is, therefore, unknown, but it is hoped that the lantern will be restored and the lighthouse opened to the public.

only after his job was terminated in 1968 that his true value was realized, as there was a marked increase in vandalism. The tower was broken into several times, and windows were smashed time after time, even shot out from the seaward side.

In September 1971, when the light was connected to commercial electrical power, the lantern was found to be badly rotted, so, as was the practice at the time, the lantern was removed down to the windowsills, decked over, and weatherproofed with fibreglass. A waterproof lantern with an acrylic lens was then mounted on the open deck.

In 1992, and again in 1994, proposals were submitted by people interested in developing local properties as recreational facilities, and wanted to include the lighthouse as part of the attraction. They proposed restoring the lantern and sharing responsibility for its care and maintenance. At the time, however, circumstances didn't allow for such an arrangement. The alternate use program recently introduced by the Coast Guard provides some hope

that a beneficial arrangement can be reached.

From Exit 13 at the east end of Seal Island Bridge on Route 105, take the road toward Boularderie and after about 7 kilometres, watch for a gravel road to the right, and follow it for about 500 metres to its end. From here, it is about a 600-metre hike to the light. Watch for and respect private property.

Kidston Island

139 The original Kidston Island light, built for the purpose of guiding vessels into Baddeck Harbour, was put into operation on November 8, 1875. The building was a small square wooden tower with a hexagonal iron lantern and three oil lamps with reflectors, which showed a fixed red light at 9.44 metres above high water for a distance of 7 nautical miles. The lighthouse was built under contract by Neil W. McKenzie for the sum of $674. The first keeper, Donald McRae, was appointed at a salary of $200 per year, which included an allowance for a boat because he lived ashore in his own home in Baddeck. The following year, a full account of the cost of the lighthouse was shown to be $1,474.63, more than double the contract price, at least partly because of the boat and a well that was dug. The light consumed about 1,436 litres of oil annually that was stored in the lighthouse instead of an oil store, which was not an acceptable practice.

This light was not a very good one from the outset—the lamps were not properly centred in the lantern and were out of focus. Several alterations didn't seem to help much, until 1910, when a glass lens was substituted for the old reflectors. However, in 1911, construction began on a new tower of a much larger size. Contracted to L. Mury of West Arichat, well-known for the many lighthouses he built in Cape Breton over the years, the new lighthouse came into operation in 1912 at a cost of $1,006.50, plus an additional $626.50 for the lantern, which was provided separately by Victoria Foundry Co. of Ottawa. The tower is 6.24 metres square at the base, tapering to 1.9 metres square at the top, surmounted by an octagonal red iron lantern with a fixed red light that could be seen from about 6 nautical miles. In 1924, a hand-operated horn was sup-

The little footbridge and the special care taken at the site has added much to the appeal of this lighthouse on Kidston Island, just a stone's throw from the waterfront of the picturesque village of Baddeck.

plied to answer vessels' signals.

In the early 1950s, the light was changed to a red flashing, battery-operated, unwatched, seasonal light, and Donald Ryan was appointed its caretaker. In 1956, the characteristic was changed to a green flashing light, a new oil store was built, and, finally, in 1959, permission was given to demolish and burn the old lighthouse that had been an eyesore and a disgrace to the community for many years. In 1962, the light once again became operational year-round, as requested by the community, to assist people crossing the ice between Baddeck and Kidston Island in the wintertime.

By 1989, the shore had eroded to within 1 metre of the lighthouse, but extensive shore protection work was done and a little arched foot bridge was built, making it a picturesque place. The island has been deeded to the community with the provision that it never be developed, and left in its natural state. The swimming beach is kept clean, but otherwise, the site remains unchanged, even to the three pairs of bald eagles that make Kidston Island their home.

Baddeck, where the Cabot Trail

KIDSTON ISLAND	
ESTABLISHED:	1875
CCG LIGHT #:	815
POSITION:	46° 05' 53" N
	60° 44' 33.5" W
	On the northeast point, at the entrance to Baddeck Harbour
LIGHT:	Fixed green
AHW:	14.6 metres
NOM. RANGE:	Unknown
HORN:	None
DESCRIPTION:	White square wooden tower with sloping sides, 15.24 metres high

begins, has a reputation as one of Nova Scotia's finest resort towns. Alexander Graham Bell had a summer home here and this is where he spent the last 37 summers of his life, before he died in 1922 at the age of 75. The local Alexander Graham Bell National Historic Site and Museum displays memorabilia and artifacts pertaining to his many accomplishments. Dr. Bell was the inventor of the telephone, developed a hydrofoil boat, and researched the education of the deaf, among other humanitarian projects. It was also in Baddeck that the first airplane flight in the commonwealth occurred. On February 23, 1909, Bell's associate, J. A. D. McCurdy, took off in

Kidston Island West

the Silver Dart and made history.

The lighthouse is only about 400 metres from the Baddeck government wharf, from which a shuttle boat service is operated during July and August by the local Lions Club. At other times, a water taxi can take you to the island.

140 Baddeck has an ever-increasing population of boaters who come to enjoy the pleasure of sailing in the protected and, for the most part, fog-free waters of the "inland sea." The harbour lies sheltered between the mainland and Kidston Island, with a channel at each end. The favoured entrance is at the northeast end, where a lighthouse has marked the way since 1875. However, as the southwest channel came into more frequent use, it became evident that an additional aid to navigation would be desirable at this location. The light on the northeast end of Kidston Island, 900 metres distant, is obscured from view to vessels approaching through St. Patrick's Channel from the west.

KIDSTON ISLAND WEST	
ESTABLISHED:	1976
CCG LIGHT #:	815.1
POSITION:	46° 05′ 33″ N
	60° 45′ 03.7″ W
	Southwest end of the island
LIGHT:	Fixed red
AHW:	11.5 metres
NOM. RANGE:	Unknown
HORN:	None
DESCRIPTION:	White circular fibreglass tower, 9.1 metres high, with two red horizontal bands, one at the top and the other about halfway down

The existing fibreglass tower first showed a light in March 1976. The prefabricated tower is secured to a concrete pad with stainless steel bolts through a flange at the bottom. Electricity supplies the 150-watt high-pressure sodium lamp, which is in a 200-millimetre gas lantern that had been converted to electricity, and has a red lens. It is a seasonal aid, operating from May 1 to December 15.

At the other end of Kidston Island is this common fibreglass tower, made necessary by the increase in boaters who use the southwest channel.

View the light from the beach at the west end of town, or for a closer view, take a water taxi from the marina.

Gillis Point

141 Gillis Point lighthouse marks the geographical centre of Cape Breton. It was built to provide guidance to vessels navigating the lake located east of Grand Narrows Bridge to and from Barra Strait. It also marks the south entrance to Maskell's Harbour, which is 640 metres wide and provides excellent small craft anchorage. The lighthouse was built by N. W. McKenzie under contract for $1,323. The first lightkeeper was F. X. McNeil, who was paid $120 per year, followed by Philip E. McNeil, who served from January 1, 1896, until December 18, 1897.

The original lighthouse was a square wooden tower with sloping sides surmounted by a red iron hexagonal lantern with an overall height of 11.3 metres. Near the end of construction, the decision was made to build a small attached dwelling for the lightkeeper, increasing the cost to $1,714.24. Further changes were made shortly after: attached to the north side of the tower, was an addition measuring 8.38 by 3.66 metres by 7.62 metres high, and on the west side, a 3.96-metre-square, 7.62-metre-high addition.

Hector McLean was the keeper from 1898 to 1916, at which time he died and left his wife in charge until 1939, when their son, Andrew M. McLean, took over the job until 1967. Andrew had known no other home, and when his wife died in 1959, he was left to raise six children, ages 1 to 15. He stayed on in the lighthouse as caretaker until October 1967, when he had to move out to a rented house in Iona. McLean qualified for a 25-year service award, but no official took the time to present it to him. He therefore had to request it, and the award arrived by mail three and a half years later.

In August 1978, plans were made to remodel the lighthouse, which included removing the living accommoda-

GILLIS POINT	
ESTABLISHED:	1895
CCG LIGHT #:	832
POSITION:	46° 01' 23" N
	60° 46' 39" W
	On south side of entrance
	to Maskell's Harbour
LIGHT:	White flashing, F0.5/E3.5
AHW:	22.6 metres
NOM. RANGE:	5 nautical miles
HORN:	None
DESCRIPTION:	White wooden
	pepper-shaker-type tower,
	11.3 metres high

Before 1978, this Gillis Point lighthouse had two good-size additions on the adjacent north and west sides, providing living accommodation for the lightkeeper and his family until it was de-staffed.

tions, so that only the tower remained—a free-standing structure, completely renovated, and covered with vinyl siding. The work was awarded to Cummings Construction Ltd. of Port Hastings and all work was completed by December 1, 1978.

Since 1984, the light has been operated seasonally from May to December. A 1995 review of aids to navigation in the Bras d'Or Lakes area indicated that it was likely that the lighthouse would be discontinued and declared surplus, with the land and buildings going to Crown Assets for disposal. If the feder-al, provincial and municipal governments have no use for the lighthouse or property, it will go to public tender at real market value.

From Iona, drive about 8 kilometres to Maskell's Harbour and watch for a narrow dirt road with a mailbox marked Boulaceet Farm. Proceed down this dirt road about one kilometre to the lighthouse.

Little Narrows

Cameron Island

142 Little Narrows channel is about 1,400 metres long and barely 70 to 80 metres wide in some places, and connects St. Patrick's Channel and Whycocomaugh Bay. The channel enables vessels to ply these waters between Whycocomaugh and Sydney. Little Narrows light marks the south side of the east entrance, and is just a short distance from a small chain ferry that takes cars and passengers across the narrow channel.

The lighthouse erected in 1880 was a white, wooden, pepper-shaker-type tower 10.67 metres high, with a hexagonal iron lantern, all supported on a foundation of hemlock posts. The $390 contract was awarded to Neil McKenzie, who had the light ready to put into operation at the opening of the 1881 navigation season. John Ferguson of Little

LITTLE NARROWS	
ESTABLISHED:	1881
CCG LIGHT #:	830
POSITION:	45° 59' 45.6" N
	60° 58' 52.8" W
	On Curlew Point, south
	side of east entrance to
	Little Narrows
LIGHT:	Fixed white
AHW:	10.5 metres
NOM. RANGE:	10 nautical miles
HORN:	None
DESCRIPTION:	White circular fibreglass
	tower with two red
	horizontal bands; one at
	the top and the other
	about 3 metres from the
	top of the 9.1-metre tower

The little chain ferry that carries vehicles across Little Narrows probably doesn't really need this light as a navigation aid!

Narrows was paid $120 annually to keep the light.

In 1951, the oil lamp was changed to a battery-operated flashing white light with a sun switch to turn it on and off—and made unwatched. Like all unwatched lights, it suffered the usual effects of vandalism and soon showed signs of neglect. But by 1980, the tower had developed a noticeable list as a result of the foundation posts rotting away. Extensive repairs were not considered to be cost-effective, so the tower was declared surplus and offered for sale, to be removed from the site. After a few months, there being no interest in

the tower, and no salvage value to it authority was given to demolish it. In October 1980, a temporary light was rigged on a 7.62-metre mast, 9 metres from the old lighthouse, which was then torn down and burned. Two months later, the existing 9.1-metre-high fibreglass tower was erected with a 115-volt, 175-watt mercury-vapour lamp showing a fixed white light, turned on and off by a sun switch.

This light can be seen about 200 metres from the Little Narrows ferry. On my last visit, the access road was grown over and barely recognizable, but with a little effort, the tower is still accessible. Watch for bald eagles.

143 This lighthouse was established as a new navigation light on Cameron Island on July 1, 1977; however, records show that the tower was built in 1903 as one of the range lights at Clarke Cove, the harbour for the community of Marble Mountain. But because vessels had to run a dangerous and complex course through many small islands and a myriad of shoals and reefs to bring the range lights in line for safe passage into the cove, it was decided that a lighthouse was needed on Cameron Island. It would provide a reference for mariners looking for the safest entrance into Clarke Cove, a narrow buoyed channel passing north of the island. So after 74 years, the range lights were discontinued and the front tower was moved to

CAMERON ISLAND	
ESTABLISHED:	1977
CCG LIGHT #:	838
POSITION:	45° 48' 52" N
	61° 00' 28" W
	On the northeast end of
	Cameron Island
LIGHT:	Green flashing, F0.5/E3.5
AHW:	9.7 metres
NOM. RANGE:	6 nautical miles
HORN:	None
DESCRIPTION:	White wooden pepper-
	shaker-type tower,
	9 metres high

Cameron Island.

This lighthouse was built in 1903 by day labour under foreman Whebby. In 1977, when it was moved, the lantern was found to be rotted from the roof down to the windowsills. This part was removed and decked over to form an open lantern deck on which the watertight marine lantern was mounted. It contained an automatic, four-place lamp changer with 12-volt lamps supplied by a battery and flasher to pro-

Cape George

Cameron Island is in the West Bay part of Bras d'Or Lake. It is a pretty but seldom-visited island, as there is little attraction other than the light tower itself—unless you're looking for solitude, peace, and quiet.

vide the flashing green light that is still the characteristic today. No lightkeeper is required.

In May 1988, the system was fitted with a solar-charging panel and a sun switch to turn the light on and off as required; it also became operational only from May to December.

Because this lighthouse is on an island, the only way it can be seen without a boat is from about two kilometres distance, viewed from the Bras d'Or Lakes scenic drive along the north shore of West Bay at the small community of Marble Mountain.

144 This lighthouse was built for the purpose of assisting in the navigation of St. Peters Inlet, and providing access to St. Peters Canal. The original lighthouse was a square wooden tower with sloping sides surmounted by a 10-sided wooden lantern, and had a dwelling attached. Duncan McRae was the builder at a contract price of $590. The Murray family kept the light for the entire 94 years it was watched, beginning with Norman Murray, who was appointed on August 3, 1875, and ending with William L. Murray, who served 39 years, from 1930 to 1969.

In 1894, an oil store was built, and by 1899, considerable work had to be done. Stone foundations were built under the new oil store and a portion of the dwelling. A tar roof was laid over the bedroom, and the covering of the lantern roof and deck was renewed. The lantern base had to be rebuilt and flushed. The light room, two bedrooms, and the porch were lined with spruce, and the kitchen and porch floors were relayed—all under the supervision of foreman McLellan.

As early as 1937, plans were being made to replace the lighthouse, but it was not until 1949 that a decision was

This Cape George lighthouse is at Bras d'Or Lake, Richmond County, not to be confused with Cape George lighthouse in Antigonish County.

CAPE GEORGE	
ESTABLISHED:	1875
CCG LIGHT #:	840
POSITION:	45° 44' 05" N
	60° 48' 40.7" W
	South side of the lake, west side of the entrance to St. Peter's Inlet
LIGHT:	White flashing, F0.5/E3.5.
AHW:	12.4 metres
NOM. RANGE:	5 nautical miles
HORN:	None
DESCRIPTION:	White wooden pepper-shaker-type tower, 8.2 metres high

made to go ahead. In June 1949, H. E. McDonald got the contract to build a single wooden dwelling and a separate light tower, and to demolish the old lighthouse. However, simultaneous contracts for this lightstation, Jerseyman Island, and Arichat delayed construction, which was not completed until March 1950. The dwelling was 10.36 by 7.92 metres by 6 metres high, and the lighthouse is the existing pepper-shaker-type tower. By 1959, the

Bourgeois Inlet

tower had taken a 10-degree list to the west, causing the glass in the lantern to break. It had been built on concrete piles instead of a frost wall, and had to be levelled on new concrete posts.

In 1968, the light was changed from an oil lamp to a battery-operated flashing light powered by 10 large single-cell batteries, a four-place lamp changer and flasher, and was classified as semi-automated. The following year, William Murray left the station after 39 years of service, and the station became fully automated. When the dwelling, oil store, and barn were declared surplus in 1975 and put up for sale, Murray took them, even though he had to remove them from the site—which he did by September 1975.

In 1988, the lighthouse tower had to be relocated a few metres to the southwest, and was again mounted on eight concrete posts, but this time with 15-centimetre by 20-centimetre wooden sills the full length of each of the four sides. Only two small 12-volt batteries are now needed for the flashing white light because a solar panel fitted on the south side of the lighthouse keeps the batteries charged.

About 10 kilometres north of St. Peter's on the Bras d'Or Scenic Drive, you will find a sign for Lighthouse Campground. A distance of about 1 kilometre will take you through a small trailer park to a gravel bar. Park here and a leisurely 10-minute walk will get you to the lighthouse beside the shore. You can see Gregory Island light about 3 kilometres to the south-southeast across the water.

145 On the north side of the east entrance to Lennox Passage, Bourgeois Inlet is an extensive arm of the sea, 4 kilometres long with an average width of only about 350 metres. The very narrow entrance is no more than 50 metres wide, and the water is just 2.1 metres deep at low tide. This is further complicated by strong tidal currents. Inside, the inlet provides good shelter. A population of about 600 people have settled along the shore of the inlet—the main community is River Bourgeois.

In 1902, construction began on a small wooden lighthouse tower on the east side of the mouth of the inlet, on the extremity of a low gravel point where the channel is narrowest. The work was done by Edward Doyle of Poulamon, under contract for $415. Put into operation at the opening of navigation in 1903, the square, wooden, pepper-shaker-type tower had sloping sides and a square wooden lantern on top—it measured 8.23 metres high from the stone foundation to the top of the lantern. The first keeper was

At least some members of the community of Bourgeois Inlet want this lighthouse replaced and are willing to cooperate with the Coast Guard to achieve that end.

BOURGEOIS INLET	
ESTABLISHED:	1903
CCG LIGHT #:	732
POSITION:	45° 37' 32.5" N
	60° 56' 53.8" W
	On a point, east side of
	the entrance to the inlet
LIGHT:	Fixed red
AHW:	7.4 metres
NOM. RANGE:	8 nautical miles
HORN:	None
DESCRIPTION:	Triangular skeleton tower
	with red and white
	rectangular-slat daymark,
	9.6 metres high

Martin Burke, who was appointed to the position at $60 per year.

By 1962, the lighthouse was in need of major repairs and there was some question as to whether it was worth the cost, but in the opinion of the users, even in poor condition it was a valuable daymark. The lantern continued to rot away until it was beyond repair, so it was stripped down to the windowsills, decked over, and mounted with two waterproof storm lanterns.

Finally, on June 2, 1989, a new aluminum Millard skeleton tower was erected, which still stands today. The old lighthouse was burned down, but residents of the community were angry that the old pepper-shaker tower was removed without consulting them. In 1992, their councillor wrote to express the view that the community had lost an attraction that inspired visitors and photographers to visit the area, and asked whether it would be possible for the community to replace the lighthouse at no cost to the Department of Transport. The Coast Guard explained that the old lighthouse had to be removed because the timber frame and access stairs to the lantern inside were completely rotted away, which made it unsafe. The residents' initial proposal

Green Island

was not accepted, but an agreement was eventually made whereby the community would build a new lighthouse on the original site and the Coast Guard would outfit it with a light. However, changes in legislation have further complicated the situation, and nothing had been settled by 1996.

In the community of Bourgeois Inlet, drive out to Church Point and just before the church, turn left onto Leviscounte Lane. The tower on the site of the 1903 lighthouse is 300 metres at the end of the lane.

146 Green Island lighthouse is a very important coast light because of the large fishing fleet and heavy traffic that head to the Canso locks and St. Peters Bay. Twenty-three metres in elevation, the island is about 700 metres long by 300 metres wide, its length in an east-west direction. Petit-de-Grat Island lies 1.7 kilometres to the northwest.

Before this light was established on the east side of Chedabucto Bay, there was not one coast light on Cape Breton's shore between Louisbourg and the Gut of Canso. The first keeper of this light, Patrick Duane, had to retire at age 60 after only six years because of bad health. He was awarded a gratuity of $250 per year, and his son William Duane was appointed in his place on November 1, 1871, at the same salary as his father, $500 per year. He went on to serve 31 years on this light, then his son served after him. The original station consisted of a one-and-a-half-storey lighthouse/dwelling combined, with a 12-sided lantern on the roof at one end of the building, and two store buildings, one for oil and the other for the 5.18-metre station boat and other fuel. It had to show a light alternately red and white, so as to not interfere with the characteristic of other lights in the

GREEN ISLAND	
ESTABLISHED:	1865
CCG LIGHT #:	722
POSITION:	45° 28′ 41″ N
	60° 54′ 00″ W
	Summit of the island
LIGHT:	Flashing white, F2/E2/F2/E14.
AHW:	34.1 metres
NOM. RANGE:	17 nautical miles
HORN:	B2, S3, B2, S3, B2, S48
DESCRIPTION:	White circular fibreglass tower, 11.5 metres high

area.

A big change occurred at the station in 1924, when a fog-alarm building was put up and a powerful diaphone horn, along with the oil engines required to operate it, was installed. With the added responsibility this brought, an assistant had to be hired and a dwelling built for him and his family. In 1927, a new combined lighthouse/dwelling was built: a two-storey square wooden building with a red iron octagonal lantern rising from the centre of the roof—a popular design at the time.

In 1960, a new one-and-a-half-storey, three-bedroom dwelling was built. Up until 1963, the light was still being produced by a 35-millimetre incandescent oil-vapour lamp—then life changed for the better. Two 5-kilowatt diesel generators were installed and the lightstation became electrified.

A new tower was built and placed into operation on July 11, 1968. Built 13.7 metres west of the old light, the skeleton steel tower had an enclosed white fibreglass stairwell. A 2.13-metre-high octagonal aluminum lantern sat atop the tower, 12.95 metres high, base to vane. The station then consisted of a two-storey dwelling, a one-and-a-half-storey dwelling, a one-storey bungalow, a fog-alarm building, an oil stores building, a boathouse and two

This is the square two-storey dwelling that had been the Green Island lighthouse, used here to mount the foghorn emitters on the old lantern deck. The light was replaced by the fibreglass tower next to it in 1986.

Marache Point

The Green Island lightstation remains intact and in good condition, waiting for an organization to come forward with an acceptable alternate use plan.

station boats—a dory and a 7.31-metre motor boat—and a new light tower.

In October 1971, the diaphone horn was replaced by an electronic horn, so the fog-alarm engines could be dispensed with, and the station was reclassified from a three-family station to a two-family station. The lantern deck of the two-storey dwelling, having had its lantern removed, was used as an ideal place to mount the new electronic horn.

Sadly, the head keeper, Conrad Landry, passed away on April 25, 1982, after serving 30 years. He had seen the station develop into a complex three-person operation, and witnessed its decline, too, but the last chapter was yet to be written. A submarine power cable came to the island from Petit Anse in 1983, and in 1986, yet another light tower was erected—the existing round fibreglass tower. But no sooner was it put into operation, than it was de-staffed and the last keeper, Gary Landry, came ashore. Thankfully, the 1927 lighthouse/dwelling, the 1960 dwelling, and the 1968 dwelling all

remain. It is boarded up and still safe, one hopes, from the idiotic rampages of vandals who have destroyed so many of our other historic lightstations. It is not clear at this time what alternate use this station could serve, but it will require the efforts of the community to find one.

Cannot be clearly seen from the mainland.

147 Because shoal water extends 275 metres offshore from Marache Point for more than 1,400 metres in a northeast direction, a lighthouse was important to local ship owners. So important, in fact, that when they and the merchants of Arichat petitioned for one, they said that if a lighthouse wasn't erected through approba-

MARACHE POINT	
ESTABLISHED:	1851
CCG LIGHT #:	708
POSITION:	45° 28' 50" N
	61° 02' 07" W
	On the point at the south entrance to Arichat Harbour
LIGHT:	Fixed white
AHW:	10.4 metres
NOM. RANGE:	11 nautical miles
HORN:	None
DESCRIPTION:	White wooden pepper-shaker-type tower, 7.6 metres high

tion of the legislature, they wanted to put up a harbour beacon themselves. The legislature was quick to approve the offer to build the lighthouse, but shortly after building started by private means, the Commissioners of Lighthouses found it to be unsuitable. In March 1850, a grant was approved to finish the building of the lighthouse, which the commissioners stated would prove to be of great use.

The Arichat light, as it was called at that time, was completed in 1851. The first lightkeeper, Joseph DeCoste, was appointed at a yearly salary of £30 plus a fuel allowances of £8. It was a very small wooden building with a very small wooden lantern, all painted white, showing a fixed white light from two oil lamps. The keeper was unable to live in the lighthouse because there was no room. He lived in his own home about 800 metres away.

Here is another case of confusion over the name of a lighthouse. Named the Arichat light for the community it served, it was changed to Marache Point lighthouse for its location.

Generally, two people stayed in the lighthouse while it was lit. One small room was used as a bedroom, but it was not permanent accommodation. After an inspection in 1866, the superintendent of lighthouses, Thomas P. Jost, stated that the lighthouse showed a very inferior light, burning only two lamps without reflectors, and that the building was leaky, unworthy of the name lighthouse, and scarcely worth repairing. He recommended that a new lighthouse be built, but further stated that as it was only used as a guide into the harbour, an inexpensive building would be sufficient. A two-storey

dwelling that would show a light from a three-sided window and a separate building for an oil store were constructed for a total cost of $1,519.55. It was put into operation on October 1, 1869, and although the dwelling was commodious, the Department of Marine and Fisheries was reluctant to spend any money on comfort or quality. Eight years after it was put into operation, a report stated that the upper storey was unfinished and the foundation wall had to be taken down to the ground and rebuilt properly with flat stones. The keeper was said to be anxious to have the upstairs bedrooms completed.

In 1949, the station was rebuilt, consisting of the existing lighthouse, a new one-and-a-half-storey bungalow, a stores building, and a boathouse. A hand-operated horn was used to answer vessels' signals. Commercial power was brought to the light in September 1954. In April 1970, the horn was discontinued and a 12-volt battery-supplied standby system was installed in case of a power failure. Fully automated, there was no requirement for a lightkeeper, so on May 13, 1970, the station was de-staffed. On July 28, 1970, all buildings except the lighthouse were declared surplus and offered for sale. All three buildings were quickly sold and removed from the property in accordance with terms of the sale, and all that remains is the lighthouse. The name of the lighthouse was officially changed on September 28, 1970, from Arichat light, which it had been called for 119 years, to Marache Point lighthouse.

To get to the lighthouse, follow the road along the harbour front at the end of Arichat Harbour, and along Cape Auget Bay, to the very end of the road, which is blocked by a gate. At this point, you have to leave your vehicle and hike about 650 metres to the point.

148 Jerseyman Island is really three islands in one. The east and west islands are connected by a shingle isthmus and both are connected by another isthmus to a smaller island. This smaller island is about 500 metres long by 250 metres wide, and the lighthouse is located at the north-

JERSEYMAN ISLAND	
ESTABLISHED:	1872
CCG LIGHT #:	707
POSITION:	45° 30' 13" N
	61° 03' 22" W
	On Beach Point,
	Arichat Harbour
LIGHT:	Fixed red
AHW:	11.9 metres
NOM. RANGE:	7 nautical miles
HORN:	None
DESCRIPTION:	White wooden pepper-shaker-type tower, 7.6 metres high

east end on Beach Point. The whole island stretches 1,800 metres across the bay, and shelters Arichat Harbour, which in the 1930s was considered the most important fishing seaport on the Atlantic coast of Nova Scotia east of Halifax.

The lighthouse, built by F. S. Cunningham for $1,200 plus $778.95 for the lantern and illuminating apparatus, was put into service on July 10, 1872. The first keeper was Charles C. Boudrot, who was appointed at a yearly salary of $250. The tower was 8.53 metres high with a small dwelling attached. There was also a small shed built alongside the dwelling, and an oil store separate from other buildings.

A storm on August 24, 1873, pushed the oil store 15 metres from its foundation, and the water rose to within 60 centimetres of the floor of the lighthouse, but no further damage was done. As a result, however, it was decided to "stay" the lighthouse with wire

Jerseyman Island lighthouse with the village of Arichat across the harbour in the background.

rope and a ballasted cribwork built on three sides of the lighthouse foundation. A 5.48-metre station boat was also provided at this time.

Aside from the usual technical advances in light and fog alarm systems, the only significant change came in 1895, when a 3-metre extension was added to the dwelling, the cellar floor was cemented, and the rooms were sheathed, all for the purpose of making barely tolerable living conditions just a bit more comfortable.

Everything finally just wore out, and in 1950 a new lighthouse and dwelling were required. Construction was complete on March 23 of that year much to the gratification of lightkeeper Irving R. Latimer and his family, who had served part of their 20 years at a time when the lighthouse was falling down around them. The tower and a new one-and-a-half-storey wooden dwelling were built separately this time. There was also a boathouse and a stores building; a dory served as the station boat.

The oil store was repaired and moved to a new location, but all the other buildings were demolished. The new lighthouse tower is the one that exists today. There had always been a hand-operated horn to answer vessels' signals in fog or thick weather, but in 1961, the decision was made to install a battery-operated horn designed to constantly blow a 2-second blast every 20 seconds. But in a short time complaints were coming in fast and furious, especially from the Notre Dame de L'Assomption convent in Arichat, which was close by on the shore. Everything was tried—from discontinuing the horn during clear weather to trying different types of horns—but satisfying the local residents simply infuriated the mariners, who complained that the horn couldn't be heard. A compromise was finally reached, though to no one's satisfaction. In 1965, the light was changed to a 6-volt battery-operated system.

In 1972, a submarine power cable was laid from the mainland to the island and life became much more comfortable. However, it also led to reclassifying the station to semi-auto-

matic and the prospect of de-staffing. In 1978, after all the years of trying to satisfy everyone with a horn that would serve the purpose of guiding the mariner and not annoy the local residents, the horn was discontinued permanently. The boathouse was renovated for use as an engine room for an automatic emergency diesel generator, and the station was de-staffed, bringing to an end Abel LeBlanc's 23 years as Jerseyman Island's last lightkeeper.

In January 1980, the dwelling was declared surplus and offered for sale. Of all the complaints over the years concerning the foghorn, nothing compared to the angry complaints expressed over the proposed removal of the dwelling. However, the dwelling has been sold and removed, and all that remains is the lighthouse.

There is a beautiful scenic view of the

Grandique Point

island and lightstation from Route 206, which runs along a high embankment by the harbour, about 600 metres above the island. Many folks stop to take photographs of the lighthouse, which still shows a fixed red light from May to December.

149 The increased traffic since the opening of St. Peters Canal and, especially, the increased number of steamers carrying passengers and mail between Port Mulgrave and Sydney through the canal have rendered the establishment of lights a necessity for the safe navigation of this route. During the summer of 1884, lights were placed at several key positions; each showed a fixed red light from a small lantern hoisted atop a 7.62-metre pole, with a small white shed at the base for daytime storage of the light and associated materials. Each light was expected to be seen from 8 kilometres away. One of these pole lights was built at Grand Dique beach. It was in about 1960 that the name was written in the official records as one word, Grandique. The first keeper was Daniel Clough, appointed at $54 per year.

GRANDIQUE POINT	
ESTABLISHED:	1884
CCG LIGHT #:	729
POSITION:	45° 35' 37.9" N
	61° 01' 22.2" W
	On the beach
LIGHT:	Fixed green
AHW:	8.8 metres
NOM. RANGE:	Unknown
HORN:	None
DESCRIPTION:	White wooden pepper-shaker-type tower, 8.4 metres high

Tidal currents were stronger around the spit at Grandique than any other part of the passage. Erosion soon placed the mast and shed in jeopardy, so they were moved to a safer place in 1900. Six years later, a decision was

Grandique Point lighthouse is situated in the picturesque Lennox Passage Provincial Park. Every lighthouse should have a park.

made to build a proper lighthouse. Built under contract by Lawrence Mury of West Arichat for the price of $452, the existing lighthouse was ready for the opening of navigation in 1907.

In October 1961, the lighthouse was fitted with two parallel banks of five large single-cell batteries to provide a modified 6-volt system for the light, a flasher, and a sun switch to turn the light on and off—watched over by a caretaker. In 1963, due to storm damage and the washing away of the pebbly beach, the tower once again had to be moved, this time to new foundation about 15 metres away. When commercial power was connected to the lighthouse in 1977, these minor lights became seasonal, maintained from May 1 to December 15. Shortly after, the job of caretaker became redundant.

After crossing the bridges on Route 320 to Isle Madame, keep left and continue about 3.6 kilometres past the

junction of routes 320 and 206, where you will see the entrance on your left to Lennox Passage Provincial Park. Turn into the park and continue about 700 metres to the lighthouse, situated on a picturesque point that juts out into Lennox Passage.

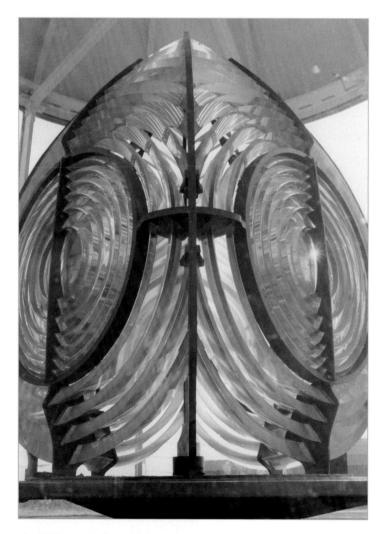

The 25.4 mm. airport beacon replaces this third order Fresnel lens in the Cape North Lighthouse.

Sunrise Trail

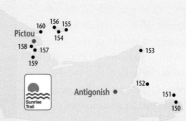

164•
• Amherst
163
Pugwash •
161•
  • 162
160 156 155
Pictou • 154
158• 157•
  159•
  • 153
• 152
Antigonish • 151•
  • 150

Sunrise Trail

150	North Canso	164
151	Havre Boucher Range	165
152	Pomquet Island	166
153	Cape George	167
154	Pictou Island South	168
155	Pictou Island East	169
156	Pictou Island West	170
157	Pictou Bar	171
158	Pictou Harbour Range	172
159	Trenton Range	173
160	Caribou	174
161	Mullins Point	175
162	Wallace Harbour	176
163	Pugwash	177
164	Coldspring Head	178

North Canso

150 This light was established early on, indicating its importance, especially in the days of sailing ships, which were difficult to manoeuvre within the confines of a narrow strait. Without a light, the dark high land to the south made it hard to distinguish the entrance to the Strait of Canso. A report from February 8, 1841, indicates that a survey had been made of the coast near the Gut of Canso, resulting in the recommendation that a lighthouse be erected at the west side of the north entrance with a grant for £1,000. The lighthouse was described as a dwelling and lighthouse combined. The square, white, wooden building was topped by a 10-sided iron lantern glazed on 8 sides, leaving the 2 land-facing west sides dark.

NORTH CANSO	
ESTABLISHED:	1842
CCG LIGHT #:	883
POSITION:	45° 41' 29.5" N
	61° 29' 20.5" W
	On the west side of north
	entrance to the
	Strait of Canso
LIGHT:	White flashing, F1/E2.
AHW:	38.1 metres
NOM. RANGE:	15 nautical miles
HORN:	None
DESCRIPTION:	White circular fibreglass
	tower, 10.4 metres high,
	with two red horizontal
	bands, one at about two
	thirds the height of the
	tower and the other at
	the top

From the base to the weathervane on the lantern measured 10.66 metres. The first keeper was George McKay, who served at this station for 39 years. Every inspection report extolled his proficiency in keeping the station, stating that the light had a very good reputation for always being well kept, and that the keeper was very attentive to his duties.

The North Canso light looking over the north entrance to the Strait of Canso between mainland Nova Scotia and Cape Breton Island.

The lighting apparatus was continually improved throughout the years, without any significant structural changes or need for major repairs until 1891, when the old lantern was condemned and the deck was found to be decayed beyond repair. Thus it was all rebuilt and a new iron lantern was fitted. A corner of the foundation was taken down and rebuilt, the barn was re-shingled, the road to the boat landing was repaired, and the chimney was built up to clear the top of the new lantern—all for $950 by foreman James McKay and local labour.

In 1960, the light was changed to electric power and made unwatched. J. X. DeCoste was appointed caretaker until November 1, 1964. With no further need of the dwelling supporting the light, and considering the light-

house was then 118 years old, a decision was made to replace it. In 1966, the existing circular fibreglass tower was bolted into position on a concrete pad and fitted with a 25.4-centimetre rotating airport beacon supplied by commercial power. The airport beacon was later changed to a 300-millimetre weatherproof lantern mounted on the open deck at the top of the tower, with a sun switch to turn it on and off, and a flasher to give it the proper characteristic. The lamp changer holds six 250-watt tungsten-halogen lamps, which rotate into place whenever a lamp burns out.

From Route 4, about 350 metres into East Havre Boucher, watch for a lane on your right, which leads to the lighthouse. Depending on the season, extreme caution should be taken when driving down this lane. Walking is recommended—it's about 1,600 metres to the light tower, where there's a magnificent view out over the strait.

Havre Boucher Range

151 It was spelled Harbour au Bouche in 1878, when tenders were invited to build beacon lights at the entrance to indicate the dredged channel. It was critical that even vessels with shallow draft keep inside the narrow channel, which at low tide was only 1.2 metres deep amid stoney points. Once inside this snug little harbour, the water depth increased to slightly more than 4 metres at low tide. The overall size of the harbour is about 1,700 metres long and 800 metres wide, but in recent years, the wharves and small boat services are only located about 300 metres inside the entrance on the west side.

There was never a lightstation here, as such, because the lightkeepers always lived in their own homes nearby. Aside from regular care and maintenance, little change of any significance occurred at these lights for about 65 years. In 1954, a new concrete foundation was poured under both towers.

Except for nine years between 1915 and 1924, these lights were kept by the Webb family. In October 1962, the last lightkeeper, J. K. Webb, retired after 38 years of service. Seward A. Crispo was hired as caretaker at $100 per year, and the lights were converted to battery power on November 4, 1963, replacing the duplex kerosene-oil lamps. A year

HAVRE BOUCHER RANGE	
ESTABLISHED:	1879
CCG LIGHT #:	884 and 885
POSITION:	45° 40′ 55.1″ N
	61° 31′ 39.7″ W
	On the southwest shore
	of the harbour.
	The rear tower is
	435 metres from the
	front at 194° 24′
LIGHT:	Fixed green
AHW:	Front, 9.4 metres;
	rear, 34.1 metres.
NOM. RANGE:	Unknown
HORN:	None
DESCRIPTION:	Both are white wooden
	pepper-shaker-type
	towers, 9 metres high,
	each with a vertical red
	stripe on the seaward side

A close view of the front tower of Havre Boucher range. Note rear tower in the distance.

The front tower can be reached by a lane to the railway yard, and from there, it's just a short walk. Please respect the private property surrounding the rear tower. To see both towers in range, as mariners would as they head into the channel, stand on the beach by the front tower and look up the hill towards the rear tower.

The towers were built to specification by William Kaulbach of Harbour au Bouche for $575, and first showed a light in October 1879. With the addition of a lighting apparatus and other extras, the final cost came to $1,309.14. On September 26, 1879, W. J. Webb took up the lightkeeping duties at a yearly salary of $200.

In 1914, the name Harbour au Bouche became Havre Bouche, and in 1917, Havre Boucher.

later, the lights were turned over to the Canso Canal staff. Commercial electric power was connected to the rear light in July 1969, and to the front light in July 1970.

In July 1987, the towers were covered with colourlok siding, and 91-centimetre-wide plywood was installed the full height of the towers on the seaward side and painted fluorescent orange as a daymark.

The towers are highly visible from the Trans-Canada Highway. Take Exit 38 into the village, from where you will readily spot the rear tower up the hill and the front tower down by the shore.

Pomquet Island

Spelled "Pomket" Island from 1868 to 1877, this light helped sailing vessels caught in the contrary winds of St. Georges Bay, make safe harbour in Bayfield. The island is also known by some, even to this day, as Bayfield Island because of

its proximity to the community. This red sandstone island is about 700 metres long by 270 metres wide, 15 metres high, and thickly wooded, mostly with spruce. Every tree on the north end of the island, however, has been killed by cormorants, hundreds and hundreds that built their nests in the treetops. Great flocks of black-backed gulls also nest on this island. A reef extends from the southwest point of the island all the way to Pomquet Point about 500 metres away. The reef dries at low tide more than half way to the point, leaving a passage with little more than a metre of water. Shallow water also extends to the northeast about 700 metres, and a reef with a large rock at the end dries at low water to about 270 metres off the east point of the island.

The lighthouse was a combined one-and-a-half-storey dwelling/lighthouse with a hip roof and five rooms. The light was shown from a three-sided dormer window with iron sashes and glazed with plate glass. There was also a small oil store building. John E.

Atwater was appointed lightkeeper at $350 per year.

In 1893, a small kitchen was built onto the main building, but it didn't last long because reports show that by 1905 it was already in bad condition and it would probably be cheaper to

Gulls and cormorants have taken over Pomquet Island. Note the basement ruins of the old lighthouse/ dwelling beside the lighthouse.

POMQUET ISLAND	
ESTABLISHED:	1868
CCG LIGHT #:	888
POSITION:	45° 39′ 27″ N
	61° 44′ 53″ W
	Northeast end of
	the island
LIGHT:	White flashing, F0.5/E3.5.
AHW:	9.1 metres
NOM. RANGE:	Unknown
HORN:	None
DESCRIPTION:	White wooden pepper-shaker-type tower, 8.5 metres high

rebuild than to make such extensive repairs. Despite a roof and windows that leaked so badly that the place was almost uninhabitable, it still took another five years before anything was done. In September 1910, a lighthouse tower was attached to the dwelling, measuring 2.44 metres square by 7 metres high. With the lantern added, it was 10.36 metres high. The six-room dwelling underwent much-needed repairs at this time.

In 1944, the lightkeeper got a new boat for the station. Its specifications were: 4.26 metres long, with a beam of 1.32 metres, and a 48-centimetre draft; stem and stern made of black spruce, ribs of juniper, and planking of black spruce; two coats of paint, two pairs of oars, and watertight. Cost: $50.

Before lightkeeper George Miller retired in 1960, plans were underway for the construction of a small separate tower with automatic lights for an estimated cost of $4,000. A letter to light-keeper Miller dated May 11, 1959, asked him to board a crew of 4 or 5 men for approximately six weeks—the government would supply the bedding. The letter also asked him to provide a horse to haul supplies at a suggested rate of $4 per day. The new lighthouse tower was completed in July 1959.

The old dwelling/lighthouse and oil store building were declared surplus on January 21, 1960, and put up for sale. After almost three years there were no takers, so on October 4, 1962, they were torn down, leaving only the existing lighthouse tower. James Boyle of Bayfield was appointed caretaker on April 7, 1960, at $475 per year, and continued in this position until 1968.

Several changes in the lighting apparatus occurred between 1960 and 1988, at which time it consisted of an acrylic 250-millimetre lantern containing a four-place lamp changer fitted with 12-volt bulbs. The bulbs were supplied by two 12-volt parallel batteries, which were kept charged by a solar panel and turned on and off by a sun switch.

On the wharf at Pomquet Point, you are only 400 metres from the island, but the lighthouse is obscured by the trees. Consequently, the only view of this lighthouse, unless you are in a boat, is from the road east of Bayfield, about 3.5 kilometres away.

Cape George

153 Cape St. George, as it was called until 1908, is a high headland rising to 182.9 metres above the sea at the northwest point of St. Georges Bay. Shallow water extends over 450 metres from the cape, dropping abruptly to a depth of 35 metres, so depth soundings provide little warning of shallow water. Because it is the turning point for a great many vessels entering and leaving St. Georges Bay en route to and from the Strait of Canso, the Committee on Navigation Securities recommended in April 1861 that a lighthouse be built there.

The lighthouse/dwelling was built during that same summer and was lit on November 1, 1861. An out-building for oil storage was also built at the time.

CAPE GEORGE	
ESTABLISHED:	1861
CCG LIGHT #:	892
POSITION:	45° 52' 27" N
	61° 54' 05" W
	On the extremity
	of the cape
LIGHT:	White flashing,
	F1/E2/F1/E2/F1/E5
AHW:	123.1 metres
NOM. RANGE:	18 nautical miles
HORN:	None
DESCRIPTION:	White octagonal
	reinforced-concrete tower
	with sloping sides,
	13.7 metres high

The lighthouse had an octagonal iron lantern placed on top, making it 11.88 metres high from the base to the top of the lantern. The light was visible 25 nautical miles from its position 106 metres above high water. The first keeper was David Condon, appointed at $469 annually.

In 1866, the superintendent of lighthouses, Thomas P. Jost, remarked that the revolving apparatus should be changed to a fixed light because in

The present-day light at Cape George, Antigonish County.

heavy gales the building shook so badly that the rotation did not work regularly. Additional wooden supports were built to help strengthen the building "for security against the storms which blow over the Cape in fearful gusts." Then in 1885, wire-rope stays were finally fitted to the lantern to prevent it from vibrating during stormy weather.

By 1908, the old lighthouse had apparently run the course of its life and a new lighthouse was built with a separate dwelling. The tower was octagonal, wooden, with sloping sides, and topped by a round iron lantern. It was 13.4 metres high from the base to the apex of the lantern. A beautiful third-order triple-flash Fresnel lens was installed, giving a bright flashing light that could be seen in every part of St. Georges Bay and across the Northumberland Strait to Cape Bear on Prince Edward Island, a distance of 30 nautical miles. The lens was rotated by a clockwork mechanism driven by weights descending in a shaft the full height of the tower. The six-room dwelling was of frame construction, placed on a concrete foundation. E. F. Munro of Westville was hired for the job at a contract price of $3,097.

Electrical power was brought to the station in 1954 and the 55-millimetre oil-vapour burner that had provided the light was replaced by a 500-watt bulb—the oil burner was kept on standby.

Once again, in 1967, a new lighthouse was proposed for Cape George and tenders were invited to construct a 10.66-metre reinforced-concrete tower, which is the existing lighthouse. The contract was awarded to Northumberland Construction Ltd. on October 12, 1967. The light in the new lighthouse was first shown on June 6, 1968, and de-staffed shortly after. The last lightkeeper, William W. Clark, having reached the age of 60 on January 22, 1967, was no doubt glad to retire after spending the last several years with his family in the old dilapidated house. He had kept this light since April 1, 1951.

The beautiful old lantern and third-order Fresnel lens were dismantled and taken away, and the old tower, in poor condition, was supposed to be demolished as part of the contract. However, in 1969, the North Antigonish County Tourist Co-Op Ltd. leased the land,

Pictou Island South

A stubby wooden tower at Cape George with a classic round iron lantern and third-order triple-flash Fresnel lens, which served mariners on the northwest point of St. George's Bay from 1908 to 1968. Note the cover over the lens—these types of lenses had to be covered every morning to prevent the sun's rays from being magnified by the prisms and starting a fire or damaging the optics.

dwelling, and old lighthouse for five years with the idea of developing an historic site. But after a few more years of indecision, the buildings were eventually bulldozed on September 7, 1978.

Happily, the first-order lantern and third-order Fresnel lens from Cape George's 1908 lighthouse are now on display at the Gateway Centre located at the Prince Edward Island end of the Confederation Bridge between Cape Tormentine, New Brunswick, and Borden, Prince Edward Island.

Cape George lighthouse is easy to find. About 35 kilometres north of Antigonish on Route 337, you will see a sign for Lighthouse Road. A gravel lane leads to the lighthouse about 800 metres from the highway.

154 Pictou Island is located at the east end of the Northumberland Strait between Nova Scotia and Prince Edward Island, about 9.65 kilometres from the Nova Scotia mainland and 16 kilometres from P.E.I. It is about 8 kilometres long in an east/west direction, and an average of about 2 kilometres wide. Composed of clay and sandstone, the island rises to a height of 46 metres near its centre. The north side is wooded and the coast is formed of low cliffs. A reef extends 800 metres from the east extremity of the island, and from the west end, Pictou Banks extends three quarters of the way across the channel to Caribou Island. A narrow

PICTOU ISLAND SOUTH	
ESTABLISHED:	1907
CCG LIGHT #:	898
POSITION:	45° 48' 14" N
	62° 35' 14" W
	On the southwest coast
	of the island
LIGHT:	Isophase white flashing,
	F2/E2
AHW:	9.8 metres
NOM. RANGE:	Unknown
HORN:	None
DESCRIPTION:	White wooden pepper-
	shaker-type tower,
	7.9 metres high

gravel road, like a spine, runs almost in a straight line along the southern portion of the island, for its full length. At one time there were about 48 families, over 300 people, living here, spread out along the length of the road. There was a church, a school, community hall, fire hall, and post office in the settlement. After World War Two, the population declined until, by 1970, there were no more than two dozen residents living there. By 1986, the population had increased to about 45 people and is probably double that in the summer months.

This harbour lighthouse is on the south shore about 1.3 kilometres from the west light and 6 kilometres from the east light. At the time it was built in 1907, it was called the Pictou Island West Wharf lighthouse because it was located on the top of a bank near the government wharf, about 10.66 metres from the water's edge. The work was carried out by day labour under the direction of the Nova Scotia Agency (a division of the Department of Marine and Fisheries) at a cost of $1,926.28. The first lightkeeper was Hugh McLean, who was paid $100 per year.

There are three lights on Pictou Island, this lighthouse in the harbour and a light tower at each end.

Pictou Island East

In 1951, a red steel skeleton tower with a white daymark consisting of a fluorescent red diamond in the centre was established on the southwest corner of the east breakwater. It would serve as the front light in conjunction with the existing light to create a pair of range lights, 126 metres apart, to guide vessels into the harbour. It then became known as the Pictou Island West Wharf range.

Discontinued as range lights in 1974, this lighthouse then became the Pictou Island South lighthouse. In 1993, the light was a 250-millimetre marine lantern, with battery-operated 12-volt lamps in a four-place lamp changer, and a small solar panel mounted on the south side of the gallery to keep the batteries charged.

The small Pictou Island ferry is for pedestrians only, and the schedule is subject to change. To get up-to-date information, call Nova Scotia's "Check-in" service at 1-800-565-0000.

155 In February 1852, funding was placed at the disposal of the lieutenant-governor to erect one or two lighthouses on Pictou Island, provided Prince Edward Island would help erect and maintain them. A year later, an agreement was reached and a lighthouse was built at the east end of the island. The building was square and painted white—a combined dwelling and lighthouse similar to other lighthouses of the day, but with an addition authorized by the Board of Works to be made more comfortable than the others. The first keeper was William Hogg, appointed at a yearly salary of £60 with a fuel allowance of an additional £20.

When the winter ice in the strait

PICTOU ISLAND EAST	
ESTABLISHED:	1853
CCG LIGHT #:	899
POSITION:	45° 48' 55" N
	62° 30' 53" W
	On the southeast point of the island
LIGHT:	White flashing, F1/E3.
AHW:	17.7 metres
NOM. RANGE:	Unknown
HORN:	None
DESCRIPTION:	Red skeleton tower, 8.4 metres high, with red and white rectangular slats for a daymark

closed navigation, this station light was discontinued until open water occurred in the springtime. The keeper was supplied with a 3-metre boat that was far too small and dangerous to use by a station that was 16 kilometres from the mainland.

On the night of April 19, 1876, a fire occurred, which the lightkeeper described as follows: "I lit the lamps at the usual hour immediately after sundown. At half past ten o'clock, a few minutes before my usual time of visiting the lantern, I was awakened by a loud explosion followed by several others. Upon rushing to the doors, I found the lantern to be one sheet of flame. After about twenty minutes of hard work we succeeded in subduing the fire although we had scarcely any hope of succeeding when we commenced. All the lamps were destroyed, the window glass broken, the ventilator blown off and broken, the lamp stand burned down and the woodwork charred. The copper floor was also destroyed. A piece of the lamp that had exploded was thrown through the window a distance of about 40 yards." No one was injured and the damage was quickly repaired, but it could have been much worse.

A new station boat was finally provided in November 1877, and in 1885, the record shows that a lifeboat was also placed at the station.

A second lighthouse was built here in

The east light, Pictou Island

1930: a white rectangular wooden dwelling surmounted by a red iron lantern, 12.2 metres high from base to vane. The fixed white light characteristic was changed to flashing white, one flash every 3.5 seconds, placed 17.68 metres above high water, from where it could be seen as far as 12 nautical miles in clear weather. This lighthouse was relatively short-lived, as the trend

Pictou Island West

toward automation of minor lights had started to take effect. In 1962, it was changed to the existing red steel skeleton tower on concrete piers, with three white slatwork daymarks on three sides and a small white building at the base for an equipment room. The light used acetylene gas, which could last a long time without care. In 1971, the daymark was changed—a fluorescent red diamond was added to the centre of the white rectangle. In 1989, the daymark became a red and white rectangle—a wide white horizontal band between two red bands. On top of the tower, there is a 300-millimetre acrylic lantern with a six-place lamp changer and a flasher, which is powered by batteries kept charged by a solar panel mounted on the roof of the equipment building. There is no sign of the previous two lighthouses.

See Pictou Island South regarding the pedestrian ferry to the island.

156 This lighthouse was a long time coming. When the east light was built in 1853 and it was discovered that it couldn't be seen from the west, another light was recommended for the west end as soon as possible. Fifty-two years later, the contract to build the lighthouse was given to Benjamin D. Huntley of Vernon River, P.E.I. for $1,470. It was a beautiful, white, octagonal wooden tower with sloping sides set securely on a 53-centimetre-thick concrete foundation wall, surmounted by a polygonal red iron lantern. The tower was 14.9 metres high, base to ventilator, shining a white flashing light from 18.6 metres above high water. The first lightkeeper was Charles D. Patterson, appointed

PICTOU ISLAND WEST	
ESTABLISHED:	1905
CCG LIGHT #:	900
POSITION:	45° 48' 14.5" N
	62° 36' 10" W
	On the west point
	of the island
LIGHT:	White flashing, F0.5/E3.5
AHW:	14.6 metres
NOM. RANGE:	6 nautical miles
HORN:	None
DESCRIPTION:	Red skeleton tower,
	6.1 metres high, with
	rectangular red and white
	horizontal stripe as a
	daymark

March 29, 1905, at $400 per year. A new dwelling was built for him in 1907, just 43 metres from the lighthouse. That work was done by day labour under the Nova Scotia Agency at a cost of $782.39.

Sixty years later, in 1965, with de-staffing and automation planned, the beautiful octagonal wooden tower was replaced by the existing red skeleton tower. It had a trapezoidal daymark with a fluorescent red diamond in the

centre of the three seaward sides. It was fitted with a battery-operated white flashing light, and made unwatched. There are two small white buildings at the base of the tower; the smaller one is unused and the larger one is the equipment room that holds the batter-

The west light, Pictou Island. Beside it, just out of the frame to the right, is the octagonal concrete foundation from the 1905 to 1965 lighthouse.

ies and associated charging equipment. A solar panel is mounted on the roof. In 1989, the flashing characteristic was changed and the daymark changed to slats on the three seaward sides, painted to show three horizontal stripes—a broad white stripe between two broad red stripes. The latest lighting apparatus is a 300-millimetre clear acrylic lantern with a six-place lamp changer and flasher to give a flash every four seconds.

The octagonal concrete foundation for the 1905 tower is still visible and in very good condition, located two metres from the existing skeleton tower. The foundation of the 1907 dwelling still exists 43 metres east of the light tower.

It is well worth a day trip to visit the three lights and this beautiful island. See Pictou Island South regarding the pedestrian ferry to the island.

Pictou Bar

157 When this lighthouse was built, only 10 others existed in Nova Scotia, which takes into account the first lighthouse, at Louisbourg, which had been destroyed by the British in 1759 and was not rebuilt until 1842. The first lighthouse here was a wooden octagonal tower painted white with red vertical stripes, measuring 16.76 metres high, base to vane. There was a dwelling built nearby for the keeper and his family. Henry B. Lowden was officially appointed in 1839 and is thought to be the station's first lightkeeper.

There were two vertically aligned lights in the tower—the top was a fixed white light, 19.8 metres above high water, and below it, a small fixed red

PICTOU BAR	
ESTABLISHED:	1834
CCG LIGHT #:	902
POSITION:	45° 41' 13.5" N
	62° 39' 51" W
	South side of the entrance
	to Pictou Harbour
LIGHT:	White flashing, F2/E3.5;
	and red quick-flashing, 60
	flashes per minute
AHW:	White, 14.6 metres;
	red, 8.2 metres
NOM. RANGE:	White light, 13 nautical
	miles
HORN:	None
DESCRIPTION:	Octagonal wooden tower
	with sloping sides,
	14.63 metres high,
	with red and white
	vertical stripes

light, which when kept west-southwest, cleared vessels by the east reefs off Pictou Island. The lights were 7.62 metres apart, and discontinued at the close of navigation in the winter, until the ice cleared in the spring.

As the buildings stood on a low sandy beach, not more than 3 metres above high water, it was necessary to build a breakwater. On August 24, 1873, a gale blew with terrific violence for about 24 hours, causing severe damage to the station. The breakwater on the east side was carried away, the dwelling house moved from its foundations, and the kitchen part of the building was totally destroyed and washed away. The sea breached the lighthouse tower, upsetting the tanks and destroying about 450 litres of oil. Immediate steps were taken to repair the station, and by September 1874, a new breakwater was ballasted with stone and brush—it was 140 metres long, 2.13 metres high, and 3.35 metres thick at the bottom tapering to 2.13 metres at the top. The total cost came to $2,507.50, which was a considerable amount of money in those days. The lightkeeper was authorized to build a small barn for his cow and was provided with a whaleboat.

Lightstations that depended on breakwaters and breastworks for protection from the sea required ongoing and expensive maintenance and repair work. And light that was produced by fire was always in danger of burning out of control, which often resulted in destruction of the lighthouse. On May 26, 1903, this lighthouse was totally destroyed by fire, though, fortunately, there were no serious injuries. A temporary 14.63-metre mast had to be erected; two anchor lights were attached to the top: one shone up the harbour and the other to seaward. A fixed red lantern was attached to the mast on the seaward side, 6 metres below the white lights. A spherical wooden cage, painted white to serve as daymark, was also attached to the top of the mast.

The new lighthouse, the existing one, is quite similar to the old one—it rests on the same site with lights of the same characteristic. This lighthouse was built by day labour under foreman E. F. Munro at a cost of $3,471.99, and was back in normal operation by the end of 1903. Aside from ongoing repairs to the breakwater, little change occurred in the following 17 years, but in 1919, a new dwelling was built. Comparatively it was a commodious two-storey house, consisting of a kitchen, living room and four bedrooms. A woodshed and veranda were attached.

On July 16, 1931, a serious fire occurred in the lantern room of the lighthouse, causing considerable damage. If it had not been for the quick action of lightkeeper William MacFarlane, the tower would most certainly have been destroyed. MacFarlane received extensive burns and was in hospital for quite a long time, during which Mrs. MacFarlane ably kept the

A beautiful octagonal wooden tower on Pictou Bar, with a daymark of bright red vertical stripes. In the dark, the tower can be recognized by the second light, a quick flashing red below the flashing white light, about halfway down.

Pictou Harbour Range

light. The lighthouse was automated in 1960, ending the 40-year lightkeeping tenure of the MacFarlane family, and passing it on to a caretaker until 1967. The job was then contracted out until July 1973, when care and maintenance were taken over by the Coast Guard in Charlottetown, P.E.I. In July 1975, the lights were electrified, and in 1980, an emergency light was added.

All station buildings except the lighthouse itself were declared surplus and disposed of in 1960/61, from which time the breakwater was no longer kept in good repair. From time to time a storm causes the sea to wash through as much as 250 metres of the bar, leaving the lighthouse on an island at high tide.

Sitting on about 1.2 hectares of shifting sand that juts out almost 1.5 kilometres into the entrance to Pictou Harbour, this lighthouse is picturesque from several vantage points. If you look carefully to the east as you cross the causeway over Pictou Harbour on Route 106, you will see the lighthouse in mid-harbour at 6.7 kilometres. Or if you proceed through Pictou out Three Brooks Road for 3.8 kilometres to Loudon Beach, you can view the lighthouse across the harbour 450 metres away. Alternatively, it can be viewed from the south side at Moodie Point in the community of Pictou Landing, 500 metres across the cove, or by proceeding to Boat Harbour, where you can leave your car and walk 1.5 kilometres out to the lighthouse. Low lying parts of the spit are sometimes flooded at high tide, but most of the time it is accessible by foot. A most enjoyable visit is assured for those who enjoy a walk on the beach, and lighthouse enthusiasts will be rewarded for their effort.

158 This pair of leading lights is situated about 1,150 metres west of the Pictou Bar lighthouse on the opposite side of the harbour. Used to guide vessels through a 122-metre-wide channel between the sand spit on the south and Murdoch's Shoal on the north side, the first lights were simply pole lights erected on the farm of Alexander Fraser. Both were fixed red

PICTOU HARBOUR RANGE	
ESTABLISHED:	1889
CCG LIGHT #:	903 and 904
POSITION:	45° 41' 18" N
	62° 40' 45" W
	On the north side
	of the entrance to
	Pictou Harbour.
	Rear tower is 141.7 metres
	from the front at 261° 50'.
LIGHT:	Fixed white
AHW:	Front, 8.5 metres;
	rear, 17.1 metres.
NOM. RANGE:	Unknown
HORN:	None
DESCRIPTION:	Both are white wooden
	pepper-shaker-type towers
	with a red vertical stripe
	on the seaward side. The
	front is 7 metres high, the
	rear is 10.4 metres high.

lights shown from reflector lanterns hoisted on masts. The front was about 180 metres in from the shore at 17 metres above high water. The rear light was 137 metres from the front at 22.8 metres above high water. Total expenditure for these lights was $159.22. The first lightkeeper was the above-mentioned Alex Fraser. Why not? The lights were on his property. He assumed his

The Pictou Harbour range lights under repair in 1994, indicating that they are still useful to mariners and likely to be around for a while yet.

duties on November 7, 1889, and his pay was $120 per year.

By 1896, these lights were no longer considered satisfactory and the decision was made to replace them with more powerful lights shown from enclosed towers. Tenders were invited but only one person responded—with the amount $826. The tender was not accepted; instead the buildings were erected under the superintendence of John Chisolm, foreman of works for the Nova Scotia Agency, which purchased materials locally and employed local labour. The total cost for the two towers was $660.22. These are the existing pepper-shaker-type towers,

Trenton Range

but built in a different location. The front tower stood immediately behind the site of the old front mast, and the rear tower stood 117 metres from the front. Both showed a fixed red light. David Lowden was appointed keeper when they were lit on July 12, 1897, and was paid $150 a year.

In 1909, the towers were moved to a new site, more to the west, where they are today. Placed on concrete foundations and securely anchored, the work was done under contract by James Arbuckle of Pictou for $816.

In 1925, the oil lamps were replaced by electric lights. Instructions for entering the harbour stated that the lights should be kept in line until the bar light was nearly abeam, at which time a 242-degree course would lead to safe anchorage in the harbour.

In 1965, the lights are listed as unwatched, but were maintained throughout the season of general navigation, as well as in winter whenever a steamship was coming into Pictou Harbour. The characteristic of the lights became fixed white in 1973. To provide a more visible daymark, the fluorescent red vertical stripes were added to the seaward side of the towers in 1986. And in 1992, they were made operational year-round.

These lights can be seen from the south side of the harbour at Moodie Point, or from Pictou Bar lighthouse. But for a close-up look, drive east 2.4 kilometres from the centre of Pictou town, turn right to Grave Point, and proceed about 400 metres to a dead end. You will see the lighthouses from here, but use your judgement when parking and walking around the site, keeping in mind that the surrounding property is privately owned.

159 The East River is navigable by small craft from Pictou to new Glasgow, a distance of 10.5 kilometres. Because the river is so silty, particular attention must be paid to the Trenton range lights to stay in the channel and reach the piers at the entrance to Stonehouse Point lock. A large power plant is situated on Stonehouse Point, and a causeway and lift bridge cross the river at the point.

First shown in 1920, both these lights were pole lights. The front was 3.65 metres high with a small tank at its base and an acetylene-gas light that showed an occulting red light, 9.1 metres above high water. The rear was 9.1 metres high with an electric fixed red light, 18.2 metres above high water. Both were unwatched. In 1923, small equipment sheds were built at the base of each light.

In 1962, the existing small white square wooden tower was built for the front light and the existing red steel skeleton tower was built for the rear

light. Both were electric and had a red diamond on their seaward face. The front was a red isophase light flashing 30 times a minute, while the rear was a fixed red light. In 1975, the front light was changed to fixed red, the same as the rear light, and in 1986, the diamond daymark was changed to vertical red stripes.

This little light can be found near the Trenton Harbour Bridge on Logan Road. Approaching Trenton from Exit 1A off Route 106, the front tower can easily be seen on the right. The rear tower is 891 metres from the front.

By day, the tiny front light tower of the Trenton range is hardly noticeable among the towers and transformers of the power station, but at night, the bright fixed red light can be clearly seen in line with the tall rear skeleton tower.

TRENTON RANGE	
ESTABLISHED:	1920
CCG LIGHT #:	910 and 911
POSITION:	45° 37' 25.5" N
	62° 38' 53.3" W
	East of Stonehouse Point.
	Rear light is 891.2 metres
	from the front.
LIGHT:	Fixed red
AHW:	Front, 7.9 metres;
	rear, 20.1 metres
NOM. RANGE:	Unknown
HORN:	None
DESCRIPTION:	Front is a white square
	wooden tower, 4.6 metres
	high, with a red vertical
	stripe on the seaward face.
	Rear is a skeleton tower,
	9.9 metres high, with a
	white daymark and red
	vertical stripe in the
	centre.

Caribou

160 The first lighthouse/dwelling at Caribou Point was a square wooden building, 7.92 metres high. Its 12-sided lantern was 2.28 metres in diameter, and contained three oil lamps with 30-centimetre reflectors fitted on a rack, back to back, with three other oil lamps and reflectors, giving a white flash once every minute at 10.66 metres above high water. The light had a nominal range of 10 nautical miles. There was a separate storehouse, and Alexander Munro, the first keeper, was provided with a small 3.65-metre station boat. He had also requested a spyglass and a flag, which were recommended, but the record doesn't show if he ever received them or not.

In the first 10 years of operation, it was noted that more than 18 metres of the bank near the buildings had been washed away leaving it only 7.62 metres from the lighthouse. Timber cribwork was built 18 metres long and two metres high, and properly ballasted with rock at a cost of $130. The following year, a further 18 metres of cribwork was added, and another 30 metres was added in 1888. The following winter, heavy gales almost totally destroyed the breakwater, raising the question of whether the lighthouse should be replaced or moved. The decision was made to move the lighthouse and tenders were called. The contract was awarded to Hugh Henderson of Pictou, who did the job for $525. The oil store was subsequently moved back at a further cost of $15.

Erosion continued, however, and in 1912, work on the breakwaters began again, continuing on into 1913. In 1916, it was decided that a new lighthouse should be built under contract to W. Talbot of Pictou at a cost of $5,103.11. The square wooden dwelling had a red octagonal iron lantern rising from the centre of the hip roof. It had an overall height of 11.58 metres, and

showed a group flashing white light from 12.2 metres above high water. The problem of erosion was ongoing, as records show that extensive repairs were made about every five years, which continued more or less until the station was automated and de-staffed.

CARIBOU	
ESTABLISHED:	1868
CCG LIGHT #:	918
POSITION:	45° 45' 52.4" N
	62° 40' 53" W
	On Caribou Point,
	northeast end of Gull
	Island
Light:	White flashing, three
	flashes every 24 seconds
AHW:	13.4 metres
NOM. RANGE:	18 nautical miles
HORN:	B3, S3, B3, S51
DESCRIPTION:	White square tower,
	10.6 metres high, on the
	corner of a white square
	building

In about 1971, the lighthouse was replaced again, this time with the existing square concrete tower on the corner of a square concrete fog-alarm building. The last keeper of this light, Foster Welsh, was light keeper at the Entry Island light in the Magdalen Islands before coming to spend nearly 20 more years as the Caribou lighthouse keeper. It was a two-person station when he arrived, but was down-

graded shortly afterward to a single-family station. After the other lightkeeper retired, his dwelling had been declared surplus, so he bought it and removed it from the site as required by the terms of sale. Welsh lived in the station's other bungalow with his wife

Despite severe erosion, extensive breastworks are protecting the lighthouse, for the time being. This lighthouse is particularly important to the Northumberland ferries sailing between Caribou, Nova Scotia, and Wood Islands, Prince Edward Island.

and six children. He fought hard to keep the station manned, citing incidents whereby the watchful eye of the lightkeeper was the difference between a life saved and almost certain tragedy. However, public meetings and petitions went unheeded, and in 1990, the station was de-staffed.

This light is of great importance to trading vessels on their way to Pictou, or heading through the Northumberland Strait to ports on the St. Lawrence River. It also helps the Northumberland ferries avoid the dangerous shoals in the vicinity, as they pass nearby, plying the strait between Caribou, Nova Scotia, and Wood Islands, Prince Edward Island.

Caribou Island is joined to the mainland by a causeway. Drive 9 kilometres on the Caribou Island Road to the lighthouse, an ideal place for a picnic lunch.

Mullins Point

161 This lighthouse was built in 1894 to replace the rear light of a pair of range lights established in 1873.

In 1873, a white, square, wooden lighthouse, 7.62 metres high, was built on Mullins Point. It had a square wooden lantern that exhibited a fixed white light 11.88 metres above high water. First lit on August 1, 1873, the light could be seen up to 11 nautical miles away. Benjamin Smith was the first keeper beginning on August 18, 1873, at an annual salary of $100, but for only eight months. Zebud Mullins built the lighthouse for $419, and in April 1874, he took over as keeper.

Before the end of the shipping season, it was realized that a set of range

MULLINS POINT	
ESTABLISHED:	1894
CCG LIGHT #:	N/A
POSITION:	45° 49' 23" N
	63° 26' 30" W
	North side of the entrance
	to Wallace Harbour
LIGHT:	No longer operational.
AHW:	Unknown
NOM. RANGE:	Unknown
HORN:	None
DESCRIPTION:	Square wooden dwelling
	and square wooden tower
	with sloping sides rising
	from the centre of the
	roof

lights could be used to good advantage in leading vessels across Oak Island Bar and into Ship Channel up to the point. By lucky coincidence, the lightkeeper's private home, about 900 metres from the lighthouse, was in a good position for displaying the rear light. The superintendent of lighthouses, therefore, quickly authorized keeper Mullins to show a fixed red light from a window in his home as rear range light, which along with the front white light in the

This Mullins Point lighthouse is unique in its construction, and deserving of heritage status. It is no longer an operational light, but the owner is committed to its restoration.

lighthouse, would guide vessels into Wallace Harbour. For his cooperation, Mullins was given a 50 percent pay increase, bringing it up to $150 per year. Shortly afterwards, Mullins was authorized to build a partition to separate the light from the rest of the house, including ventilation and metal protection.

In 1884, it was discovered that the front lighthouse shook a lot in heavy gales, which required extensive work to overcome. To steady the building, the stone wall foundation was rebuilt, and galvanized-iron rope guys were attached to the four corners. The lantern floor was covered with zinc as a protection against fire, and a gallery was built around the tower.

On June 8, 1892, Zebud Mullins died and was succeeded by James Mullins, who refused to continue the arrangement of having the rear range light in his dwelling. Thus it became necessary to build a new rear range tower, and to provide a dwelling house for the new

keeper. A temporary light was hanged from a pole, and a contract was immediately awarded to Daniel McDonald of Pictou to construct a new lighthouse in time for the next shipping season. The old oil store would also be moved to the new site, bringing the total cost of the project to $1,507. The new combined lighthouse/keeper's dwelling, the existing one, first showed a light on August 25, 1894. This one-and-a-half-storey building has a square white wooden tower with sloping sides rising from the centre of a gabled hip roof—a unique design. Similar lighthouse/dwelling combinations simply have the lantern mounted on the roof, but in this case, the extra height was needed to clear the treetops, so that the rear light would properly range with the front light. The lighthouse is 14.63 metres high base to vane, and the focal plane of the light was 25 metres above high water. The fixed red light was 449 metres, 284 degrees from the front one.

The 1965 record indicates that both lights were made unwatched after they were put on steel skeleton towers. The rear lighthouse/dwelling was declared surplus and offered for sale. It was bought in 1965 by Mr. and Mrs. John E. Sproul, who in July 1966, moved it about 1,450 metres along the shore.

This unique lighthouse is highly visible 2 kilometres across Wallace Harbour from Route 6. Alternatively, cross the Wallace Harbour Bridge, then turn right to North Wallace. The lighthouse is about 2 kilometres past North Wallace, right on the road. The building is now recognized as a Nova Scotia heritage property, but visitors to the site are reminded that it is private property.

Wallace Harbour

162 With an entrance 1,100 metres to 2 kilometres wide, Wallace Harbour appears to have sufficient room for large vessels. When the narrowest part between Palmer Point and Caulfield Point has been safely navigated, however, shallow water severely restricts the movement of larger vessels in the channel, which is, at its widest part, only 300 metres wide. Two range lights were established on MacFarlane Point on October 20, 1904, to lead vessels safely into the harbour. They were shown from typical pepper-shaker-style

The front light of the Wallace Harbour range was discontinued as a range light when the back light became obscured from view by trees.

wooden towers with sloping sides, and topped by square wooden lanterns. The front tower, 8.5 metres high, stood on the northeast extremity of the point, on the south side of the harbour, about 6 metres back from the edge of the bank. The rear tower was 13.7 metres high and 567 metres from the front one. Both showed fixed red lights and could be seen as far as 4 nautical miles. Both buildings were constructed under contract by John D. Reid of Wallace Bay for $2,400. The first keeper of this range was George Boyle, who was appointed on May 23, 1905, at $150 per year.

Both lights were electrified in 1958, and although the record is not clear, it seems that in 1977, the characteristic was changed to fixed yellow, and in 1986, a red vertical stripe was added to both towers to enhance their visibility in the daytime. This didn't do much for the rear tower, however, as it was obscured by trees and bushes growing between the two towers. On April 30, 1986, a letter and petition with 41 names requested that the rear light be made visible because several vessels had gone aground after dark the previous year. The

[ABOVE] The Wallace Harbour range light was reconfigured to install a sector light. [BELOW] The rear tower of the Wallace Harbour Range, converted into a private summer home.

WALLACE HARBOUR	
ESTABLISHED:	1904
CCG LIGHT #:	924
POSITION:	45°48' 46.7" N
	63° 27' 45.9" W
	On MacFarlane Point
LIGHT:	White, red, and green sector
AHW:	12.4 metres
NOM. RANGE:	Unknown
HORN:	None
DESCRIPTION:	White square wooden tower with sloping sides, 8.5 metres high, with two red horizontal stripes on the seaward side

owner of the property on which the offending trees and bushes grew refused permission to clear them away, and after much negotiation without the desired result, the Coast Guard decided to discontinue the rear light and make the front one a sector light. In 1990, the configuration was changed somewhat on the original 1904 tower to accommodate the sector light apparatus. The familiar square lantern was removed and a new one was built—rectangular and offset from the centre both fore and aft, as well as from side to side, for reasons unknown. The vertical red stripe on the seaward side was changed to two horizontal red stripes.

After the rear tower was evaluated and found to have no heritage value, it was declared surplus and offered for sale. It was bought by Graham Long in March 1994, and in September 1995, it was cut into three sections and moved on a flatbed truck, one piece at a time, about 18 kilometres away to Malagash Point, where it is being renovated and remodelled for use as a summer home.

The front tower remains where it was built in 1904, at the east edge of the community of Wallace, on Route 6, virtually on the shoulder of the road.

Pugwash

163 Pugwash Harbour, in the entrance to Pugwash River, is small and sheltered, but with a difficult channel and currents that can run up to 4.5 knots. Pilotage is compulsory. Frequent dredging is carried out in the channel, which is well marked, but the lighthouse is necessary to guide vessels into the approaches.

PUGWASH	
ESTABLISHED:	1871
CCG LIGHT #:	926
POSITION:	45° 52' 16" N
	63° 40' 45" W
	On Fishing Point
LIGHT:	Red isophase, F3/E3
AHW:	17.1 metres
NOM. RANGE:	15 nautical miles
HORN:	None
DESCRIPTION:	Red skeleton tower with enclosed upper portion and sloping sides, 15.2 metres high

The old Fishing Point lighthouse was replaced by this structure, which is different from any other lighthouse in Nova Scotia.

This Pugwash lighthouse was moved from Fishing Point, and now sits in a farmyard with no apparent plan to preserve it as a heritage building.

The contract for a lighthouse on Fishing Point was given to John B. Reed for $1,195. The work was completed during the summer, and a fixed red light was first exhibited on August 1, 1871, from a square wooden tower, 13.4 metres high, with a dwelling attached. The total cost up to June 30, 1872, was $1,676.91. The first keeper was Rufus F. Bent, appointed at a yearly salary of $200. An oil store was also built at the station, and a 4.87-metre boat was provided.

Although ship masters proclaimed this light to be a good one, seen at least 12 nautical miles offshore, an 1874 report stated that the lantern was entirely too small and it was not possible to replace it with a larger one because the top of the tower wasn't large enough.

But as the bank was quickly washing away, this had to be the first consideration. In 1878, a stone protection was built along the bank about 106 metres long and one metre high to protect against ice and wash of the sea. In 1880, the gallery deck was finally rebuilt to support a larger octagonal iron lantern and more powerful optic.

Erosion was always a problem, creating a lot of work and costing a lot of money over the years. About every second year, more protection work was required, so it was not surprising that in about 1958, the decision was made to build a new tower, and to make it a square skeleton design for the bottom two thirds, with the top one third and the lantern enclosed. This would alleviate some concern about flooding during stormy weather and the occasional unusually high tide. The light's isophase characteristic is achieved with a rotating shield inside a fourth-order drum lens.

The old lighthouse/dwelling was declared surplus and bought by the Mundle family, who moved it about 2.5 kilometres down the road to where it now sits on the corner of Eldon Mundle's farm.

The village of Pugwash is proud of its Gaelic heritage and early Scottish settlers. So much so that all the village street signs are bilingual, English and Gaelic. There is an annual gathering of the clans held July 1 in Eaton Park, which was donated to the community by Cyrus Eaton, the Pugwash-born financier who started the famous Pugwash conferences at Pineo Lodge back in 1957. Called the "thinker's conference," it has attracted worldwide attention and is now held in different countries every year.

Both lighthouses are easy to find at the entrance to the harbour, and both can be photographed from the road.

Coldspring Head

164 The north side of the entrance to Baie Verte is marked by Indian Point, 1.6 kilometres south of Cape Tormentine. Across the mouth of the bay, 14.5 kilometres south of Indian Point, Coldspring Head lighthouse is perched on the head, 30 metres back from the 9-metre-high bank at the shore. The ever-dangerous Aggermore rock and Laurent shoal lie 5 metres beneath the surface of the water, about 6.5 kilometres north-northeast of Coldspring Head.

Coldspring Head is a well-maintained, still-operational lighthouse.

At the time this lighthouse was being built in 1890, the Chignecto Ship Railway was also under construction, with its Northumberland Strait terminus at Tidnish, about 11 kilometres to the west. This railway was to have carried ships up to 2,700 tonnes across the Chignecto Isthmus from Cumberland Basin to Northumberland Strait, but after five years had to be stopped because funding ran out. Coldspring Head lighthouse would no doubt have played an important role in guiding ships in and out of the North Terminus had it been completed and put into operation.

This lighthouse was built under contract by J. Harvey Brownell of nearby Northport for the sum of $894. Although construction was complete in 1889, it was not put into operation until the opening of the 1890 navigation season in these waters. The contractor, J. Harvey Brownell, applied for the position of lightkeeper and was appointed on April 12, 1890, at $100 per year. He resigned 13 months later and was succeeded by Alfred Brownell, thus keeping it in the family.

Recent records for this lighthouse are not available, but aside from several

COLDSPRING HEAD	
ESTABLISHED:	1890
CCG LIGHT #:	941
POSITION:	45° 57′ 45″ N
	63° 51′ 57″ W
	On the north side
	of the head
LIGHT:	Flashing white, F0.2/E4.8
AHW:	18.3 metres
NOM. RANGE:	15 nautical miles
HORN:	None
DESCRIPTION:	White wooden pepper-shaker-type tower, 11 metres high

changes in the lighting apparatus over the years, little seems to have changed in the tower itself. In 1997, it appeared to be well maintained and in excellent condition—still in operation and showing a flashing green light.

At 1.2 kilometres north of the community of Northport on Route 366, you will find "Lane 26." Proceed on this lane for about 600 metres to a community of cottages with lanes winding through a well-treed area. Keep right and then go left for 100 metres or so, and you will find the lighthouse in an open field. It's usually easy to find someone local to help with the directions.

Glossary

Characteristic: Lighthouses can be identified by sight in daylight hours; by configuration, colour and/or pattern; by light, colour and duration of flashes or fixed beam; by sound of horn if fitted; by length and number of blasts.

Daymark: Any object that is clearly visible in daylight, such as a lighthouse.

Fathom: 1.8288 metres (six feet).

Flashing light: For example, code F5/E10/F5/E40; F=Flash and E=Eclipse, all in seconds.

Focal plane: Horizontal level at the centre of the optic.

Fresnel lens: A beehive shaped lens invented by french physicist Augustin Fresnel in 1823, consisting of prisms radiating outward from a central lens to refract and reflect 83 percent of light source into a horizontal plane.

Gallery: A deck with guard rails around the outside of the lantern.

High water: The mean level of maximum vertical rise of tide.

Lantern: The glazed room at the top of the tower that houses the optic and light source.

Lights: Fixed lights have a continuous steady light, while with flashing lights the duration of light is shorter than the duration of darkness. Occulting lights have a longer duration of light than darkness, and isophase lights have the same duration of light and darkness. Finally, sector lights show three colours, which indicate the mariner's position in relation to the channel.

Low water: A plane below which the tide seldom falls.

Nautical mile: One minute of arc of latitude at the meridian, or 6080 ft.

One degree (indicated by: °) is 60 nautical miles at the meridian.

One minute (indicated by: ′) is 01 nautical mile at the meridian.

One second (indicated by: ″) is 1/60 of a nautical mile at the meridian.

Pepper-shaker: A name given to describe the many small wooden lighthouses in Nova Scotia that are square with sloping sides and surmounted by a square wooden lantern.

Shapes: In addition to square and round lighthouses, there are also hexagonal (six-sided), and octagonal (eight-sided) lighthouses in Nova Scotia. The lanterns are usually the same shape as the tower; however there are some multi-sided lanterns, usually with 10 or more sides (polygonal).

Tides:

Ebb: the horizontal movement of water associated with a falling tide.

Flood: the horizontal movement of water associated with a rising tide.

Neap: occurs at quarter moons and is lower than average low water.

Spring: occurs twice monthly on the full moon or new moon and is higher than the average high water.

Tower: Some of the measurements relating to lighthouses are confusing. The height of the tower is usually measured from ground level to the top of the ventilator or the weathervane on the roof of the lantern. Sometimes, however, it is the distance from ground level to the gallery deck and the lantern height is added. The focal plane of the light is sometimes measured from the tower base, though it is more properly the distance between the focal plane and high water.

LENSES are classified in "orders." The order depends upon the focal length, which is half the diameter of the lens at the focal plane. Listed below are the six main orders of lenses, an additional two orders of the smaller drum lenses, and three other less common lens sizes.

Size of lens	Focal length	Diameter
Hyper-Radial	1,330 mm	2,660 mm
Meso-Radial	1,125 mm	2,250 mm
First Order	920 mm	1,840 mm
Second Order	700 mm	1,400 mm
Third Order	500 mm	1,000 mm
Third Order (small)	375 mm	750 mm
Fourth Order	250 mm	500 mm
Fifth Order	187.5 mm	375 mm
Sixth Order	150 mm	300 mm
Seventh Order	100 mm	200 mm
Eighth Order	75 mm	150 mm

Catoptric: a system of projecting light by curved reflectors plated with silver. Only 17 percent of the light is effective.

Dioptric: a system of projecting light by means of lenses that refract and reflect the light in a horizontal beam. Eighty-three percent of the light is effective.

Drum: usually smaller lenses, molded or cut into a cylindrical or drum shape, sometimes having individual prisms fitted at top and bottom.

Bibliography

Appleton, Thomas E. *Usque Ad Mare, A history of the Canadian Coast Guard and Marine Services*. Ottawa: Department of Transport, 1968.

Armstrong, Bruce. *Sable Island*. Halifax: Formac Publishing, 1987.

Beaver, Patrick. *A History of Lighthouses*. Secaucus, NJ: Citadel Press, 1971.

Bush, Edward F. *The Canadian Lighthouse*. Ottawa: Parks Canada, Indian and Northern Affairs, 1975.

Findlay, Alexander George. *Lighthouses of the World and Fog Signals*. London: Richard Holmes Laurie, 1896.

Hague, Douglas B. and Rosemary Christie. *Lighthouses, Their Architecture, History and Archaeology*. Wales: Gomer Press, 1975.

Hichens, Walter. *Island Trek*. Hantsport, NS: Lancelot Press, 1982.

Keough, Pat and Rosemary. *Wild and Beautiful Sable Island*. Fulford Harbour: Nahanni Productions Inc., 1993.

Mills, Chris. *Vanishing Lights*. Hantsport, NS: Lancelot Press Ltd., 1992.

Pullen, Hugh F. *The Sea Road to Halifax*. Halifax: The Nova Scotia Museum, 1980.

Raddall, Thomas H. *Halifax, Warden of the North*. Toronto: McClelland and Stewart Ltd., 1971.

Raddall, Thomas H. *Hangman's Beach*. Garden City, NY: Doubleday, 1966.

Richardson, Evelyn M. *We Keep a Light*. Toronto: Ryerson Press Ltd., 1945.

Richardson, Evelyn M. *B — Was For Butter*. Halifax: Petheric Press Ltd., 1976.

Rigby, Carle A. *St. Paul Island: The Graveyard of the Gulf*. Hartland Publishers Ltd., 1979.

Slocum, Joshua. *Sailing Alone Around the World*. New York: Dover Publications, 1956.

Stephens, David E. *Lighthouses of Nova Scotia*. Hantsport, NS: Lancelot Press, 1973.

Stevenson, D. Alan. *World's Lighthouses Before 1820*. London: Oxford University Press, 1959.

Wallace, Frederick William. *Wooden Ships and Iron Men*. London: Hodder and Stoughton Ltd., 1925.

Wickens, Sonia. *Seal Island, an Echo from the Past*. Yarmouth, NS: Sentinel Printing Ltd., 1988.

Witney, Dudley. *The Lighthouse*. Toronto: McClelland and Stewart Ltd., 1975.

Canadian Coast Guard List of Lights; *Canadian Geographic* Jun./ Jul. 1982, Mar./Apr. 1992; *Canadian Geographical Journal*, Jan. 1948, Mar. 1957, Feb. 1975; Cape Breton's Magazine, various; *Halifax Chronicle-Herald*, various; Bruce, Harry, *Imperial Oil Review*, Spring 1991, pp. 1-9; *Journal and Proceedings of the House of Assembly of the Province of Nova Scotia*; National Archives of Canada, various; Nova Scotia Pilot, seventh edition-1930, United States Navy Department Hydrographic Office, Washington; Nova Scotia Pilot, second edition-1944, Department of Mines and Resources, Ottawa; Nova Scotia (S. E. Coast) and Bay of Fundy Pilot, Fourth Edition-1966, "The Canadian Hydrographic Service; Sailing Directions," Gulf of St. Lawrence, Fisheries and Oceans-1992; Sailing Directions, Nova Scotia, Fisheries and Oceans-1990; Lucas, Zoe, Sable Island Papers, various; Parliamentary Sessional Papers, Annual Reports; Provincial Archives of Nova Scotia, various.

Index

#	LIGHT .PG
001	Apple River 2
002	Ile Haute 2
003	Cape d'Or 3
004	Spencers Island 4
005	Port Greville 4
006	Cape Sharp 5
007	Parrsboro 6
008	Five Islands 7
009	Bass River 8
010	Burntcoat Head 9
011	Walton Harbour 10
012	Mitchener Point 12
013	Horton Bluff 12
014	Black Rock 13
015	Margaretsville 13
016	Port George 14
017	Hampton 14
018	Prim Point 15
019	Digby Gut 16
020	Victoria Beach 16
021	Bear River 16
022	Schafners Point 17
023	Annapolis 17
024	Boars Head 18
025	Grand Passage 19
026	Brier Island 19
027	Peter Island 20
028	Gilbert Point 21
029	Belliveau Cove 22
030	Church Point 22
031	Cape St. Mary 23
032	Cape Forchu 23
033	Bunker Island 26
034	Green Island 28
035	Candlebox Island 28
036	Pease Island 29
037	Seal Island 30
038	Tusket River 32
039	Whitehead Island 32
040	Abbott's Harbour 33
041	Pubnico Harbour 34
042	Bon Portage Island 35
043	Stoddart Island 36
044	Woods Harbour 37
045	West Head 37
046	Cape Sable 38
047	Seal Island Light Museum .39
048	Baccaro Point 40
049	The Salvages 41
050	Cape Negro Island 42
051	Cape Roseway 43
052	Sandy Point 44
053	Gull Rock (Lockport) 45
054	Carter Island 47
055	Little Hope Island 47
056	Port Mouton 48
057	Western Head 50
058	Coffin Island 50
059	Fort Point 52
060	Medway Head 53
061	Port Medway 54
062	Mosher Island 55
063	West Ironbound Island . . .56
064	Battery Point Breakwater . .57
065	Cross Island 58
066	Gunning Point Island 59
067	Westhaver Island 60
068	Kaulbach Island Range 61
069	Quaker Island 61
070	East Ironbound Island 62
071	Pearl Island 64
072	Indian Harbour 65
073	Peggy's Point 66
074	Betty Island 67
075	Terence Bay 68
076	Pennant Harbour 70
077	Sambro Harbour 70
078	Sambro Island 71
079	Chebucto Head 75
080	Maugher Beach 76
081	Georges Island 78
082	Devils Island 79
083	Musquodoboit Harbour Range 82
084	Jeddore Rock 83
085	Egg Island 84
086	Spry Bay 85
087	Sheet Rock 86
088	Sheet Harbour Passage Range 87
089	Beaver Island 87
090	Liscomb Island 89
091	Redman Head 90
092	Port Bickerton 91
093	Fisherman's Harbour 92
094	Isaac's Harbour 93
095	Country Island 94
096	Berry Head 95
097	Charlos Harbour Range 96
098	Hog Island 97
099	White Head Island 98
100	Sable Island West 101
101	Sable Island East 102
102	Cranberry Island 103
103	Canso Range 105
104	Queensport 106
105	Guysborough 107
106	Eddy Point 108
107	Balache Point Range 112
108	Henry Island 113
109	Mabou Harbour 114
110	Margaree Island 115
111	Margaree Harbour Range .116
112	Chéticamp Harbour 117
113	Enragee Point 118
114	Caveau Point Range 119
115	St. Paul Island 120
116	Cape North 122
117	Neil's Harbour 125
118	Ciboux Island 126
119	Carey Point Range 127
120	Great Bras d'Or Range . . .128
121	Black Rock Point 129
122	Point Aconi 130
123	Sydney Range 131
124	Sydney Bar 132
125	Low Point 133
126	Glace Bay North Breakwater 135
127	Flint Island 136
128	Scatarie 138
129	Louisbourg 140
130	Main-à-Dieu 142
131	Gabarus 143
132	Rouse Point 143
133	Guyon Island 144
134	Fourchu Head 146
135	Jerome Point 147
136	Gregory Island 148
137	McNeil Beach 149
138	Man of War Point 150
139	Kidston Island 151
140	Kidston Island West 152
141	Gillis Point 153
142	Little Narrows 154

143	Cameron Island 154
144	Cape George 155
145	Bourgeois Inlet 156
146	Green Island (CB) 157
147	Marache Point 158
148	Jerseyman Island 159
149	Grandique Point 161
150	North Canso 164
151	Havre Boucher Range 165
152	Pomquet Island 166
153	Cape George 167
154	Pictou Island South 168
155	Pictou Island East 169
156	Pictou Island West 170
157	Pictou Bar 171
158	Pictou Harbour Range . . .172
159	Trenton Range 173
160	Caribou 174
161	Mullins Point 175
162	Wallace Harbour 176
163	Pugwash 177
164	Coldspring Head 178

Light / # . . . . .PG

Abbott's Harbour / 040 33
Annapolis/ 023 17
Apple River / 001 2
Baccaro Point / 048 40
Balache Point Range / 107 112
Bass River / 009 8
Battery Point Breakwater / 064 57
Bear River / 021 16
Beaver Island / 089 87
Belliveau Cove / 029 22
Berry Head / 096 95
Betty Island / 074 67
Black Rock / 014 13
Black Rock Point / 121 129
Boars Head / 024 18
Bon Portage Island / 042 35
Bourgeois Inlet / 145 156
Brier Island / 026 19
Bunker Island / 033 26
Burntcoat Head / 010 9
Cameron Island / 143 154

Candlebox Island / 035 28
Canso Range / 103 105
Cape d'Or / 003 3
Cape Forchu / 032 23
Cape George (Richmond) / 144 . .155
Cape George (Antigonish) / 153 . .167
Cape Negro Island / 050 42
Cape North / 116 122
Cape Roseway / 051 43
Cape Sable / 046 38
Cape Sharp / 006 5
Cape St. Mary / 031 23
Carey Point Range / 119 127
Caribou / 160 174
Carter Island / 054 47
Caveau Point Range / 114 119
Charlos Harbour Range / 097 96
Chebucto Head / 079 75
Chéticamp Harbour / 112 117
Church Point / 030 22
Ciboux Island / 118 126
Coffin Island / 058 50
Coldspring Head / 164 178
Country Island / 095 94
Cranberry Island / 102 103
Cross Island / 065 58
Devils Island / 082 79
Digby Gut / 019 16
East Ironbound Island / 070 . . .62
Eddy Point / 106 108
Egg Island / 085 84
Enragee Point / 113 118
Fisherman's Harbour / 093 92
Five Islands / 008 7
Flint Island / 127 136
Fort Point / 059 52
Fourchu Head / 134 146
Gabarus / 131 143
Georges Island / 081 78
Gilbert Point / 028 21
Gillis Point / 141 153
Glace Bay
   North Breakwater / 126 135
Grand Passage / 025 19
Grandique Point / 149 161
Great Bras d'Or Range / 120 128
Green Island / 034 28
Green Island (CB) 146 157
Gregory Island / 136 148

Gull Rock (Lockport) / 053 45
Gunning Point Island / 066 59
Guyon Island / 133 144
Guysborough / 105 107
Hampton / 017 14
Havre Boucher Range / 151 165
Henry Island / 108 113
Hog Island / 098 97
Horton Bluff / 013 12
Ile Haute / 002 2
Indian Harbour / 072 65
Isaac's Harbour / 094 93
Jeddore Rock / 084 83
Jerome Point / 135 147
Jerseyman Island / 148 159
Kaulbach Island Range / 068 61
Kidston Island / 139 151
Kidston Island West / 140 152
Liscomb Island / 090 89
Little Hope Island / 055 47
Little Narrows / 142 154
Louisbourg / 129 140
Low Point / 125 133
Mabou Harbour / 109 114
Main-à-Dieu / 130 142
Man of War Point / 138 150
Marache Point / 147 158
Margaree Harbour Range / 111 . .116
Margaree Island / 110 115
Margaretsville / 015 13
Maugher Beach / 080 76
McNeil Beach / 137 149
Medway Head / 060 53
Mitchener Point / 012 12
Mosher Island / 062 55
Mullins Point / 161 175
Musquodoboit
   Harbour Range / 083 82
Neil's Harbour / 117 125
North Canso / 150 164
Parrsboro / 007 6
Pearl Island / 071 64
Pease Island / 036 29
Peggy's Point / 073 66
Pennant Harbour / 076 70
Peter Island / 027 20
Pictou Bar / 157 171
Pictou Harbour Range / 158 172
Pictou Island East / 155 169

Pictou Island South / 154 168
Pictou Island West / 156 170
Point Aconi / 122 130
Pomquet Island / 152 166
Port Bickerton / 092 91
Port George / 016 14
Port Greville / 005 4
Port Medway / 061 54
Port Mouton / 056 48
Prim Point / 018 15
Pubnico Harbour / 041 34
Pugwash / 163 177
Quaker Island / 069 61
Queensport / 104 106
Redman Head / 091 90
Rouse Point / 132 143
Sable Island East / 101 102
Sable Island West / 100 101
The Salvages / 049 41
Sambro Harbour / 077 70
Sambro Island / 078 71
Sandy Point / 052 44
Scatarie / 128 138
Schafners Point / 022 17

Seal Island / 037 30
Seal Island
   Light Museum / 047 39
Sheet Harbour
   Passage Range / 088 87
Sheet Rock / 087 86
Spencers Island / 004 4
Spry Bay / 086 85
St. Paul Island / 115 120
Stoddart Island / 043 36
Sydney Bar / 124 132
Sydney Range / 123 131
Terence Bay / 075 68
Trenton Range / 159 173
Tusket River / 038 32
Victoria Beach / 020 16
Wallace Harbour / 162 176
Walton Harbour / 011 10
Western Head / 057 50
Westhaver Island / 067 60
West Head / 045 37
West Ironbound Island / 063 56
White Head Island / 099 98
Whitehead Island / 039 32
Woods Harbour / 044 37